Health Informatics

(formerly Computers in Health Care)

Kathryn J. Hannah Marion J. Ball
Series Editors

For other titles published in this series, go to
www.springer.com/series/1114

Tim Benson

Principles of Health Interoperability HL7 and SNOMED

 Springer

Tim Benson
www.abies.co.uk
Thatcham RG 18 9WL
UK

ISBN 978-1-84882-802-5   e-ISBN 978-1-84882-803-2
DOI 10.1007/978-1-84882-803-2
Springer London Dordrecht Heidelberg New York

British Library Cataloguing in Publication Data

A catalogue record for this book is available from the British Library
Library of Congress Control Number: 2009941467

Printed on acid-free paper

Springer is part of Springer Science+Business Media (www.springer.com)

This book is dedicated to my sons
Laurence, Oliver, Alex and Jamie.

Foreword

Health data standards are a necessary component for interoperability in health care. Aggregation of health-related data mandates the use of standards, and aggregation is necessary to support safe and quality care. The American Recovery and Reinvestment Act (ARRA) includes $19 billion in direct funding and an additional $18.5 billion in returned savings tagged to the use of health information technology (HIT). The resulting expanding use of HIT has engaged a growing number of stakeholders, many of whom are now realizing the value of standards.

All aspects of the process of creating and effectively using electronic health records (EHRs), which meet the requirements of "meaningful use," require standards. From the planning stages of effective use of HIT through reference information models, data models, use cases, story boards, and domain analysis models; to defining the data elements with common terminologies, definitions, data types, units and other attributes; to templates, clinical statements, clinical documents and data interchange; and to the EHR, its functional requirements in multiple sites and presentations; to decision support standards; and including standards for security and privacy. These standards extend beyond definition standards, to use standards for linkage among disparate systems to standards for reports (claims, infectious disease reports, patient summaries).

With the increasing demand for individuals knowledgeable in what standards are available and when and how to use those standards, this book is most welcome. The author, Tim Benson, has been engaged in the creation of standards since the beginning. His experiences span organizations – including HL7, CEN, and ISO, and terminologies such as SNOMED and LOINC. He has engaged the global community and understands similarities as well as differences among the global community. He has a top reputation as a teacher and writer within the international community. I know no other individual who is more qualified to write this book than Tim Benson.

In *Principles of Healthcare Interoperability HL7 and SNOMED*, Tim focuses on major contributors to the set of required standards. In the first section, he lays out a framework for why interoperability is important and what is needed to accomplish that interoperability. Although there are several contributing Standards Developing Organizations (SDOs) in the global community, Health Level Seven is perhaps preeminent. Its standards are widely used, and cover the full spectrum of applications. Its membership is international (currently including over 35 countries) and includes the major HIT vendors and representatives of the full set of stakeholders. The International Healthcare Technology Standards Developing Organization (IHTSDO) is rapidly promoting SNOMED CT as the preferred terminology in health care. But at the same time, while focusing on HL7 and SNOMED CT, he includes much useful information on other standards and other organizations.

Readers will find this book easy to read, even if it is their first exposure to standards. In this rapidly changing field, this book is a must for anyone who is involved or has interest in the use of health information technology – and who is not.

W. Ed Hammond, Ph.D.
Professor Emeritus, Department of Community
and Family Medicine, School of Medicine
Professor Emeritus,
Department of Biomedical Engineer,
Pratt School of Engineering
Adjunct Professor,
Fuqua School of Medicine
Duke University,
Durham North Carolina
Founding Member of Health Level
Seven (1987)Chair, HL7 (1991, 1996-1997,2008-2009)

Preface

Health care has to cross the quality chasm, to become safer, more efficient and effective (Institute of Medicine 2001). The transformation of health care depends critically on interoperability, enabling computers to share information and deliver information from where it originates to where it is needed.

When interoperability is commonplace, patients, clinicians, managers, and researchers will enjoy secure access to the right information at the right time and the at right place; they will make more soundly based decisions, leading to better patient outcomes and fewer mistakes. Interoperability is a prerequisite for the process reengineering that will reduce the waste of unnecessary costs, errors, delays, and futile repetition.

There is nothing new in this (Blum and Duncan 1990; Hayes and Barnett 2008). Why has it not happened? At a technical level it cannot take place until we agree, implement, and deploy the sort of stringent standards that are needed for plug and play between the disparate computer systems found in health care.

These standards will almost certainly be based on HL7 and SNOMED CT working together as a tightly specified language for exchanging health-care information. All languages depend on grammar and words. HL7 provides the grammar as standardized structures for healthcare communication, rather like English or French grammar, while SNOMED CT provides a comprehensive clinical terminology, analogous to a dictionary.

The documentation of HL7 and SNOMED runs to tens of thousands of pages and creates a steep learning curve and barrier for entry. This book sets out to provide an introduction to these standards, focusing on the core principles in a way that is understandable to the average analyst, student, clinician and manager.

About the Author

Tim Benson graduated from the University of Nottingham as a mechanical engineer, was introduced to health-care computing at the Charing Cross Hospital in London (now part of the Imperial College Healthcare NHS Trust), where he evaluated the socioeconomic benefits of medical computing systems. In 1980, he founded Abies Informatics, Ltd. as one of the first GP computer suppliers. There, he needed a coding system to record consultation details and, with James Read and David Markwell, developed a proprietary system, which became known as the Read Codes. In 1987, a working party set up by the British Medical Association and the Royal College of General Practitioners recommended that this become a national standard in the UK and it went on to become one of the two main tributaries of SNOMED CT. In 1988, he was invited to lead a European project team to examine the need for open standards in health informatics, which led to 2 decades of work on interoperability standards and collaboration with HL7.

Tim is founder of Abies Ltd. and Routine Health Outcomes Ltd. He is an honorary Senior Research Fellow at UCL CHIME (Centre of Health Informatics and Multi-professional Education).

Acknowledgments

Many people have contributed to my understanding of health-care interoperability, HL7 and SNOMED. First, I want to single out David Markwell, my friend and collaborator for 25 years, who has made an enormous personal contribution to both clinical terminology and health-care interoperability. In the HL7 space, I want to acknowledge my debt to Ed Hammond, Mark Schafarman, Jack Harrington, Clem McDonald, Woody Beeler, Charlie Mead, and Bob Dolin. I also want to acknowledge the members of the HL7 Education Committee including Mike Henderson, Abdul-Malik Shakir, Virginia Lorenzi, and Rene Spronk, and members of HL7 UK, notably Charlie McCay, Leo Fogarty, Andrew Hinchley, Martin Whittaker, and Ann Wrightson. In clinical terminology I have learnt much from Alan Rector, Kent Spackman, Ed Cheetham, and Tom Marley. I would also like to thank Roddy Neame, Sigurd From, Georges de Moor, Seref Arikan, and David Ingram.

Series Preface

This series is directed to Health-care professionals, who are leading the transformation of health care by using information and knowledge. Historically, the series was launched in 1988 as Computers in Health Care, to offer a broad range of titles: some addressed to specific professions such as nursing, medicine, and health administration; others to special areas of practice such as trauma and radiology; still other books in the series focused on interdisciplinary issues, such as the computer-based patient record, electronic health records, and networked health-care systems. Renamed Health Informatics in 1998 to reflect the rapid evolution in the discipline known as health Informatics, the series continued to add titles that contribute to the evolution of the field. In the series, eminent experts, serving as editors or authors, offer their accounts of innovations in health Informatics. Increasingly, these accounts go beyond hardware and software to address the role of information in influencing the transformation of Health-care delivery systems around the world. The series also increasingly focused on the users of the information and systems: the organizational, behavioral, and societal changes that accompany the diffusion of information technology in health services environments.

Developments in health-care delivery are constant; most recently developments in proteomics and genomics are increasingly becoming relevant to clinical decision making and emerging standards of care. The data resources emerging from molecular biology are beyond the capacity of the human brain to integrate and beyond the scope of paper-based decision trees. Thus, bioinformatics has emerged as a new field in health informatics to support emerging and ongoing developments in molecular biology. Translational informatics supports acceleration, from bench to bedside, i.e., the appropriate use of molecular biology research findings and bioinformatics in clinical care of patients.

At the same time, further continual evolution of the field of Health informatics is reflected in the introduction of concepts at the macro or health systems delivery level with major national initiatives related to electronic health records (EHR), data standards and public health informatics such as the Healthcare Information Technology Standards Panel (HITSP) in the USA, Canada Health Infoway, NHS Connecting for Health in the UK.

We have consciously retained the series title Health Informatics as the single umbrella term that encompasses both the microscopic elements of bioinformatics and the macroscopic aspects of large national health information systems. Ongoing changes to both the micro and the macro perspectives on health informatics will continue to shape health services in the Twenty First Century. By making full and creative use of the technology to tame data and to transform information, health Informatics will foster the development and use of new knowledge in health care. As coeditors, we pledge to support our professional colleagues and the series readers as they share advances in the emerging and exciting field of Health Informatics.

Kathryn J. Hannah
Marion J. Ball

Contents

Part I
Principles of Interoperability

Chapter 1
The Health Information Revolution

Healthcare quality improvement is an economic and moral necessity. The transformation, which is needed to improve productivity and effectiveness, will rely on computer interoperability to deliver information when and where required, support soundly-based decision-making, eliminate unnecessary repetition, reduce delays and avoid errors.

Interoperability is one of the core themes of the US Federal Health Information Technology Strategic Plan, which states: "to effectively exchange health information, health IT systems and products must use consistent, specific data and technical standards."[1]

Health interoperability has been given a massive impetus in the 2009 Health Information Technology for Economic and Clinical Health (HITECH)[2] initiative, which encapsulates in its name the economic and clinical necessities for healthcare IT. The nominal focus is to deliver the promise of an interoperable electronic healthcare record (EHR) for all Americans by 2014, but the real goal is to improve value for money (Blumenthal 2009).

Before receiving HITECH payments, each doctor (or other eligible professional) has to demonstrate that he or she is a meaningful user of a certified interoperable EHR system. The early focus is on:

- e-Prescribing, including decision support
- Information exchange including laboratory and radiology reports, demographic and administrative data, and visit summaries
- Quality data sets

Tom Daschle, President Obama's original nominee as Secretary of Health, describes the problem being addressed:

> Our health care system is incredibly primitive when it comes to using the information systems that are common in American workplaces. Only 15 to 20 percent of doctors have

---

[1] The ONC-Coordinated Federal Health Information Technology Strategic Plan: 2008–2012: Using the Power of Information Technology to Transform Health and Care. Department of Health and Human Sciences, 3 June, 2008.

[2] Part of the American Recovery and Reinvestment Act, 2009 (ARRA).

T. Benson, *Principles of Health Interoperability HL7 and SNOMED*, HI, DOI 10.1007/978-1-84882-803-2_1, © Springer-Verlag London Limited 2010

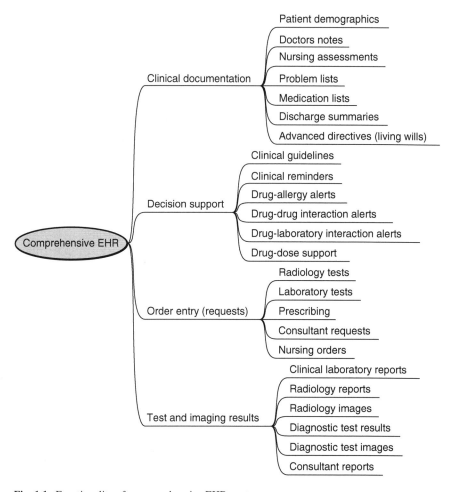

Fig. 1.1 Functionality of a comprehensive EHR system

computerized patient records and only a small fraction of the billions of medical transactions that take place each year in the United States are conducted electronically. Studies suggest that this weakness compromises the quality of care, leads to medical errors, and costs as much as $78 billion a year. (Daschle 2008)

Only 1.5% of US hospitals have comprehensive electronic health records (EHR) systems of the type called for in the HITECH Act; a further 7.5% have basic systems (Jha et al. 2009). What is a comprehensive EHR? An expert consensus view of the functionality required suggested 24 core functions (see Fig. 1.1) in four main groups:

- Clinical documentation
- Test and imaging results

- Decision support
- Computerized provider-order entry

In ambulatory care (doctors' offices), the proportion of doctors using comprehensive and basic EHR systems are 4% and 9%, respectively (DesRoches et al. 2008).

The problem is not one of technology. In the United Kingdom, all GPs (yes, 100%) use EHRs in their consulting rooms and a large proportion work paper-free – they rely entirely on electronic records while consulting. However, GP surgeries, in which all records are electronic, are not able to share data with hospitals, primarily because the hospitals do not use computers for maintaining patient records. In 2009, most hospital doctors do not use computers for maintaining case notes in the consulting room or at the bedside.

There are several reasons why GPs use computers but hospital doctors do not (Benson 2002). Incentives have played a big part. Over a 40-year period, the leaders of the GP profession worked with the government to provide incentives and to remove barriers to computerizing practices. By 1996, 96% of British GPs were already using computers.

The story of the computer-printed prescription form used in England FP10 (comp) provides a good example of the way that governments can remove barriers to computerization. The computer form is twice the width of a standard prescription, with a large blank area on the right-hand side. The original reason for the blank space was that narrow tractor-feed printers were not available when the form was developed (for use in one practice only) in the mid-1970s. The blank right-hand side was later used to provide each patient with a record of his or her medication; this is so useful that no one has seriously considered doing away with it. In 1981, the Department of Health approved the national use of the form, in spite of well-founded reservations that the wider form would be more expensive and computers would make it easier to prescribe more, hence increasing costs. This simple regulatory change was critical in enabling the development and spread of GP computing, where computer-assisted repeat prescribing saves time and improves legibility and safety. In most other countries computer-printed prescriptions remained illegal for many more years, slowing their uptake of computing.

On the other hand, hospital computing has been treated as an administration overhead (a cost to be contained), and doctors have not been offered incentives or other encouragement to become involved. At a time when almost 100% of prescriptions written by GPs are computerized, the proportion of computerized hospital prescriptions is tiny (probably less than 2% but likely to increase rapidly).

One issue has been resistance by hospital doctors and managers. This is not new. Based on his experience in implementing comprehensive EHR systems during the early 1970s, Melville Hodge wrote:

> Success has repeatedly been demonstrated to be the consequence of each doctor, one at a time, coming to see how his performance is enhanced by investing his always scarce time in learning how to use the system efficiently. Similarly hospital managers must participate in and buy into a carefully designed benefits realization program before they can be reasonably expected to act. (Hodge 1990)

There are other difficulties also. What works well in GP surgeries does not scale to work in acute hospitals. Attempts to replicate the success of GP computing in hospitals have failed repeatedly. You cannot shoehorn a system that works well for one specialty into another.

GPs work as individuals working mainly in a single consulting room, but hospital clinicians work as teams and are highly mobile; their work is more diverse and specialized than that of general practice. Hospitals need excellent communication within the work-group, between doctors, nurses, and other professions. For example, about 70% of the tasks performed by junior hospital doctors are done together with another member of staff, usually another doctor (Westbrook et al. 2008).

The information systems used by each specialty need to work together, which requires the deployment of stringent interoperability standards for each use case. Many of the standards required have not been agreed; many of those that have been agreed have not yet been deployed.

The NHS Informatics Review, 2008,[3] sets out a vision to support patient-centered care in a way that empowers patients to be more involved in their care and staff to improve NHS performance (Fig. 1.2).

To help achieve buy-in from hospital doctors the review identified five key features, which are referred to in the report as the "Clinical 5":

- Patient Administration System (PAS) with integration with other systems and sophisticated reporting
- Order Communications and Diagnostics Reporting (including all pathology and radiology tests and tests ordered in primary care)
- Letters with coding (discharge summaries, clinic, and Accident and Emergency letters)
- Scheduling (for beds, tests, theaters, etc.)
- e-Prescribing including "To Take Out" (TTO) medicines

The review also identified that a major program of standards development would be needed to enable these goals to be achieved.

1.1 Health Care is Communication

Health care is a communications industry. Most healthcare processes involve exchanging information; billions of documents are generated. Consider four different types of communication, based on the physical distance that the information has to travel:

- Within the work-group, to record and manage the care of individual patients
- Between specialized diagnostic and treatment departments, to request services and to report results

---

[3] Health Informatics Review. DH July 2008, Ref 10104

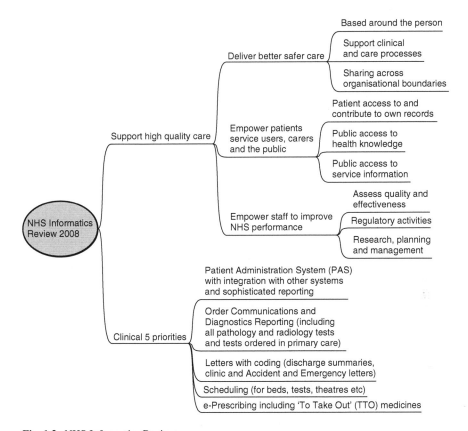

Fig. 1.2 NHS Informatics Review

- Across organization boundaries between hospital doctors GPs and community staff, to ensure continuity of care
- From the care provider to payers and regulatory agencies, for revenue and accountability

These four categories of communication are listed in decreasing order of information volume yet in increasing order of use of information technology. It is like a banana republic that invests in airports and motorways, but does nothing to improve transport for the millions in the cities.

Historically, healthcare information systems have been organized hierarchically, with the government or payer at the top, then provider organizations such as hospitals, followed by departments, clinicians, and ultimately the patient (GP computing in the UK is a notable exception to this model). This hierarchy reflects the flow of money, authority, and power, but has little in common with the natural flow of healthcare information needed to care for individual patients; patient care has more in common with a social network, with each individual patient at the centre of their own net.

1.2 Patient-Centric Health Care

The patient is the sole reason for healthcare activity, and so we should focus on meeting the patient's needs. Each patient wants to live longer, feel well, and be able to do what he or she wants. Health care is changing from a paternalistic model to one of partnership between patients and healthcare professionals.

In 2001, the Institute of Medicine's *Crossing the Quality Chasm* set out a manifesto for transforming healthcare systems to become safe, effective, patient-centered, timely, efficient, and equitable. It called for urgent action to automate all clinical, financial, and administrative information, and to share that information electronically among clinicians, patients, and appropriate others within a secure environment (Institute of Medicine 2001).

In the traditional healthcare model, care was based around discrete visits and episodes of care; professional autonomy led to variability as each care professional decided on investigations and treatment based on their own training and experience. Safety was an individual responsibility; the patient record was primarily a record of what had happened and was kept secret. The system as a whole defended professional demarcation, focused on cutting costs, reacted to patient needs as and when they arose. This model is disappearing fast, but we still rely on information systems that were originally conceived and designed for that environment.

The new patient-centric model is quite different: care is based on continuous healing relationships, customized according to individual patient needs and values, with the patient as the ultimate source of control. Knowledge is shared, information flows freely, and decision-making is evidence-based. Transparency and collaboration are virtues, patient needs are anticipated, and effort is devoted toward reducing waste (that is, any activity that delivers no benefit to the patient) (Fig. 1.3).

This change toward partnership and patient-centered care involves changes in information systems architecture, more along the lines of social networking than the traditional enterprise-centric systems that have been implemented over the last 30 years or so. A prerequisite of personal health records (PHR) systems is data liquidity using open standards. Unfortunately, most existing EHR systems have incompatible means of acquiring, processing, storing, and communicating data (Mandl et al. 2001).

Most patients, doctors and other healthcare professionals find it surprising that when so much of what we do is performed over the Internet, we are still not able to share information seamlessly to provide joined-up patient-centric care. Coiera has pointed out that health systems are socio-technical systems, involving the interaction of people and technology and that we cannot design organizational and technical systems independently of each other, nor expect to reinvent healthcare systems successfully without a thorough understanding of the technology needed to make all the parts interoperate smoothly (Coiera 2004).

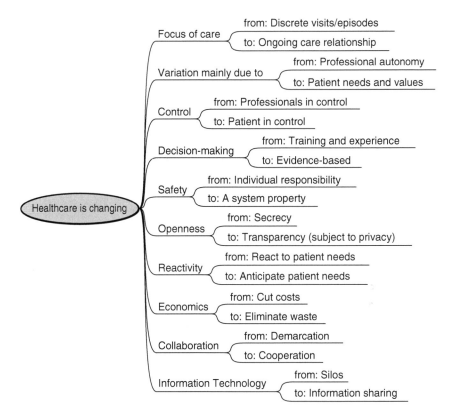

Fig. 1.3 Differences between traditional and patient-centric health care

1.3 Stages of Information Handling

Let us go back to basics. Information handling has evolved over several thousand years through four distinct stages as originally set out by Marshall McLuhan in *Gutenberg's Galaxy* (McLuhan 1962).

In the first stage, information and knowledge was held only in the human brain and transferred from one person to another by speech. Oral tribal culture provides an example. Access depends on the presence of the person with the knowledge, which is lost forever when a person dies. A good deal of one-to-one health care still relies on the human memory and speech.

The second stage began with the invention of handwriting. Handwritten records are formatted at the time of writing, cannot be replicated without transcription, and often illegible. Modern health care, involving teams of doctors and nurses, each doing a specialized task, would be impossible without written records.

The third stage was triggered by the invention of printing by Johannes Gutenberg around 1455, which provided the means to replicate and broadcast information widely. This led to the Renaissance, the Age of Enlightenment, the Industrial Revolution and the Information Society. The impact of this top-down broadcasting and dissemination of knowledge on medical education has been massive, but there has been little impact on how people perform routine health care and maintain care records.

The fourth and last stage, the electronic age, has its origins in the development of electronic computers and information science during World War II and has been gathering pace exponentially ever since, driven by the Laws of Moore and Metcalfe, leading to the explosive development of the Internet, the Web, mobile phones, and social networking.

Moore's Law is the prediction made in 1965 that the power of computer devices would continue to double every 2 years; this has held good for almost 60 years and shows few signs of stopping yet.

Metcalfe's Law is based on the twin observations that the cost of adding each user to a network is linear but the value each user obtains from that network depends on the number of users they can link to. Thus, as networks grow, the value to each user continues to increase and the total value of the network increases exponentially.

It is surprising that health care, the largest and quintessential information-based industry, has failed to harness these forces and become joined-up for so long. The oral tradition and handwritten manuscripts remain prevalent throughout most of the sector (Fig. 1.4).

Health professionals are overwhelmed by information. Herbert Simon noted:

> Information consumes the attention of its recipients; a wealth of information creates a poverty of attention and a need to allocate that attention amongst the overabundance of information sources that might consume it. (Simon 1971)

The value of information lies in its use, which falls into two main categories: clinician support at the point of care, and service management.

Clinician support includes all of the tasks needed to support clinical decision-making, to order tests and treatment, to correspond with patients, hospital specialists, GPs, community and social care services, and to review clinical performance. The nature of clinical care is ultimately determined by the natural history of disease processes, which are highly complex but do not change. Clinical care is task-oriented. At any moment a clinician is performing one of a number of well-defined tasks, which differ considerably from specialty to specialty, with some overlap. Clinical care comprises thousands of discrete tasks, each of which has its own information and communication needs and requires systems, terms, and classifications tailored to the needs of the task.

Service Management is focused on meeting the contractual obligations of commissioners and regulators, which, unlike clinical processes, are subject to frequent and regular change. Managers do not need to understand every detail of clinical care. They focus on providing a safe, courteous, and efficient service, by enabling the smooth administration of each patient's stay or visit, monitoring the quality of care provided in terms of safety, patient experience, and effectiveness,

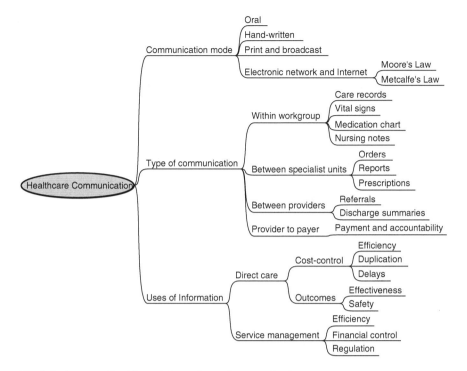

Fig. 1.4 Aspects of healthcare information and communication

costs and opportunities to improve efficiency. Management information is invariably classified into a relatively small number of discrete groups.

Clinical decisions, such as ordering tests, therapy, referrals, and care, determine the cost and outcome of care. Only a small proportion of cost variance in health care can be attributed to service efficiency (doing things right). Most cost and outcome variance is the result of differences in clinical management, individual doctors' patterns of treatment and investigation (doing the right things). It is always important to do tests efficiently, but if the test is inappropriate (e.g., it is repeated without good reason), it is a waste of resources irrespective of how efficiently it is performed.

Donald Berwick has written:

> The ultimate measure by which to judge the quality of a medical effort is whether it helps patients (and their families) as they see it. Anything done in health care that does not help a patient or family is, by definition, waste, whether or not the professions and their associations traditionally hallow it. (Berwick 1997)

Paper-based patient records are widely recognized as not fit for purpose. For example:

> The medical record is an abomination … it is a disgrace to the profession that created it. More often than not the chart is thick, tattered, disorganised and illegible; progress notes, consultants notes, radiology reports and nurses notes are all co-mingled in accession

sequence. The charts confuse rather than enlighten; they provide a forbidding challenge to anyone who tries to understand what is happening to the patient. (Bleich and Lawrence 1993)

A paper record can be used only in one place by one person at a time and is often not where it is needed. Once to hand, it is hard to find what you want in a disorganized, illegible, inconsistent, incomplete, badly sorted bundle of paper. The user has to do all of the work to glean any useful information.

The electronic patient record is key to improved clinical decision-making and accountability. Information quality is a paramount concern. Computer-based patient records are legible and the information can be displayed in many different ways to suit the task at hand. Several people can work on it at different places at the same time, saving the delays and effort required to locate, retrieve, and transport paper. Prompts can improve quality and safety, prevent key data being omitted, and save time by not needing to record the same data time and again.

1.4 Health Care Is Complex

Health care is inherently fractal. The more closely you look, the more complexity you find. The information in hospital medical records is enormously varied; it includes: referral and discharge letters from different doctors; investigation findings from laboratories and diagnostic imaging departments, medication charts, nursing notes, ECG traces, plus the history, examination, progress notes, and plans kept by each doctor.

It is easy to overlook just how flexible paper-based patient records are, in spite of their deficiencies.

Healthcare communication and information flow patterns involve many people over a wide geographical area and diverse subject matter. For example, over 30,000 GPs in England refer over 15 million patients a year to 60,000 hospital and community doctors and receive more than 40 million clinic and discharge letters in return. Each primary care doctor can refer patients to any specialist and each specialist can receive referrals from any GP (Fig. 1.5).

Each doctor also communicates with a multitude of specialized investigation and treatment services, community care agencies, administrative and funding bodies. This complex many-to-many communication pattern is prevalent throughout the health and social care services.

The workflow is varied, depending on what is the matter with the patient and at what stage they are in the process; it changes from one patient to another and from one care setting to another. The half-life of information (how long a piece of information has any value) differs enormously in different contexts, such as in outpatient clinics, on the wards, in intensive care, and during an operation in an operating theatre.

Each class of clinician has its own needs. The Department of Health recognizes more than 60 clinical specialties for doctors plus a similar number of other nursing,

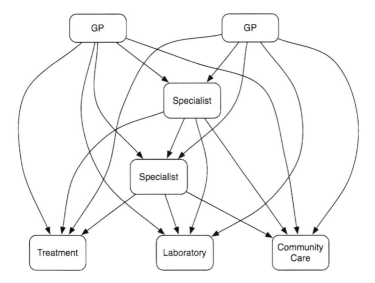

Fig. 1.5 Information flows

therapy and investigation specializations. Each specialty has its own governance, education, and quality assurance requirements, speaks its own dialect and has its own ways of working. Clinical heterogeneity helps explain why many successful electronic patient record systems are limited to single specialties, such as general practice, maternity care, or renal dialysis, where the needs are relatively homogeneous and well-understood.

The situation is exacerbated because most healthcare professionals are mobile and can be found on any ward where they have patients, in clinics, at any one of several hospitals, on domiciliary visits in the community, in laboratories, or in their own office.

The concept of the one-size-fits-all patient record has not been very successful except where great efforts have been made to tailor the system to individual needs and management has been able to mandate its use, such as in the Veterans Administration hospitals, where clinicians were offered no choice as to whether or not to adopt it.

1.5 Looking Back

Sometimes it pays to stand back and take the long view. We now have almost 40 years experience in implementing EHRs and know what works and what does not. There is no excuse for not learning the well-documented lessons of history

1.5.1 Problem-Oriented Medical Records

The Problem-Oriented Medical Record (POMR), first described by Larry Weed in 1968 (Weed 1968), was one of the first and most influential attempts to improve the structure of the patient record.

Weed's POMR divides the record into two parts. The first, called the database covers the patient's social, family, and past medical history. The second main section is the progress notes. Progress notes are organized under problems.

A problem is anything that causes concern, not only a diagnosis. The problem list is a list of all the patient's problems indicating those that are active and those that have been resolved.

Each progress note has a problem heading and four subheadings, using the acronym SOAP:

S – Subjective, meaning the information provided about history and symptoms by the patient or relative.
O – Objective, meaning information obtained by direct examination of the patient or from clinical investigations (laboratory, radiology, etc.).
A – Assessment, meaning the clinicians assessment about what is the matter with the patient (diagnosis), prognosis, etc.
P – Plan, meaning the future plan of action, including investigations and treatment (drug prescriptions, physiotherapy, surgery, and so on). Drugs prescribed are also listed in a separate medication list. This section is a problem-specific care plan.

From 1967 to 1982 Larry Weed was funded by the US government to implement a remarkable problem-oriented electronic patient record system known as PROMIS, based on the use of touch-screen terminals. This pioneering project was implemented for many years on medical and gynecological wards at the University of Vermont, but it was withdrawn after federal funding ceased (Schultz 1988). Weed went on to develop problem-knowledge couplers (PKC), which match detailed patient information with an extensive medical database to provide guidance tailored to individuals (Weed 1991).

The POMR concept was taken up in primary care in the United Kingdom where most GP systems are problem-oriented, linking medication and tests with problems (Fig. 1.6).[4]

---

[4] The first widely used problem-oriented GP system in the was Abies System 5, introduced in 1987, distributed by AAH Meditel, and one of the ancestors of iSOFT's Lorenzo system.

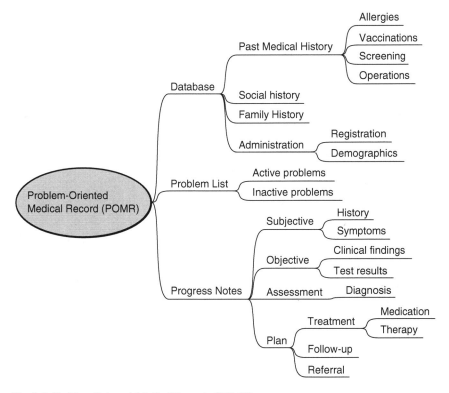

Fig. 1.6 Problem-Oriented Medical Records (POMR)

1.5.2 El Camino Hospital Project

The first hospital to implement a comprehensive EHR was the El Camino hospital in California, which went live in 1971. This was subjected to a detailed 6-year evaluation that compared its costs and other outcomes with those of control hospitals. Such detailed long-term evaluations are rare, but other studies have shown similar findings. Introducing electronic health records into a large hospital i difficult and time-consuming, but the scale of efficiency improvements can be large.

The following quotes come from an account of the experience by Melville Hodge, who led the project for the supplier (Hodge 1990).

The project met:

> massive resistance from important segments of the medical staff, spreading quickly to ... national newspaper headlines. This resistance, initially justified in part by early system shortcomings, seemed intractable.

Hodge warns:

> Never forget that introduction of [EHR] into a hospital impacts a <u>human</u> organization to perhaps an unparalleled degree. If the need to manage the change process is ignored, resistance and even rebellion may be reasonably predicted.

The resistance was overcome:

> by effective leadership of the more visionary El Camino physicians.

The outcome was that 10 years later, the hospital chief executive could claim:

> [T]he hospital inpatient cost per case is 40% less than the county average for 13 similar community hospitals.

1.5.3   The NHS National Programme for IT

The English National Health Service National Programme for IT (NPfIT) demonstrates the need for appropriate standards to be fully deployed (Brennan 2005). The central recommendation of the Wanless Report, which led to the creation of the program was for:

> a doubling of spending on ICT to fund ambitious targets of the kind set out in the NHS Information Strategy. To avoid duplication of effort and resources and to ensure that the benefits of ICT integration across health and social services are achieved, the Review recommends that stringent standards are set from the centre to ensure that systems across the UK are fully compatible with each other. (Wanless 2002)

More detail was provided in a Strategy document 3 months later, which stated:

> The core of our strategy is to take greater control over the specification, procurement, resource management, performance management and delivery of the information and IT agenda. We will improve the leadership and direction given to IT, and combine it with national and local implementation that are based on ruthless standardisation. (DH 2002)

The vision of integration across health and social services and cross-UK compatibility had been quietly dropped. The focus was to provide a centrally procured set of one-size-fits-all systems. However, the NHS is not a monolithic organization, but may be better thought of as comprising thousands of units linked by a single payer. It is more like an industry sector than a single service. Linking such an ecosystem requires integration standards to be deployed everywhere.

The Strategy listed ten key elements of the national program, the final one being to:

> create national standards for data quality and data interchange between systems at local, regional and national levels. (*op cit* paragraph 2.3.2)

At the outset, the National program underestimated the requirement to develop and deploy the standards needed to enable interoperability at all levels and focused attention on providing only those needed to support links to national services.

The Strategy even implied that the relevant standards were already available.

Work is already underway on a strategy for electronic Clinical Communications and a report is due at the end of March 2002 (sic). This will guide the implementation of the electronic pathology results to GPs and GP to GP record transfer (both due in December 2002); radiology reporting and electronic discharge summary implementation due to commence in March 2003; and the standards for the electronic transfer of prescriptions will be available later this year. (*op cit* paragraph 4.2.2)

The first phase of the project, between April 2002 and March 2003, was to be used to:

define the data and data interchange standards we will require in the future. (*op cit* paragraph 1.2.3)

These targets were missed. One of the reasons was that at that time the responsibility for standards development was spread across several independent organizations with responsibility for strategic direction, defining standards, ratifying standards and certification testing. No one was in control of the whole picture. These national functions were eventually brought together under NHS Connecting for Health, but this took until April 2005 and by then many key decisions on scope, technology, and budgets had been set.

A major effort was directed toward the development of data interface specifications for national services using HL7 Version 3, but the specification and deployment of local and regional services was left to the Local Service Providers who adopted different releases of Hl7 Version 2.

In Canada, the Health Infoway project has learnt some of these lessons and in 2006 established a centrally funded Infoway Standards Collaborative, to:

support and sustain health information standards and foster collaboration to accelerate the implementation of pan-Canadian standards-based solutions.[5]

In the United States, the HITECH Act has established a statutory Health Information Standards Committee as well as a budget of $2 billion to support the Office of the National Coordinator for Health Information Technology (ONCHIT) to build the requisite infrastructure; develop health information exchange capabilities at the regional and state levels; and provide grants to assist with implementation, education adoption, and interoperability.

1.5.4 Lessons from Denmark

The development and deployment of healthcare interoperability standards are hard, but important lessons can be learnt from experience in Denmark, which has been uniquely successful in linking primary care doctors with laboratories, hospitals, and pharmacies.

---

[5] http://www.infoway-inforoute.ca/lang-en/standards-collaborative

In 1994 the Danish Government established MedCom as a national public project collaborating with public authorities, healthcare organizations, and private firms. Initially, a small group of experts developed a set standards for referrals, discharge letters, laboratory and radiology requests and reports, prescriptions, and reimbursement claims, which were based on European standards developed by CEN TC251. Between 1994 and 1996 these specifications were piloted in 11 independent locally managed projects, revised and retested in a further 15 projects. The experience gained was brought together in voluminous documentation:

> in such detail and so accurately and precisely that the overwhelming opinion is that MedCom's standards can indeed be used from Gedser to Skagen (from one end of Denmark to the other). (MedCom 1996)

Unfortunately, the early optimism (hubris) was not justified. The information sent was not always displayed or was misinterpreted due to ambiguity in data definitions of data elements, local coding schemes, and lack clarity about which elements were mandatory or optional. These issues were tackled in a 3-year consolidation project leading to revised standards and compulsory certification. By the end of 2002, 53 software versions had been certified and the error rate reduced by more than 70% (Johansen et al. 2003).

By 2008, all Danish GPs receive discharge summaries and lab results electronically; most prescriptions and referrals are also sent electronically. One of the key lessons is that success has taken time to achieve (Fig. 1.7) (MedCom 2008).

Three factors contributed to the Danish success.

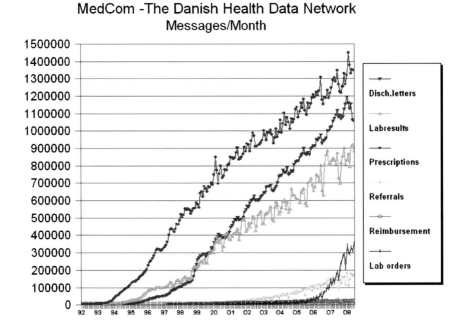

Fig. 1.7 Rise in interoperability in Denmark over the 16-year period 1992–2008. Source: Medcom

Steady political support was provided over many years, even when things went badly. Central support kept the stakeholders together and enabled modest direct financial incentives for participants. As in the United Kingdom, the use of computers by GPs is voluntary, but appropriate incentives produced high participation.

Second, the project was established as a formal collaboration between government, industry, and healthcare providers. Funding is provided one-third each by the state, the County Association, and other sources including doctor's organizations and industry (Protti and Johansen 2003).

Third, the project was proactive and innovative in training suppliers to understand the specifications in precisely the same way. For several years, usually in winter when the weather is bad in Denmark, a few programmers from each software supplier were invited to a special workshop on the Mediterranean coast. These workshops achieve high levels of attendance, collaboration, and bonding.

1.6   Evidence-Based Medicine

Evidence-based medicine (EBM) is one of the most important developments in the clinical use of information over the last 20 years, representing a sea change in the way that clinicians are taught to think. EBM addresses the challenge of finding a way to ensure that clinicians base their day-to-day decision-making on current best evidence. All too often clinicians are unaware of the available evidence or fail to apply it. Even those who are aware of the evidence risk making the wrong recommendations if they do not involve patients in the decision-making process (Guyatt et al. 2004).

EBM is the conscientious, explicit, and judicious use of current best evidence in making decisions about the care of individual patients. The practice of evidence-based medicine requires the integration of individual clinical expertise with the best available external clinical evidence from systematic research and our patient's unique values and circumstances (Straus et al. 2005).

The practice of EBM has five steps:

1. Convert our need for information (about prevention, diagnosis, prognosis, therapy, causation, etc.) into an answerable question
2. Track down the best evidence to answer the question
3. Critically appraise the evidence for validity and applicability
4. Integrate the critical appraisal with our clinical expertise and our patient's unique biology, values, and circumstances
5. Evaluate our performance

The first step is to identify the answerable questions.[6] There are two main types of questions – background and foreground.

Background questions occur when we have limited knowledge of the subject. These usually begin with a question root (who, what, where, when, how, why), followed by a verb and a disorder, e.g., "what causes Lyme disease?"[6]

---

[6] Lyme disease is an infectious disease transmitted by ticks.

Foreground questions ask for specific knowledge about managing patients with a disorder and are usually specific to a patient's problem, intervention (treatment, test, exposure, perception, etc.), comparison interventions (if relevant) and clinical outcomes of interest.

These questions can be grouped into ten central issues in clinical work:

- Clinical findings – history and physical examination
- Aetiology – causes of disease including iatrogenic forms
- Clinical manifestations – how often and when a disease causes clinical manifestations
- Differential diagnosis – possible causes (likely, serious, and responsive to treatment)
- Diagnostic tests – selection and interpretation of tests to confirm or exclude a diagnosis
- Prognosis – likely clinical course and possible complications
- Therapy – appropriate treatments
- Prevention – risk factors and screening
- Patient experience and meaning – empathy with the patient's situation
- Self-improvement

This classification of types of clinical question could be used to classify access to answers in electronic knowledge tools, using appropriate icons or color codes.

Detailed advice of a general in guidance needs to be tested for issues that make the instructions locally impractical, such as

- Burden – is the frequency too low to warrant action?
- Beliefs – do the risks outweigh the benefits?
- Bargain – are there better uses of our resources?
- Barriers – are there insurmountable barriers (geographic, organizational, traditional, etc.) to adoption?

These are referred to as the "killer Bs."

In her survey of implementing evidence-based findings, Greenhalgh notes that "standard issue" guidelines and protocols and didactic education are usually ineffective, while high-quality, computerized decision support and interactive hands-on education are much more effective (Fig. 1.8) (Greenhalgh 2001).

1.7 EHR System Functional Model

In this field, as in many others, one of the difficulties is definition of terms. What do we mean by the terms such as e-prescribing or clinical decision support? We need an agreed set of definitions so that users, regulators, purchasers, and suppliers can be sure that they are all talking about the same thing.

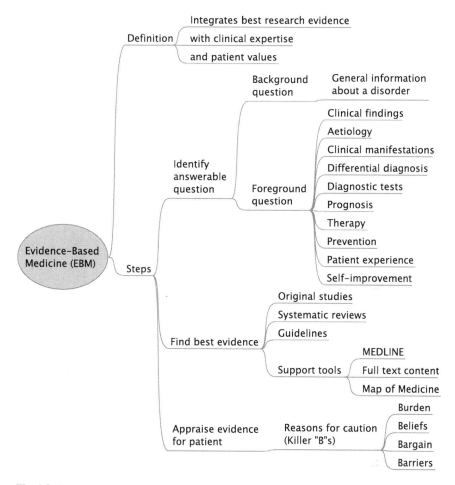

Fig. 1.8 Evidence-based medicine

The need for shared understanding of meaning is the core problem of health interoperability and is the central theme running through the whole of this book.

A comprehensive hierarchical breakdown of the capabilities of EHR systems has been developed by HL7 as the EHR System Functional Model (EHR-S FM). At the top level, there are three groups of functions[7]:

- Direct care: functions used for providing direct health care, or self-care, to one or more persons
- Supportive: functions that use EHR data to support the management of healthcare services and organizations
- Information Infrastructure: backbone elements of security, privacy, registry, interoperability, and terminology

---

[7]HL7 EHR System Functional Model: A Major Development Towards Consensus on Electronic Health Record System Functionality. A White Paper, 2004

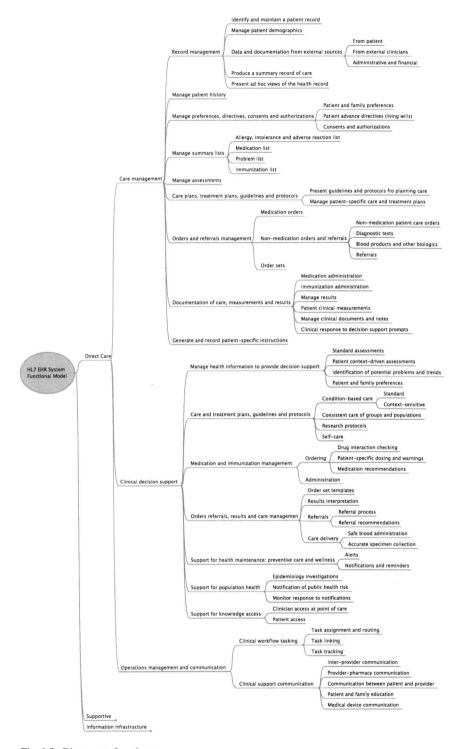

Fig. 1.9 Direct care functions

The whole HL7 EHR System Functional Model taxonomy is shown as an Annexe to this chapter; it provides an overview of the scope of health informatics in general and EHRs in particular. It provides a reference list of over 160 functions that may be present in an Electronic Health Record System (EHR-S).

The function list is described from a user perspective with the intent to enable consistent expression of system functionality. This EHR-S Functional Model, through the creation of Functional Profiles, enables a standardized description and common understanding of functions sought or available in a given setting (e.g., intensive care, cardiology, office practice in one country or primary care in another country).

The EHR-S FM is not a list of specifications for messaging, implementation, or conformance. Nor is it a specification for an actual EHR-S. However, the EHR-S FM is a valuable resource for industry, healthcare providers, governments, and other organizations to uses as a common language (tool) for discussing the functionality of electronic health records (Figs. 1.9–1.11).

Fig. 1.10 Supportive functions

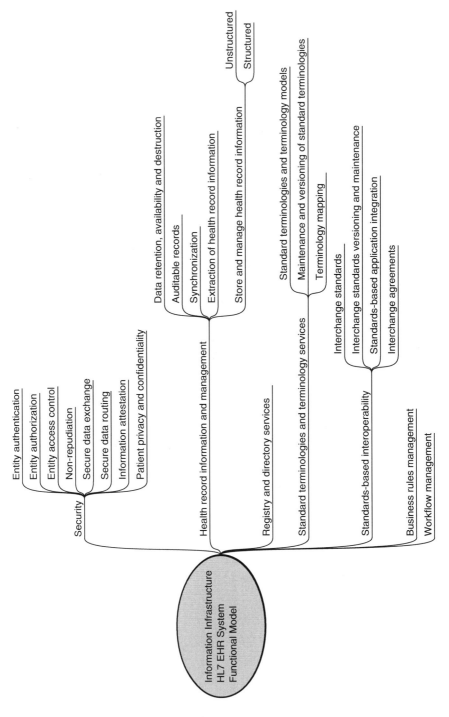

Fig. 1.11 Information infrastructure functions

Chapter 2
Why Interoperability is Hard

2.1 What is Interoperability?

The term interoperability means different things to different people. For example, the *HIMSS Dictionary of Healthcare Information Technology Terms, Acronyms and Organizations* lists 17 definitions, from the strictly technical factor to social, political, and organizational factors (HIMSS 2006).

A widely used definition is:

> Interoperability is ability of two or more systems or components to exchange information and to use the information that has been exchanged. (Institute of Electrical and Electronics Engineers 1990)

The HL7 EHR Interoperability Work Group has developed a framework, which covers three different points of view (Gibbons et al. 2007):

- Technical interoperability
- Semantic interoperability
- Process interoperability

These concepts are interdependent, and all three are needed to deliver significant business benefits.

Technical interoperability moves data from system A to system B, neutralizing the effects of distance. It is domain-independent. It does not know or care about the meaning of what is exchanged. One of the foundations of technical interoperability is Claude Shannon's information theory, which proved that it is possible to achieve 100% reliable communication over a noisy channel (Shannon 1948).

Semantic interoperability ensures that system A and system B understand the data in the same way. It allows computers to understand, interpret, and use data without ambiguity. This is specific to domain and context and usually involves the use of codes and identifiers. Semantic interoperability is at the core of what we usually mean by healthcare interoperability.

Process interoperability coordinates work processes, enabling the business processes at the organizations that house system A and system B to work together. Process interoperability is achieved when human beings share a common understanding, so that business systems interoperate and work processes are coordinated. They obtain benefits only when they use the new system in their day-to-day work; if it is not used as intended, for whatever reason, it is a failure. The importance of reengineering work processes to take full advantage of electronic systems has long been recognized, but the lessons have not been well-learnt.

The more we know about the three types of interoperability, the less likely we are to underestimate what is required to make health systems interoperable.

2.2 Benefits

The benefits of joined-up health care, to provide the right information at the right time and place, are predicated on deploying and using standards that enable computer systems to exchange information in a way that is safe, secure, and reliable.

The problem with standards is not that there are so many to choose from, but that we have not deployed those we have and that there is no regulator to make deployment happen. Standards that are not deployed are a waste of time and effort.

The center of the star at the right of the figure below indicates a single specification being used for linking the six domains (Fig. 2.1). This replaces the 15 separate specifications shown on the left-hand side.

The benefits increase exponentially and more parties are involved, because the number of interfaces needed to connect N systems increases using the formula (N^2–N)/2. Without using a standard in this way, linking two nodes needs only a single interface, which can easily be agreed by people sitting around a table; linking six nodes requires 15 interfaces; but linking 100 nodes requires 4,950 interfaces (Fig. 2.2).

Examples of functions needing interoperability cover a wide range:

- Requests for investigations such as laboratory tests and radiology
- Prescriptions for medication and other therapy in hospitals and in the community
- Orders for nursing care, equipment, meals, and patient transport
- Investigation reports from laboratories, radiology, and other diagnostic departments

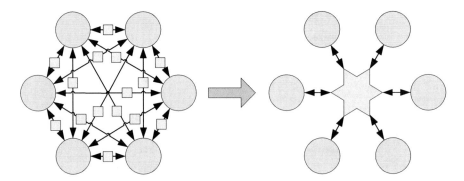

Fig. 2.1 The benefits of one standard

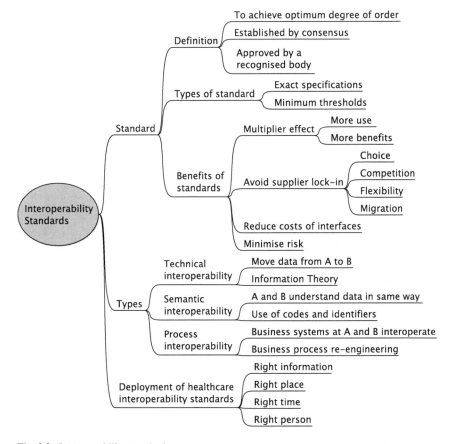

Fig. 2.2 Interoperability standards

- Administrative data such as patient registration and identification, clinic appointments, admissions, discharges, and transfers (ADT)
- Letters and memos from one clinician to another, including referral, clinic and discharge letters and opinions exchanged between hospital specialists, GPs, and community services
- Transfer and merging of electronic medical records between GPs and within and between hospitals and community services
- Information used for management, audit, and monitoring
- Commissioning, billing, and accountancy data

The numbers of transactions in healthcare systems can be vast. For example, in 2007 a single system (the EHR system) at one large hospital (the Mayo Clinic in Rochester, MN) processed 660 million HL7 messages or about two million messages a day.[1]

---

[1] Anthony J., Personal Communication.

2.3   Need for a Lingua Franca

Problems begin because each computer system stores data internally in a different way. This means that to communicate, data has to be translated from one format or internal language into another. The solution is often achieved by translating to an intermediate *lingua franca* (such as a version of HL7) that is understood by each party.

There are two translations in any interchange; first from the native language of System A to the lingua franca; second, from the lingua franca to the native language of System B.

When we talk about a language we mean both the syntax, grammar or information structure of the language and its semantics, vocabulary, or terminology.

The Rosetta stone from ancient Egypt, now in the British Museum, provides an analogy. The Rosetta stone contains the same proclamation in three languages, used by the priests (Hieroglyphic), the court (Greek), and the people (Demotic). In our context, the three languages could be those used by a sending system, the receiving system and a common lingua franca used for information interchange, such as HL7. The meaning of a message is precisely the same in each language but the notation is quite different.

The inscribers of the Rosetta stone only needed to perform their translation once, but in computer interoperability, each and every message has to be translated from one format to another without error. The choice of interchange language is not sufficient to ensure interoperability. Each transaction needs to be defined in unambiguous detail as part of a complete, consistent, coherent, and computer-readable set of specifications for interoperability between the machines to minimize any possibility of error.

2.4   Electronic Health Records

Clinical information is complex, but before exploring the variety let us look at ways in which clinical information is similar.

In their seminal paper, Rector, Nowlan, and Kay (Rector et al. 1991) describe how an electronic health record (EHR) is best thought of as a collection of statements, which is a faithful record of what clinicians have heard, seen, thought, and done. The EHR is not a collection of facts, but a set of observations about a particular patient, which have been made by clinicians, each at a specific time and place for some purpose.

Because each clinical statement is an observation, it is quite possible for two statements about the same event to disagree with each other, but this can be resolved if the context or provenance of each statement (who stated it, when, and where) is recorded. As with a work of art, a statement without provenance is of doubtful validity.

The ISO 13606 Reference Model for electronic health record communication sets out a useful hierarchy of clinical information in the context of exchanging clinical information between parties.[2]

- Extract: The top-level container of all or part of the electronic health record (EHR) of a single subject of care (patient) is known as the EHR Extract.
- Composition: The EHR is made up of Compositions. The Composition is a key concept; it is the set of information committed to one EHR by a clinician relating to a specific clinical encounter. Progress notes, laboratory test reports, discharge summaries, clinical assessments, and referral letters are all examples of Compositions.
- Folder: Compositions may be grouped together into Folders and sub-Folders. Folders may be used as containers for various purposes, grouping together the records by episode, care team, clinical specialty, condition, or time period.
- Entry: Each Composition comprises a number of Entries, also known as Clinical Statements. An Entry is the information recorded in the EHR as a result of a single clinical action, observation, interpretation, or intention. It may be thought of as a line in the record. Examples include the entries about a symptom, a laboratory result, a diagnosis, or a prescribed drug.
- Section: Entries may be grouped together in Sections. A Section is a grouping of related data within a Composition usually under a heading such as Presenting History, Allergies, Examination, Diagnosis, Medication, and Plans. Sections may have subsections.
- Element: The leaf node of the EHR hierarchy is an Element, which is a single data value, such as systolic blood pressure, a drug name, or body weight.
- Cluster: Related Elements may sometimes be grouped into Clusters. For example, systolic and diastolic blood pressures are separate Elements, but may be grouped into a Cluster (e.g., 140/90), which represents one Item in an Entry (Fig. 2.3).

Each clinical specialty has its own way of working. The grand vision of joined-up health care is predicated on the notion that patient records can be shared electronically between clinicians from different specialties. Historically, this has been largely wishful thinking. There have been few successes and many failures. Yet, this is the promise of President Obama's HITECH Act and was a specific but largely unrealized objective of the NHS National Program for IT, which was established in 2002. Every success has depended on the certified use of agreed standards.

First, we must recognize that it is difficult to share information between different computer applications even within the same specialty. This is because each computer application stores data in a different way and may use different internal codes. The GP2GP project in England illustrates the point. Patients in England have a lifelong

---

[2] ISO 13606-1:2008. Health Informatics – Electronic health record communication – Part 1: Reference Model

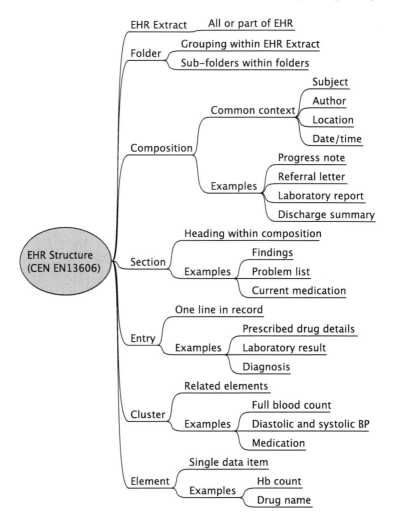

Fig. 2.3 CEN EN13606 EHR Structure

medical record, which follows them when they move from one GP to another. In an ideal world, each patient's records would be sent electronically from their old practice to the new in a manner that minimizes risk and avoids the need to reenter information.

The GP2GP project set out to do just that, although the project's leaders recognized that it could a poisoned chalice.[15] The work has been every bit as difficult as predicted and each record has to be carefully quality-checked before transmission and on receipt; but after 7 years work it is a qualified success story, but not the Holy Grail.

Even within the same specialty, the information about an outpatient visit differs greatly from that about an elective surgical operation or inpatient discharge summary following an emergency admission.

For example, consider the following types of document. At one level each of these could be regarded as a discharge summary, written from a hospital to a GP, summarizing the outcome of a visit or episode of care. At another level each is very different.

- An elderly patient discharged home after a fracture
- Mother and baby following birth
- A family after a course of counseling by a psychologist
- Consultation report from an ophthalmologist notifying a proposed operation for cataract
- Letter to GP notifying that a patient has been diagnosed with cancer
- Discharge from hospital following coronary artery bypass grafts
  Postmortem report

Each of these is a composition which relates to a discharge event, but the information contents are extremely diverse.

Similarly, people sometimes talk about clinical laboratory reports as if they were homogeneous, but the content of each type of clinical laboratory report is quite different, as is the work done in each type of laboratory. Histopathology examines cells with a microscope; microbiology grows bacteria to identify them; haematologists count blood cells; and clinical chemistry measures chemical concentrations by measuring the intensity of color changes when chemical are added. The only commonality is that they all work with specimens extracted from patients. Yet, the specimen workflow is not fixed; sometimes the requester supplies the sample, sometimes the sample is taken by the laboratory, and sometimes the patient is required to be present in person.

2.5   Analysis is Paramount

Much of the hard work involved in interoperability lies in teasing out the hundreds or thousands of different use cases. Information technology analysts, and those who pay them, tend to focus on the high-volume transactions, which are common across all specialties and prefer not to deal with the specific needs of the smaller specialties. Yet, the common stuff is not usually the most important clinically. The value of any piece of information is, like a piece of art, often related to its rarity.

Even apparently simple concepts such as name and address become complex on closer inspection and in spite of years of effort, there are still no satisfactory international standards for name and address. Even the order in which names and addresses are written varies substantially between countries.

One person may have several names and several addresses, which they can change at will. For example, a woman may use both her maiden and married names in different contexts. One person may use several addresses (home, work, previous, holiday, etc.) and each address may also be associated with different people, such as family members, friends, or colleagues.

The naming rules for addresses are complex in themselves. For purposes of addressing, buildings have names or numbers or both; they can be subdivided into units, apartments, or rooms. Multiple factors identify the physical location of each building, including its street, locality (village, part of a town or district), town or city, state (county or region), country, and postal code, as well as supplemental data such as map-grid references and instructions on how to find the house.

One way to simplify the problem is to distinguish clearly between information that needs to be processed by computer and that which needs to be read and understood by human users. Computer processing is essential when data elements need to be identified, matched, retrieved, or counted. This type of information must be structured, complete, unambiguous, and validated. These are relatively few but important.

Human readers, responsible for any aspect of the care of an individual patient, need information in a format that they can understand. This does not have to be highly structured, although it needs to be easy to read and accompanied by supporting contextual data such as who wrote it, when, and where, and for what purpose. Humans are good at judging the significance of small discrepancies, but digital computers are unforgiving of a single unexpected bit.

2.6   Complex Specifications Create Errors

Building a single link to exchange data between two computers is relatively straightforward. Everyone sits around a table and works out what they are going to do. This approach works for very small projects, where each person is co-located, but it does not scale. One alternative approach is to develop rigorous implementation guidelines, but these are often complex and voluminous. For example, in the NHS Pathology Message Implementation Project (PMIP), which was a successful national project to send clinical chemistry and hematology laboratory test reports to GPs in England, the implementation guidelines consisted of 185 separate Word documents, running to almost one million words. The endeavor to be rigorous leads to errors caused by the sheer length and complexity of the specifications.

A different sort of problem arises when the domain experts (such as doctors, nurses, and managers) are unable to fully understand these specifications due to the complexity of language or simply the time it takes to read them. As a consequence, these specifications may not be reviewed or checked at the specification stage as thoroughly as is required.

Errors multiply according to the:

- Probability of misunderstanding any part of the specification, which depends on difficulty of language and domain and technical knowledge of participants (people with high levels of both technical and domain knowledge are rare).
- The length of specification: In a long specification, exactly the same idea may be presented in different ways in two places, but each may be understood differently. If large blocks of information are replicated in different sections, with small but important differences, these differences may be missed.

- Number of options permitted.
- Number of times different implementations to be made: Each implementation involves mapping or translating the specification into the local implementation language.

Misunderstanding inevitably leads to error; errors increase costs and reduce quality, create delays, and hit profits and reputation.

Successful specifications avoid errors by limiting scope, being easy to understand, relatively short, and simple, with few if any options.

Many problems are caused by inadequate thought and preparation by both users and suppliers. If time is running out, it is all too easy to be vague in a specification or offer the implementer a choice of options depending on the local context.

2.7   Users and Suppliers are both Guilty

Often, both users and suppliers genuinely believe that they are in full agreement until the moment when users try to use the final product. Problems lie on both sides.

Users do not fully understand what they want, let alone what other parties can or cannot provide; they do not commit enough time or effort up-front to fully review written requirements specifications; they then will not commit to these, and insist on new features after the schedule and budget have been fixed. Most users are technically unsophisticated, do not understand the development life cycle, and are simply unable to perform the sort of scrutiny which is demanded of them. This is one of the reasons why users need a far higher level of education in health informatics than has been provided in the past.

Suppliers are equally guilty. They often try to shoehorn the users' requirements to fit their existing systems or patterns, believing that it will be quicker, cheaper, and lower-risk to reuse what already exists, while failing to grasp that the user will never be happy with it and really needs something else. Suppliers may also lack the specialized domain knowledge to fully understand the user's business processes at the required level of detail. This is one other reason why most suppliers focus attention on the high-volume aspects of health informatics, because they do not have the domain knowledge to deal with the idiosyncrasies of each and every specialty.

2.8   Shared Meaning

Shared meaning between computers requires shared understanding between all of the human participants.

An analogy is the purchase of a new kitchen. The kitchen designer prepares a plan of the new kitchen. This plan is checked, reviewed, and signed off by the customer and is the basis of the contract. All of the details that are important to the user (sizes, color, etc.) are specified precisely and agreed with the customer in a way that is also understood by the manufacturer (implementer). This plan uses a precise technical notation, which provides a means of communicating precisely the user's needs to the implementer (manufacturer), in a form that can be understood by both. Manufacture only begins after the customer has agreed the specification.

Manufacture uses a different but related set of plans, which specify the exact materials and products to be used down to the precise specification of every last screw.

The challenge in interoperability is harder; it is to ensure understanding horizontally across business processes, which may be in different organizations (between domain expert and domain expert) and vertically within computer systems suppliers, between users and developers who speak different dialects (Fig. 2.4).

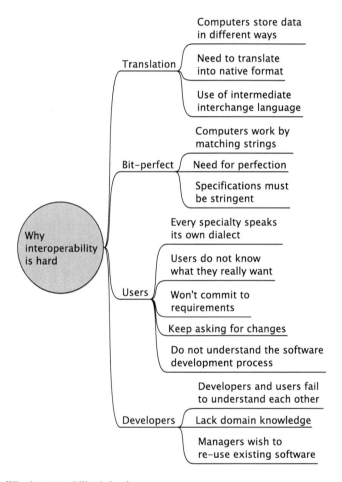

Fig. 2.4 Why interoperability is hard

Chapter 3
Models

A deep understanding of what it means to create or apply a model underpins the way we interact with the world and how likely we are to be successful in achieving our goals. Models define the way we learn about the world, interpret what we see, and apply our knowledge to affect change, whether that is through our own actions or through the use of technology like a computer.

Enrico Coiera (Coiera 2003)

3.1 Modeling Basics

Models play a central role in interoperability, and a clear understanding of modeling is an important foundation skill. Most people can learn to understand models quite easily, but it is much harder to create good models.

Models are either representations of aspects of interest in the real world, such as maps, or specifications for things that have not yet been built, such as blueprints used by architects and engineers. Each model is a simplified representation of aspects of the real world or the world we wish to create.

For example, an architect produces hundreds of different drawings or diagrams when designing a building – each diagram having a specific purpose and relating to a single project. Any single type of diagram shows only certain aspects of a situation – everything else is ignored. This simplification provides both the power (it makes the situation understandable) and the weakness of diagrams (each diagram has a limited scope and some things are left out).

If a single model is used to document each major stage of a project, then each diagram is a single view of that model, ensuring that all parts are coherent. Each component is recorded only once, irrespective of how many diagrams it is used in. This makes it easier to make changes and to ensure that the whole model and its diagrams retain coherence and consistency.

T. Benson, *Principles of Health Interoperability HL7 and SNOMED*, HI, DOI 10.1007/978-1-84882-803-2_3, © Springer-Verlag London Limited 2010

3.1.1 Model Driven Architecture

In addition to models of the real world (AS IS) and specifications (TO BE), we can build models at different levels of abstraction. The Object Management Group (OMG), which is the group responsible for the major information modeling standards, has defined Model Driven Architecture (MDA) as a framework for the development of object-oriented software (Mellor et al. 2004). MDA uses four types of model, with mappings between them:

- Computational-Independent Model (CIM)
- Platform-Independent Model (PIM), which describes the conceptual design of a system
- Platform-Specific Model (PSM), which specifies the implementable design
- Code, the actual software code written, sometimes referred to as "wire-format"

A key feature of MDA is formal mapping between each of the deliverables: CIM to PIM, PIM to PSM, and PSM to Code. This provides traceability between each stage in the process.

In healthcare, Mead has argued that computable semantic interoperability needs four pillars (Mead 2006). These are:

- A common model across all domains of interest
- This model to be grounded on robust data type specification
- Methodology for binding elements of the model with terms from concept-based terminologies
- A formally defined process for defining specific structures to be exchanged between machines – the data interchange standard itself

3.1.2 The CEN Model

The European working group responsible for healthcare communications and message standards (CEN TC251 WG3) was one of the first groups to adopt this approach.[1] The story of how it came about is worth recounting. The problem was how to choose an interchange format (syntax) to be used in European interoperability standards. At that time, there were plenty of candidates. This was a time of "syntax wars," with a range of competing standards and observers such as Tanenbaum could quip: "the nice thing about standards is that there are so many of them to choose from."[2]

A project team was established to investigate the problem. First, it created a small set of technology-neutral general message specifications (GMD), using an object model similar to UML. Secondly, the team tested whether each GMD could

---

[1] The author was the founder convenor of CEN TC251 WG3 from 1991 to 1997, when the work described here was performed

[2] Tanenbaum A, *Computer Networks Second Edition*. http://en.wikiquote.org/wiki/Andrew_S._Tanenbaum

be implemented in each of five target interchange languages, by developing an implementable message specification (IMS) in each target interchange language (CEN Report 1993).

The main conclusion of the study was that whilst none was ideal, each interchange format was adequate for current needs and that the "selection of an interchange format was not the largest obstacle for realizing message exchange in healthcare."

While doing this, the project team recognized the power and value of the GMDs. They proposed, and CEN TC251 accepted, that the specification of syntax-independent specifications (GMDs) should be the core of message standardization. These could then be implemented in any syntax of choice, such as EDIFACT or HL7.

The approach was further developed over the following years to identify three main types of specification (CEN Report 1996):

- A single domain-wide model, which acts as a reference for all others. This is now referred to as a reference model.
- Technology-independent message specifications, each of which is a constraint on the domain wide model. These specifications may have various levels of granularity and scope from the broad and general to the narrow and stringent.
- Implementable message specifications, which are direct mappings from the technology-independent message specifications into the selected syntax.

These ideas were also adopted and modified by HL7 in the development of HL7 Version 3 (Beeler 1998) and are also found in ISO 13606.

3.1.3 Modeling Maturity

Human beings find it easier to work with formal graphical models and diagrams than with unstructured narrative. For example, if you wish to describe a place to someone else, it can be done in various ways:

- A face-to-face conversation
- A text narrative
- A structured narrative with headings and sections
- Ad hoc diagrams and pictures
- A formal map using standard conventions

It needs little imagination to recognize that these are listed in increasing order of preciseness and ability to convey meaning accurately and reliably. The same applies to specifications, which is why engineers use formal blueprints to specify how a machine is to be built. Computer engineers and analysts also use models.

Kleppe and Warmer (Warmer and Kleppe 2003) classify the role of modeling in a project using six Modeling Maturity Levels (0–5).

- Level 0: No specification; the specification of software is not written down. It is kept in the minds of the developers. At this level we find conflicting views between developers and users and it is impossible to understand the code if coders leave (and they always do, sooner or later).

- Level 1: Textual specification; the software is specified by a natural language text (e.g., English), written down in one or more documents. Such specifications are usually ambiguous, because natural language is ambiguous; it is impossible to keep this type of specification up-to-date when code is changed.
- Level 2: Text with models; a textual specification is enhanced with several models to show some of the main structures of the system. This is easier to understand, but still difficult to maintain.
- Level 3: Models with text; the specification of software is written down in one or more models. In addition to these models, natural language text is used to explain details, the background, and the motivation of the models, but the core of the specifications lies in the models.
- Level 4: Precise models; the specification of the software is written down in one or more models. Natural language can still be used to explain the background and motivation of the models, but it takes on the same role as comments in source code. At this level, coders do not make business decisions and incremental development is facilitated by direct transformation from model to code.
- Level 5: Models only; the models are precise and detailed enough to allow complete code generation. The code generators at this level have become as trustworthy as compilers; therefore, no developer needs to even look at the generated code (Fig. 3.1).

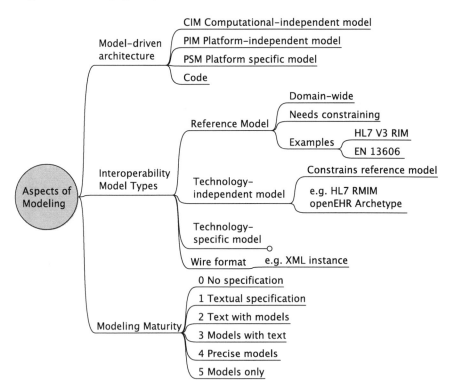

Fig. 3.1 Modeling foundation concepts

3.2 Life Cycle

The life cycles of all software development projects, including interoperability projects are broadly similar. The stages include:

- Scope and objectives
- Process analysis and design
- Conceptual design specification
- Technology specific specification
- Coding
- Testing
- Deployment, including user education, data migration, and installation
- Support and maintenance

The first step is to understand the domain and the opportunities for improvement. This phase articulates the problems which need to be solved and the benefits that can be achieved.

The next step is to refine the scope and define the detail needed to deliver the benefits in a logical, platform-independent way. At this stage a range of alternative implementation platforms may be considered. In MDA terms, this defines the platform-independent model (PIM).

Only when all stakeholders have agreed and accepted the PIM, should we start to work on the platform specific implementation. Interoperability requires a shared understanding of what we are trying to do, shared between all interested stakeholders including users, such as clinicians, sponsors, and software developers.

This is difficult. It is a challenge to achieve a shared understanding on a human-to-human level between one user and one developer, but the challenge is enormously greater as the number of parties grows. An underlying assumption of computable semantic interoperability is that both sender and receiver share the same understanding of what each and every data element means (Fig. 3.2).

3.3 Preliminary Business Analysis

The preliminary business analysis may have four main deliverables, which may form a single report:

- Scope statement provides the big picture of what it is all for, including the case for action, objectives, and scope delineation.
- Story-boards provide an intimate view of how individuals use the system to obtain value.
- Requirements description provides a structured description of the most important aspects of the system using activity diagrams and class diagrams.
- Glossary and value sets.

Fig. 3.2 Project life cycle

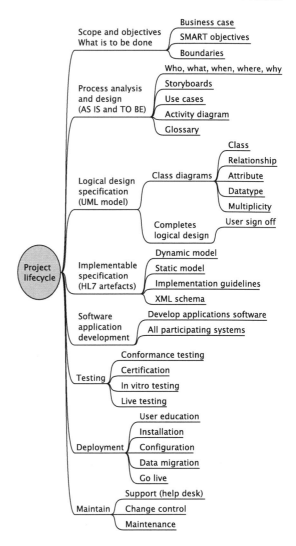

3.3.1 Scope

The scope statement provides a management summary of the whole project. It summarizes why the project is needed, what it should achieve, and what is excluded, showing the boundaries and responsibilities of the system of interest. Many problems with both systems and stakeholders occur when developers set the boundaries and/or responsibilities differently from those expected by the users.

Any change in scope must be incorporated into the scope statement, to prevent scope creep. However, changes in scope are an inevitable part of most projects, as more is understood about the domain and the user needs. It can be useful to set out the Scope Statement under the three subheadings: the case for action, objectives, and scope delineation.

- The case for action is a concise, comprehensive, and compelling case for why the project is needed. It describes the context, the problem, user needs, and the consequences of doing nothing.
- The objectives provide a clearly stated focus of what this particular project is about. These should be SMART goals:
- Specific, clearly stating what you want to achieve
- Measurable, with a means of measuring whether or not you are achieving the objectives
- Attainable within the available resource constraints
- Relevant to the organization's needs
- Time-bounded, with clearly dated milestones
- Scope delineation clearly shows the boundary of the project – what is in or out of scope. This may also include constraints such as standards and other work that must be used, as well as functionality that are explicitly outside the scope.

3.3.2   Storyboard

Storyboards provide a useful means of capturing domain knowledge, providing specific detail, as opposed to the high level of the scope statement. They provide examples of the participants involved, the information flow, real-world situations where the services may be used and provide an informative overview, which assists in the whole development process. Storyboards may also provide a starting point for the development of test data.

Several different storyboards should be developed to cover each of the ways the system may be used.

Each storyboard is a story, told in the present tense, describing in detail how a set of named actors use the system to carry out a single instance of a task. Storyboards do not contain options. If there are two ways of doing something, then two storyboards are needed, one for each option.

Storyboards describe situations that represent either typical or extreme cases. They provide useful context that everyone can understand and also provide a starting point for developing test data.

Each storyboard can be written by a domain expert, checked by a business analyst, revised, and then discussed in a group to ensure that it captures the process accurately. Storyboards of the AS IS situation should not change, but TO BE storyboards may well need to be updated as the design of the system evolves.

Storyboards generate documentation that is useful at all stages of the development. For example, storyboards illustrate the participants involved, indicate variances in information flow, describe real-world situations where the services may be used and provide an informative overview.

An example of a story board for breast cancer triple assessment is the following:

Jane Sharp attends the One Stop Breast Clinic, having been referred urgently by her GP after noticing a lump in her breast. She sees Dr Lee who takes her history (presenting symptoms, appropriate medical, and family history) and performs a physical examination. Jane then proceeds to mammography, where a fine needle aspirate (FNA) is also collected. The mammograph is reported by a radiologist and a pathologist reports the FNA. Jane is asked to return later to hear the result of these tests. On her return she is relieved to find out that the results are negative.

The development of storyboards provides an opportunity to gather information concerning representative forms and information sets currently being used; the functionality of existing computer applications, including details of data dictionaries; relevant standards and specifications from national and international bodies; regulatory constraints, including security and data protection requirements; and future developments and the potential to simplify and rationalize communications.

3.3.3   Business Analysis

Clear understanding of the business information flow is critical; mistakes made here affect everything else. Failure to fully nail down and specify the exact information flows now and in the future system is one of the most common causes of systems failure.

It is useful to prepare two documents; a description of the present system (AS IS) and a separate description of the proposed system (TO BE). The AS IS description is an accurate description of what happens now and can be easily checked by existing users as to whether it is right or wrong. The TO BE system does not yet exist, so it is much harder to check. Some people find it useful to visualize and test out how imaginary systems will work using storyboards (see below).

The business analysis is best done as collaboration between one or more business analysts and domain experts, such as users. The requirements are not frozen finally, but continue to evolve, being updated as more is learnt and understood about the domain.

There is no one right or wrong way to understand and elucidate the business processes. Each experienced analyst uses his or her own approach. One approach I have used and found useful to capture key aspects of the business processes is to use structured narrative descriptions, under the headings of service overview, transactions, participants, locations, identification, evidence, transaction outcome, and rules:

1. *Service Overview* elaborates the domain scope, describes each service provided and expected to be of value. A service typically represents the outermost use case of interest. Each service can be decomposed into sub-services and transactions

(see below). The broad scope of the service needs to be considered to ensure that the whole system is developed in a joined-up way, avoiding silos.

2. Each of the main *Transactions* (when) is described, together with an indication of its timing, origin, trigger event and pre-conditions, destination, purpose, volume, and outcomes. Transactions are the main use cases of interest. Each transaction is typically an exchange of information with a common set of participants, requiring evidence and generating some outcome(s); each transaction achieves some useful goal for the primary actor and has a trigger event and pre-conditions.

3. *Participants* (who) are the parties, things, and systems that are involved and how these relate to one another. Participants may be physical such as people, things (e.g., specimens), machines (e.g., computer systems), or abstract such as organizations. They are the things about which information is recorded, whether they are active participants in transactions or third parties.

4. *Locations* (where) are physical or virtual places associated with a service or transaction, such as where things take place or the origin and destinations of data. They may be physical or virtual (on a computer network). It is particularly important to specify exactly where transactions take place when considering the differences between the AS IS and TO BE models.

5. *Identification* (what) of participants, locations, and information objects is crucial, because computers systems need unique identifiers. We need to identify what identifiers are used, who or what assigns them, and what information may be accessible as a result of knowing this identifier, including any legal restrictions in using it outside of the main purpose. Many organizations assign their own identifiers (e.g., NHS number), but there are important legal restrictions in using these outside of their main purpose. Furthermore, significant numbers of individuals do not know their assigned identifier or do not have one. Soft identifiers, such as name, address, date of birth, and gender may be needed to match up individual people. These are "soft," because people can change their names and addresses, give false dates of birth, and even change gender. An identifier may refer to an individual instance (such as a person or the serial number on a machine) or to a category of things (such as the bar codes printed on packets of corn flakes).

   (a) Computer systems need unique identifiers. In every context, we need to identify what identifiers are used, how the assigner is identified, and what information is accessible as a result of knowing this identifier. For example, we may need to know what data elements are likely to be made available to each user and what mechanism is in place to ensure that all users share the same meaning – for example, do they have access to the same reference database?

   (b) *Evidence* is the information needed to support each transaction, which needs to be known prior to the transaction being triggered; it may be obtained either by direct data input or by querying a database. Evidence is usually associated with one of the participants in the Interaction.

   (c) *Outcome* describes the possible results of each transaction, including the post-conditions and responsibilities of each participant. For example, updates to records and letter generation would be described here.

(d) *Rules* include the regulations and constraints governing the transactions, including nonfunctional requirements, security, and privacy. Rules may be legislative or policy, logical, procedural, or temporal. A Rule can be free-standing or part of a multilevel hierarchy of decision-making criteria. Rule documentation should include all rules, regulations, error handling, reference data, and coding schemes related to the Transaction, which have not been documented elsewhere. Rules are often important in determining how to handle failures and errors.

3.3.4 Glossary

A glossary of terms used is another important deliverable. It contains the name of each term, description/definition, and source (if obtained from another reference). Whenever terms are used they should always have the meaning specified in the glossary. The glossary may be populated from material such as: forms and information sets currently being exchanged, the functionality of existing computer applications in this domain, including data dictionaries and relevant national and international standards.

This process described above is iterative, with continual feedback between work on finalizing the scope statement, business process analysis, storyboards, and glossary development. This stage may be fairly short (in comparison with the total project), but it is most important. Mistakes made at this stage can be expensive to correct later.

These early deliverables should not be "frozen" but need to be reviewed regularly throughout the project and updated and necessary.

Business processes can be described using use case descriptions, activity diagrams, and sequence diagrams. The static structure is described using class diagrams. These tools are described in Chapter 4 (Fig. 3.3).

3.4 Conceptual Design

Related conceptual specifications for different use cases should be modeled as views into a larger conceptual model. A single conceptual model may contain any number of consistent specifications, each tailored for a different use case. The conceptual specification should be part of a contract for the technical work to be done later.

The conceptual design specification specifies the detailed design of each part of the system in a way that is technologically neutral and that both users and technical staff can understand, check, and sign off. This may comprise a set of UML (Unified Modeling Language) class diagrams.

Each conceptual design specification should meet the following criteria:

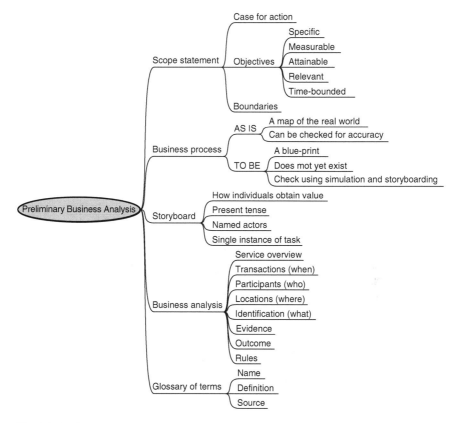

Fig. 3.3 Preliminary business analysis

3.4.1 Criteria

The following criteria (the 8 Cs) are proposed:

1. *Comprehensive.* The model should include all high-volume transactions within its scope, being sufficiently expressive and general to fully represent and describe each at different levels of sophistication. It needs to be extensible to incorporate new requirements and local needs.
2. *Context explicit.* The model should describe not only the static structure of transaction payloads, but also the business processes surrounding each transaction, specifying trigger events, delays, timing and other constraints, business rules, outcomes, and error handling.
3. *Complete in itself.* The model should represent both data structure and processes (dynamic behavior). The sequence of activities must be clearly indicated (e.g., whether the order in which tasks are performed is significant or not). The model

should be documented internally so it stands alone without need to reference other documents or manuals.

4. *Consistent.* Each term used should be defined unambiguously and the source of each definition referenced. The same concept should only have one name, avoiding synonymy, and the same term should not ever be reused for a different concept, to avoid homonyms. A common architecture, notation, and terminology should be used to define each and every element of the model. Any problem may be divided into several sub-problems, whose solution may then be pursued separately and can be expanded or consolidated.

5. *Compatible.* Data element definitions should be compatible with international standards. Platform-independent models facilitate transfer across institutions and allow different end-user suppliers to implement compatible solutions using different proprietary technologies and to migrate to new technologies in the future.

6. *Composable.* Parts may be reused and combined freely with each other to produce new ones, possibly for purposes quite different from that for which they were originally designed. There should be minimum dependency between parts, so that any change or error in one is not propagated to others.

7. *Comprehensible.* Understandable, so that each part can be understood and reviewed on its own by clinical end users, domain experts, and implementers. A simple graphical notation is ideal, which ought to be easy to learn and use. Names and definitions should be written in the language of the user. Abstract terms and neologisms (words or phrases with newly coined meaning) should be avoided. Each element needs to be able to be understood separately by a human reader without need to consult external reference manuals.

8. *Conformance-testable.* Messages based on the model need to be tested against the model to demonstrate conformance. As few alternative methods as possible should be provided for doing any business task. Navigation across associations should be in one direction only. Recursive structures should be avoided as much as possible. Many-to-many relationships should be avoided and zero-to-many multiplicities used as little as possible. Basis for test data (Fig. 3.4).

Software engineers use technology-specific specifications to design the software that creates and reads the actual messages sent. If there is any doubt as to the meaning of any part of the specification then they need to consult the whole specification (both the technology-specific and conceptual parts). The conceptual specification should be regarded as the ultimate authority, because this is what the domain experts can understand and approve.

The mapping from a conceptual specification to a technology-specific interchange language should not permit any changes in the semantic content either by addition or constraint. The technology-specific specification indicates the "wire format" that is implemented, tested, deployed, and supported.

A conceptual specification supplements the traditional technology-specific specification and can be understood by all stakeholders. The full specification should

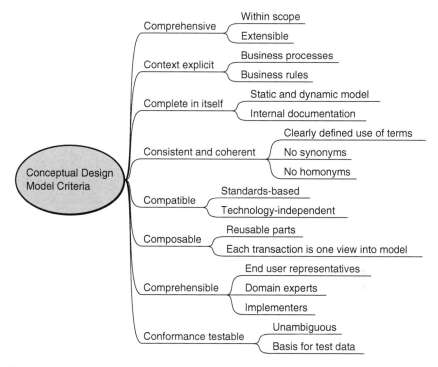

Fig. 3.4 Conceptual design model criteria

comprise both the conceptual specification and the technology-specific specification (Benson 2007).

It can be part of a contract for the technical work to be done later.

The conceptual design specification is the detailed conceptual design of what is to be provided. It is not a model of the real world or of an existing system and does not usually cover the nonfunctional requirements of the system. Being technologically neutral, it does not specify what software shall be used.

Each use case can be modeled as one view into a larger model. A single UML model can support a large number of different use cases, and the conceptual design specifications can be output in several formats including diagrams, hyperlinked documents, and as XML Metadata Interchange (XMI), which is a standard used to pass model data as XML between UML tools and software generation tools.

The crucial point about the conceptual design specification is that it is the most detailed specification that users should, with help, be able to understand, criticize, review, and sign off. It can be the basis of a contract between users and the developers. All stakeholders need to share and agree the conceptual design specification, but the technology-specific specification may be private to each developer.

3.4.2   Technology-Specific Design

The technology-specific specification sets out exactly what is to be implemented in the chosen interchange language (e.g., HL7 Version 3), including implementation guidelines and XML schema if required. This is the specification of what is to be built, tested, deployed, and supported. Technologies change and evolve much faster than the conceptual design specification. The same conceptual design can be implemented in many different ways. The mapping from the conceptual design specification to any specific implementation should not involve any changes, either by addition or constraint, in the semantic content.

The objective of business analysis is to capture the complete requirements in a form that is fully understood by users and technical staff. This feeds into the conceptual design, platform-specific specifications, and ultimately forms the basis for testing and conformance. The development of the Business Analysis is iterative with a number of parallel strands. Business Processes are documented initially using UML Activity Diagrams and Class Diagrams, supported by detailed definitions (Glossary) of every data item. UML models provide an effective and flexible way of sharing understanding about the system under consideration.

The next part of this report shows how these technologies may be applied to a simple example, Colorectal Cancer referrals.

3.5   Colorectal Cancer Referral

3.5.1   Scope and Background

This example describes the process when a GP refers a patient suffering from colorectal symptoms for urgent endoscopy to diagnose or exclude possible cancer. This example uses a two-stage process, based on NICE Guidelines (NICE 2004) and the work of Selvachandran and colleagues at the Leighton Hospital, Crewe (Selvachandran et al. 2002).

Colorectal (CR) cancer is the second most common cancer, in terms of both incidence and mortality in England and Wales. With about 30,000 cases a year, each GP is likely to come across about one new case each year. Survival is strongly related to speed of diagnosis and the research literature shows evidence of delays, often lasting a year or more, between the onset of symptoms of colorectal cancer and diagnosis. This is due to patient delay in reporting symptoms, and to a lesser extent, delays by the GP and hospital. For example, a national survey of NHS patients in 1999/2000 found that 37% had to wait over 3 months for their first hospital appointment and 13% waited 7 or more months.

The scope is limited to the business process and decision criteria used to make the "two-week possible colorectal cancer" referral decision by the GP in his or her surgery. All other aspects of the problem are out of scope. In particular, the processes used to book the GP and the endoscopy appointments, and consideration of problems other than possible colorectal cancer, are out of scope.

3.5.2 Objectives

The objectives of the process are:

1. Reduce the number of days between initial reporting of symptoms and final diagnosis. NB. Survival is strongly related to speed of diagnosis. Five-year survival is:

   (a) Eighty-three percent for Dukes Stage A (localized within the bowel wall)
   (b) Sixty-four percent for Stage B (penetrating the bowel wall)
   (c) Thirty-eight percent for Stage C (cancer in Lymph nodes)
   (d) Three percent for Stage D (distant metastases, most often in the liver)

2. Reduce the number of false negatives (cancer cases missed) and false positives (the number of urgent referrals that are subsequently shown to be free from cancer)

3. Reduce the number of appointments required

3.5.3 Participants and Locations

Referral for possible CR cancer involves not only the direct participants, suc
patient, the GP, and practice staff, but other stakeholders, notably the st
units to which the patient may be referred, including doctors, nurses,
and clerks.

The patient complains of symptoms and may have cancer. The
primary source of information about history and symptoms and mu
physical and endoscopic examinations and diagnostic imagin
providing samples of blood, feces, etc. for laboratory tests.

The second key participant is the GP, who takes the decis
to refer the patient for endoscopy. Reception and secretari
may also undertake some tasks. Although CR Cancer is th
type of cancer, each GP sees about one new CR cancer pa
of symptoms that warrant detailed assessment is not
any tools used to facilitate this need to be unobtrusive
a month present with symptoms that warrant furthe
patients a year need to be referred for urgent end

Other actors, such as the e-Booking service
outputs from the interaction, but are not invol
the patient should be referred.

Although the main interaction takes place at the GP surgery, the patient may not know some of the information at the time and may need to consult relatives about details of family history or cross-check the dates at which they first complained of symptoms. For these reasons, detailed history may be collected at the patient's home using a web-based questionnaire. Patients who cannot use a web-browser can be given a paper questionnaire, which can be scanned or transcribed. Much of the information used to make this decision is relevant to subsequent care and treatment and may be collected in a form suited for use in a referral letter.

3.5.4 Outcome

The outcome is a decision of whether or not to refer for urgent (possible cancer) endoscopy. The process can be thought of as two "yes/no" decisions.

1. Does this patient have any CR symptoms that might be indicative of CR cancer, sufficient to warrant more investigation – this "triage" decision is based on the NICE criteria, which include presenting symptoms, physical examination, and patient's age. If this decision is positive, then take detailed history.

   decision – whether to refer the patient for urgent hospital investigation detailed structured history covering: symptoms and presenting and past medical history. If this is also positive, then refer

description of how the

bowel
GP,

gests that
d at home.
set of details

up from his wife
morning, the surgery
come in and see Dr

s of his history on her
that there is some cause

for concern. Dr Price notices this and that the symptoms and history warrant urgent endoscopic investigation.

She explains the situation to John and makes a referral to the local Endoscopy Unit via an electronic booking service (Choose and Book). The information collected by the OCR scanner is sufficient to produce a structured referral letter, which Dr Price checks, authorizes, and sends.

John is naturally anxious and so Dr Price goes into an electronic reference (Map of Medicine), where it lists the main reasons for referral for possible CR cancer as well as other data. She prints out a copy of the relevant page and gives it to John.

The next day, John is contacted by the Endoscopy Unit and makes arrangements for the test to be done the next week.

Here only one storyboard has been provided, but in any real project a number of storyboards should be developed covering all of the main scenarios.

3.5.6 Business Process Diagram

The flow can also be shown as a business process diagram using the BPMN notation (Fig. 1). This is similar to an activity diagram (Fig. 3.5).

The main locations (GP Surgery, patient's home, and specialist Endoscopy Unit) are shown as pools. The GP Surgery is subdivided into two lanes (reception and GP consulting room). The rounded rectangles represent separate tasks and the circular icons represent discrete events. The diamond shapes represent decision branches and the "O" icon inside states that the branches are mutually exclusive (OR). The clock icon represents a time-specific event or delay, while the envelope icon represents a message.

The BPMN notation is a formal notation and the diagram can be exported in XML format.

The evidence and rules used to make these decisions are discussed below. We do not discuss what action to take if the answer to either question is "no."

3.5.7 Data and Rules

There are many possible causes of colorectal symptoms and it is important to take note of those combinations of symptoms that may indicate cancer and those that do not. Decision support tools may help in ensuring that the right patients are selected for urgent referral. However, the relatively low incidence of cancer means that any such tools should not be intrusive in normal day-to-day clinical activity.

NICE has listed criteria for urgent referral, based on combinations of symptoms and signs, from which a mind-map has been derived. Seven questions relate to presenting

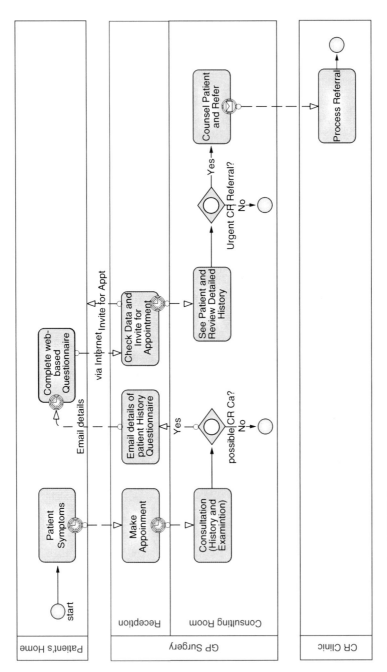

Fig. 3.5 Colorectal cancer referral BPMN diagram

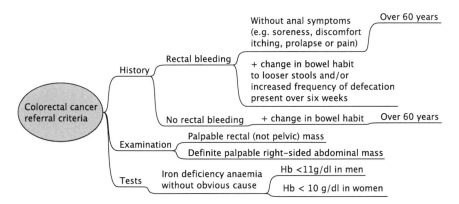

Fig. 3.6 NICE colorectal referral guidelines

history, three to physical examination, and one each for age and hemoglobin (iron deficiency anemia). The decision to refer urgently is based primarily on the patient's report of his or her symptoms and medical history, the patient's age, evidence (or lack of it) from physical examination, and blood tests (hemoglobin).

This set of criteria is used for initial triage. Although about 85% of patients with colorectal cancer meet these criteria (sensitivity), the large proportion of all patients who have these complaints do not have cancer (specificity) (Fig. 3.6).

Chapter 4
UML and XML

This chapter provides a short introduction to UML and XML, key underlying standards used in healthcare interoperability.

4.1 Unified Modeling Language

UML stands for Unified Modeling Language. The term "Unified" in the name is a clue to its origins. During the early 1990s, a number of different modeling notations were in widespread use. This was, to say the least, confusing. Between 1995 and 1997, Rational Software (now part of IBM) brought together three leading methodologists (Booch, Rumbaugh, and Jacobson) and, together with the Object Management Group (OMG), they developed a modeling notation and language, which they called the Unified Modeling Language that combined many of the best ideas of the then existing methods. UML is now the standard modeling notation used throughout the IT industry.

UML Version 1.0 was issued in 1997; a major revision, UML 2, was issued in 2003. Most of the changes in UML 2 are technical refinements, intended to support the concepts of executable UML and enable the exchange of models and diagrams between different tools.

UML is a specialized modeling language, not simply a notation for drawing diagrams. It includes a notation, which is used on diagrams, and a meta-model, which is of interest primarily to the developers of UML software tools. Simple things are simple, but complex things require the use of purpose-built tools.

UML makes a critical distinction between models and diagrams. A model is the sum of all the information held about a project in UML. Each diagram is a partial view of this model. When learning UML, it is a convenient simplification to regard a model as the sum of the diagrams. Each diagram shows a small part of the total design. The model is the sum total of all the specifications, comprising hundreds of diagrams and supporting text. This is one reason why specialized UML modeling tools are needed for building UML models. Each tool maintains an internal repository, which facilitates the reuse of common components and avoids all sorts of problems produced by describing the same thing in a different way in different places.

T. Benson, *Principles of Health Interoperability HL7 and SNOMED*, HI,
DOI 10.1007/978-1-84882-803-2_4, © Springer-Verlag London Limited 2010

Fowler (Fowler 2004) identifies three main ways in which people use UML: sketch, blueprint, and programming language. Sketches can be made using white boards or multipurpose tools such as Visio or PowerPoint. We may start off using sketches, but soon need to move on to developing blueprints. The distinction between a sketch and a blueprint is that sketches are incomplete and exploratory, while blueprints are complete and definitive. Serious modeling (blueprints rather than sketches) requires a specialized UML tool.

The step beyond blueprint is when programs are produced directly from the model. Here, UML becomes the source code for executable code. Full use of this approach will lead to automated production of conformant XML schema, documentation, and test rigs. A new generation of tools is being developed using the Eclipse Framework by collaborations such as Open Health Tools (OHT).

UML allows beginners to do simple things simply, yet also supports highly complex applications, underpinned by a rigorous formal language. No other scheme is so scalable or complete.

UML is completely independent of the software used to implement computer applications and is not tied to any development methodology. UML's independence of technology and method is one of the keys to the wide support that it enjoys throughout the IT industry. It fits into any IT organization.

UML has a number of weaknesses. Models and diagrams created using different tools cannot be imported and exported into and out of different tools reliably, although solutions to this problem have been proposed. It does not have a neat way of specifying multiple choices, decision tables or other constraints, although it does have a special Object Constraint Language (OCL), based on predicate calculus. However, this is opaque to those not trained in computer science (Warmer and Kleppe 2003). In many models, unstructured text annotations form an important part of the documentation.

A premise of UML is that no single diagram (or type of diagram) can provide, on its own, a full representation of what goes on, and so we need to use sets of related diagrams. Each type of diagram only shows certain aspects of a situation – everything else is ignored. This simplification provides both the power (it makes the situation understandable) and the weakness of diagrams (each diagram has a limited scope).

4.1.1 UML Diagrams

UML diagrams relate either to information structure or to behavior (Fig. 4.1). UML 2 recognizes 13 diagram types, although most users of UML make do using three or four types of diagram, depending on what they are using it for.

One danger point is UML's principle of suppressing information. This allows information to be omitted from any diagram in order to make it easier to understand. The corollary is that you should never infer anything from the absence of information in a diagram and that UML diagrams should not be read on their own without access to the rest of the model.

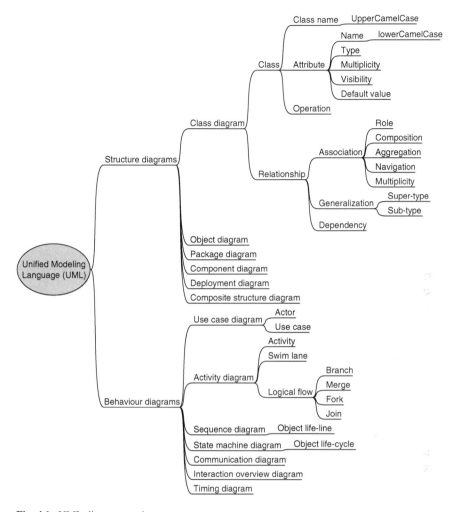

Fig. 4.1 UML diagrams and components

For example, all attributes have a default multiplicity of [1] (mandatory), but if a multiplicity is not shown against an attribute in a diagram, it may either mean that the information is suppressed or that the default value should be used. For example, no attribute multiplicities are shown in the HL7 RIM (Reference Information Model), because they are suppressed. Structural attributes in the RIM are mandatory [1] while all others are optional (but this is not shown on the diagrams). The only way to check is to look deeper into the model and see what is really there. Individual organizations often develop their own conventions about what is and is not shown on each diagram.

Diagram layout and style facilitate understanding (see Ambler 2003). Some guidelines apply to all types of diagrams, such as:

- Diagrams should be laid out so that they can be read left-to-right and top-to-bottom.
- Avoid crossed, diagonal, and curved lines.
- Document diagrams using notes.
- Use the parts of UML that are widely understood, not the esoteric parts.
- Use color coding with discretion.
- Use common naming conventions such as UpperCamelCase (e.g., ClassName) and lowerCamelCase (e.g., attributeName).
- Do not put too much on a single diagram. Restrict diagram size to a single sheet of A4.
- Use consistent legible fonts.
- Show only what you need to show. It is good practice to suppress unnecessary detail.

4.2   Structure Diagrams

4.2.1   Class Diagrams

Class Diagrams are the most widely used UML diagrams. Class diagrams show the static structure of classes, their definitions, and relationships between classes.

A class is a description of a group of objects with properties (attributes), behavior (operations), relationships to other objects (associations and aggregations), and semantics. Classes are shown as rectangles with one, two, or three compartments. The top compartment shows the class name, the second shows attributes. Attributes describe the characteristics of the objects, while operations are used to manipulate the attributes and to perform other actions. Attributes and operations need not be shown on a particular diagram.

Class names should be a singular noun and the class name is conventionally written using UpperCamelCase notation (e.g., ClassName). This class has two attributes, documented and date, and one operation – create().

Figure 4.2 shows a simple class diagram representing a prescription. Each prescription has a prescriber (author) and relates to a single patient. It has one or more prescription lines. Each prescription line includes details of a drug and may have any number (zero to many) of dosage instructions.

The arrowheads on the lines (associations) show navigation. The arrow from Prescription to Patient shows that, in this model, one goes from Prescription to Patient but not the other way round.

The notation for multiplicity, used in associations and attributes, is:

- [0..1] optional, no more than one is allowed
- [*] or [0..*] optional, any number of instances is allowed

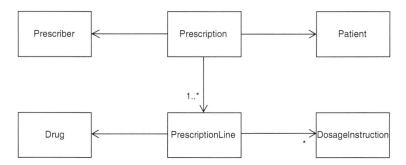

Fig. 4.2 Simple class diagram

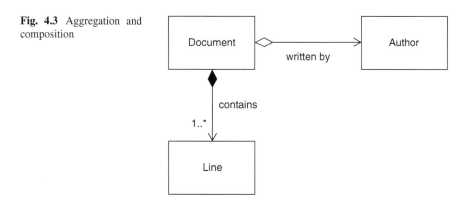

Fig. 4.3 Aggregation and composition

- [1] mandatory always one required (this is the default)
- [1..*] mandatory to have at least one instance

If no multiplicity is shown, the default assumption is multiplicity of 1, meaning that exactly one is required, although caution must always be observed when inferring anything from the absence of data on diagrams.

Figure 4.3 illustrates two notations used for showing containment.

The black diamond indicates composition between Document and Line. Each Document contains one or more Lines, but Line cannot exist independently of Document.

The hollow diamond indicates aggregation between Document and Author. Each Document has one Author, but the Author can exist independently of Document.

The multiplicities used in any diagram depend on its purpose. Figure 4.3 (above) is a Document-centric showing Document has just one Author (a one-to-one relationship), but an Author-centric diagram, Fig. 4.4 (below) shows that Author has one or more Documents (a one-to-many relationship). Both are right, it just depends on the purpose of the model.

Fig. 4.4 Author-centric diagram

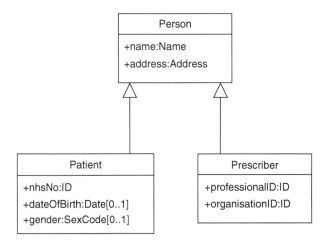

Fig. 4.5 Person specialization

The concepts of inheritance and attributes are illustrated in Fig. 4.5. Patient and Prescriber are both specializations of Person; Person is a generalization of Patient and Prescriber. The triangle arrowheads indicate that both Prescriber and Patient classes inherit the properties of Person. Patient has attributes: nhsNo, dateOfBirth, and gender, but also inherits the attributes name and address from Person. Similarly Prescriber, has attributes professionalID and organizationID, as well as the properties of Person.

Attributes have several properties. For example, the notation + dateOfBirth: Date[0..1] indicates:

- Visibility (+) is public, meaning that it is fully accessible.
- Attribute name is "dateOfBirth."
- The attribute type is "Date."
- Multiplicity is [0..1] meaning that this attribute is optional with a maximum number of occurrences of one.
- Initial values and defaults may also be specified.

Attribute names are usually written in lowerCamelCase (e.g., attributeName).

Operations implement the functionality of a software object. They are the actions that an object knows how to carry out. The syntax for operations includes:

Fig. 4.6 Simple object diagram

- Visibility
- Name
- Parameter list (in parenthesis)
- Return type
- Property string

An object is a unique instance of a class. An object diagram, such as Fig. 4.6, shows the relationships between objects. Each object may have:

- Identity (name)
- State (attributes)
- Behavior (methods)

The object name is underlined (to distinguish it from a class) and comprises the object's name, which is optional, followed by a colon and the class name (e.g., TimBenson:Author).

4.2.2 Package

Packages are used to divide up a model in a hierarchical way. Each package may be thought of as a separate name space. Each UML element may be allocated to a single package.

Packages provide a useful means of organizing the model. Classes that are closely related by inheritance or composition should usually be placed in the same package.

In Fig. 4.7, the Party package might include all classes related to people and organizations, including patients, doctors, and nurses. The Interaction package might include messages and entries in clinical records. The dashed arrow from Interaction to Party indicates that Interaction has a dependency on Party (Interactions involve Parties).

4.2.3 Deployment

The physical organization of computer systems is shown in deployment diagrams (Fig. 4.8). Each piece of the system is referred to as a node. The location of software can be shown as components.

Fig. 4.7 Package diagram

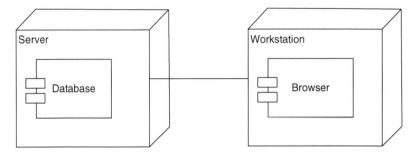

Fig. 4.8 Deployment diagram

4.3 Modeling Behavior

4.3.1 Use Case

Use cases capture the behavioral requirements of business processes and provide a common linkage across all aspects of a project from initial analysis of requirements right through development, testing, and final customer acceptance. They show how people will ultimately use the system being designed. Each use case describes a specific way of using the system. Any real system has many use cases.

Each use case constitutes a complete course of events, initiated by an actor (or trigger). A use case is essentially a special sequence of related transactions performed by an actor and the system in a dialogue.

An actor is an external party, such as a person, a computer, or a device, which interacts with the system. Each actor performs one or more use cases in the system. By going through all of the actors and defining everything they are able to do with the system, the complete functionality of the system is defined.

Each use case is a description of how a system can be used (from an external actor's point of view); it shows the functionality of the system, yielding an observable result of value to a particular actor. A use case does something for an actor and represents a significant piece of functionality that is complete from beginning to end.

The collected use cases specify all the ways the system can be used. Nontechnical personnel can understand use cases intuitively. Thus they can form a basis for

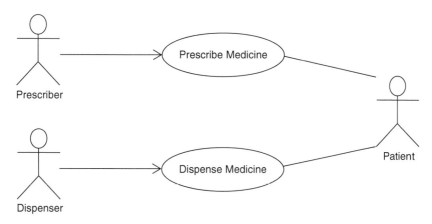

Fig. 4.9 Use case diagram

communication and definition of the functional requirements of the system in collaboration with potential users.

A simple use case diagram is shown in Fig. 4.9. Stickmen represent actors; ellipses represent use cases. In this diagram, the principal Actors are shown on the left. The arrowheads indicate the actor that initiates the use case.

Use cases are fundamentally a text form and should be documented using simple templates, such as:

- Metadata, such as use case name, unique ID, author, date, version, and status
- Scope and context
- Primary and other actors
- Preconditions and trigger event
- Main success scenario describing the normal flow of events using numbered steps from trigger through to post-conditions
- Post-conditions
- Alternative flows, e.g., when errors occur
- Importance and priority
- Open issues

A scenario is an instance of a use case. It is one path through the flow of events for the use case and can be documented using an activity diagram or a storyboard free text description (Fig. 4.10).

4.3.2 Activity Diagram

Use activity diagrams to show the important business processes undertaken by each role, such as validation and database update. Each role may be shown in a separate "Swim Lane." Transactions are communications that cross swim lanes.

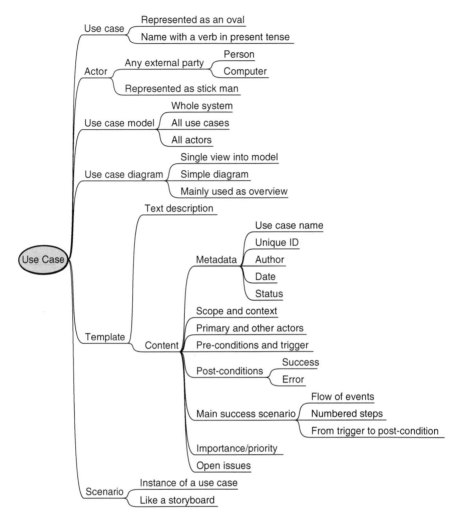

Fig. 4.10 Use cases

Activity diagrams display a sequence of actions (including alternative execution paths) and the objects involved in performing the work. They are particularly useful for describing workflow and behavior that have branches and forks. Figure 4.11 shows a simplified activity diagram for the exchange of a referral and clinic letter between GP and hospital. It is organized in swim lanes to show who or what is responsible for each activity.

Activity diagrams can be used to show logical data flows. A branch has a single entry point, but a choice of exits depending on some condition. Only one route can be taken. Branches end at a merge. A fork has one entry and multiple exits, which can be undertaken in parallel, and the order of activities is not important. A fork ends at a join.

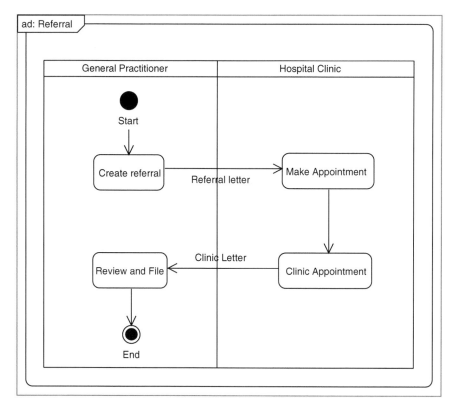

Fig. 4.11 Activity diagram

4.3.3 Sequence Diagram

Sequence diagrams (e.g., Fig. 4.12) show how objects interact with each other. Sequence diagrams show when messages are sent and received.

A Sequence Diagram is a diagram that depicts object interactions arranged in time sequence, where the direction of time is down the page. The objects, which exchange information, are shown at the top of a vertical line or bar, known as the object's lifeline. An arrow between the lifelines of two objects represents each message.

4.3.4 Statechart Diagram

An object state is determined by its attribute values and links to other objects. A state is the result of previous activities of the object. A state is shown as rectangle with rounded corners. It may optionally have three compartments (like classes) for name, state variables, and activities (Fig. 4.13).

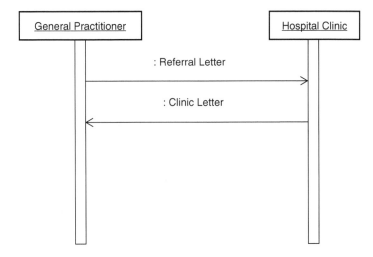

Fig. 4.12 Sequence diagram

Fig. 4.13 Statechart diagram

A statechart diagram shows an object life cycle, and can be used to illustrate how events (messages, time, errors, and state changes) affect object states over time. State transitions are shown as arrows between states.

4.4 UML Summary

UML is the standard modeling notation used for healthcare IT purposes. The basic notation is simple and quick to learn, although this hides much of the complexity that is needed for some purposes. UML is used to prepare rough sketches or to produce stringent specifications (blueprints). Specialized modeling tools are essential for serious work, involving more than a handful of diagrams.

A UML model may comprise many diagrams of different types as well as detailed documentation for each element. All of the information about a model is held in a common repository. This illustrates one of the key advantages of using a purpose-built UML tool, which facilitates reuse of work and ensures consistency.

UML facilitates the design of all types of software systems before coding. It is now one of the essential skills of health informatics.

4.5 Business Process Modeling Notation (BPMN)

Clinical processes are difficult to model with existing tools, in part because they are inherently complex, but more importantly because each patient is different and each clinician may adopt a variety of different paths, depending on the specific clinical situation of the individual patient. This requires business process specifications that take account of the full range of choices that clinicians have open at any one point in time.

BPMN (Business Process Modeling Notation) is a notation for documenting complex business processes (White and Miers 2008). The BPMN notation is understandable by end users and it is also capable of including the technical detail needed to specify messages involved in web services delivery and the generation of XML-based Business Process Execution Language (BPEL). BPMN is now part of the Object Management Group (OMG), which is also responsible for UML.

BPMN is a standard for business process modeling with a notation that is similar to that used in UML Activity Diagrams. Some commentators regard the future of BPMN as a specialized "front end" to UML.

BPMN has several advantages over standard UML activity diagrams:

- Shows explicitly who does what, where and in what sequence using the Pool and Swim-lane notation, distinguishing between messages which flow between actors from the flow of activities by a single actor or team
- Explicitly shows trigger events, delays, and messages that precede or follow on from each activity
- Allow drill down of subprocesses into greater detail of activities and tasks
- Provide additional structured and/or free text documentation for any element
- Executable output, using Business Process Execution Language (BPEL), an XML-based language, which has industry support from Microsoft, IBM, etc.

4.5.1 Activities

Activity is the generic term for Business Process, Process, Sub-Process, and Task. These have a hierarchical relationship. To use an analogy: a business process is a group of one or more trees; a process is a single tree; a subprocess is a branch (and may have further subbranches, sub-subbranches, and so on); task is a leaf, which is not subdivided further.

Business Process is the top of the Activity hierarchy in BPMN. It is defined as a set of activities that are performed within an organization or across organizations, shown on a Business Process Diagram (BPD).

Process is limited to the activities undertaken by one Participant (organization or role). Each Business Process may contain one or more Processes. A Process is an activity performed within an organization, and is depicted as a set of activities (Sub-Processes and Tasks) contained within a single Pool (see below Fig. 4.14).

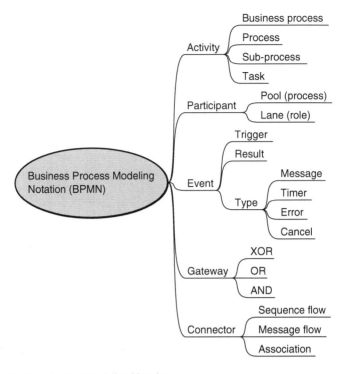

Fig. 4.14 Business Process Modeling Notation

Each Sub-Process may be expanded as a separate, linked diagram, showing its component Sub-Processes or Tasks. The facility to expand or consolidate Sub-Processes is a useful feature of BPMN.

A Task is an atomic activity, showing that the work is not broken down to a finer level of detail. Sub-Processes and Tasks are shown as rounded rectangles. Sub-Processes, which can be expanded, are shown with a "plus sign" at the bottom center of the icon.

Participants are each represented by a Pool, which may contain Lanes. Each Pool contains a single Process. A Pool may be subdivided into Lanes (like swim lanes in UML activity diagrams). Lanes may represent different roles within an organization. If a diagram contains a single Pool, the Pool boundaries need not be shown. A Pool is a container separating each Process from others and showing the Sequence Flow between activities.

Shown as a small circular icon, an Event is something that happens during the course of a business process that affects the flow. Events may represent triggers for activities to begin or their outcomes. Start, Intermediate, or End events are indicated by the thickness of the circle perimeter. An additional icon inside the circle shows the type of Trigger or Result (Message, Timer, Error, Cancel, Compensation, Rule, Link, Multiple, or Terminate).

A Gateway, shown as a square diamond, is used to control branching, forking, merging, and joining of paths. An icon inside the diamond shows the type of control (exclusive XOR, inclusive OR, parallel AND, or complex).

Connectors link the flow objects (Activity, Event, and Gateway). There are three types of Connectors:

- Sequence Flow (a solid line with arrow head) shows the order that activities are performed within a Process.
- Message Flow (a dotted line with arrow head) shows connections between Processes (crossing the boundary of a Pool).
- Association (dotted line, no arrow head) is used to associate information (such as Data Objects) and Annotations with Flow Objects.

4.5.2   Business Process Example

A complete business process from start to finish is shown in Fig. 4.15, which illustrates the traditional OP referral pattern for a patient suffering from a bowel problem.

The Pools and Lanes show clearly who does what in what order. The dotted lines represent movement of information (messages) or of information sources (e.g., the patient).

Each of the tasks shown could be represented as subprocesses and analyzed further in subsequent diagrams. Clinical care is essentially fractal and can usually be decomposed into smaller and more detailed subprocesses and tasks.

Trigger events are shown as circles, with an icon indicating the type of trigger – an envelope indicates a message and a clock indicates a time trigger, such as an appointment slot.

4.6   XML

XML (eXtensible Markup Language) is a universal format for encoding documents and structured data, which is used in interoperability between different applications. XML documents are independent of the applications that create or use them (Bos 1999).

XML is relatively modern, initially defined in 1998. XML Schema is even newer, published in 2001.

XML is derived from SGML (Standard Generalized Markup Language) which became a standard in 1986 (ISO 8879) at about the same time as EDIFACT (ISO 9735: 1987). SGML is an international standard for the definition of device-independent, system-independent methods of representing texts in electronic form. XML is strictly speaking a meta-language for formally describing a markup language. For example, XHTML is a version of HTML which is fully XML-compliant.

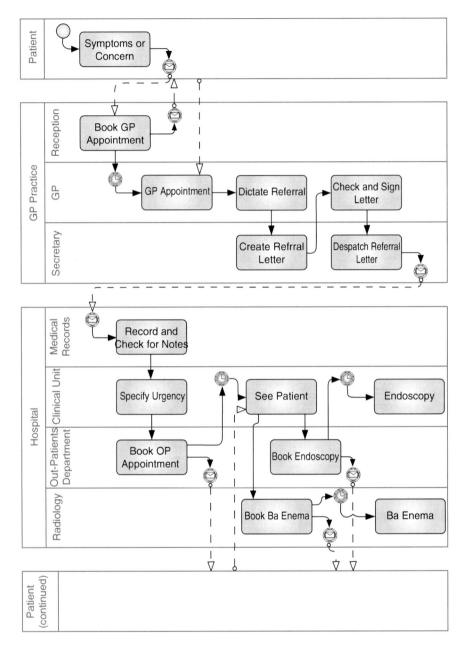

Fig. 4.15 Traditional OP referral for bowel problem

4.6.1 Markup

Markup is a term that covers any means of making explicit an interpretation of a text. In electronic documents, including all word processors, the system does this by inserting special coded instructions into the text, which are not normally seen on a printed copy. A markup language specifies:

- What markup is allowed
- What is required
- How markup is to be distinguished from text
- What the markup means

XML provides a method of doing the first three; additional documentation is required for the last. Such specifications may be extensive. The real work is in the definition of message structures.

4.6.2 Descriptive and Procedural Markup

Most word processors include markup instructions embedded within their text. However, XML differs in one vital respect from this sort of markup. XML is a descriptive markup scheme, while most schemes used in word processors and desktop publishing are procedural. A descriptive scheme simply says what something is (for instance, a heading), while a procedural scheme says what to do (for instance, print in 18 point Ariel font, bold, left-hand justified). XML specifies how to render information using style sheets, coded using related style sheet languages called CSS (Cascading Style Sheets) and XSL (Extensible Stylesheet Language).

This separation of description (providing names for parts of a document) from procedure is the secret to platform-independence and universality, which are XML's greatest strengths. A text marked up using a descriptive scheme can be processed in different ways by different pieces of software. Procedural markup can only be used in one way.

4.6.3 XML Files

XML files are text files that people should not have to read, but they are human-readable when the need arises, for example, when debugging applications. XML is verbose by design.

XML files are nearly always larger than comparable binary formats. The rules for XML files are strict, and forbid applications from trying to second-guess an error. These were conscious decisions by the designers of XML.

XML documents can include images and multimedia objects such as video and sound. The data may also include metadata – information about itself – that do not appear on the printed page.

XML and HTML are closely related. Indeed, XHTML is a version of HTML which is fully XML-compliant. Like HTML, XML makes use of tags (words bracketed by "<" and ">") and attributes (of the form name = "value"). The key difference is HTML specifies what each tag and attribute means, and how the text between them will look on a browser, but XML uses the tags only to delimit pieces of data, and leaves the interpretation of the data to the application that reads them.

An XML document is said to be well-formed if it complies with a concise set of well-defined rules. One of the most important is that all nonempty elements are delimited by both a start-tag (e.g., <tag> and a matching end-tag </tag>. Element names are case-sensitive.

4.6.4   XML Schema

The structure of an XML document is specified in a schema, which is also written in XML (van der Vlist 2001). The schema defines the structure of a type of document that is common to all documents of that type. It identifies the tags (elements) and the relationship among the data elements. This means that any document of a known type can be processed in a uniform way, including checks that all of the elements required are present and in the correct order.

The development of schemas is the central analysis and design task of working with XML. Schemas can be prepared for use with existing text and databases. Tighter rules may be specified where uniformity of document structure is desirable. The schema makes the rules explicit. XML allows data to be tagged with literally any information that may be considered useful.

Schema processing tools are used to validate XML messages or other XML documents using one or more schemas. Schema validation is applied to elements within a well-formed XML document.

Three schema languages in widespread use are W3C's Schema Definition Language (XSD), RELAX NG, and Schematron.

In XML a number of words such as *element* and *attribute* are used in specific technical ways, as described below.

4.6.5   XML Element

In XML, documents are made up of elements. Each element is tagged using a start-tag and an end-tag. For example, a diagnosis element in a text might be tagged as follows:

<diagnosis> Diabetes mellitus </diagnosis>.

Note that in HTML all of the elements are predefined; in HTML it is not possible to have a tag such as <diagnosis>.

A start-tag takes the form <name> while the end-tag takes an identical form except that the opening angle bracket is followed by a slash character </name>.

Every XML document has a hierarchical tree-structure. Elements may be nested (embedded) within elements of a different type. For example, the line of a poem may be embedded within a stanza, which is embedded within the poem, which is embedded within an anthology.

An XML element definition is a detailed specification of the form and content of an XML element, which includes the name (a generic identifier in XML terminology) for the element. A simple type contains no sub-element definitions. A complex type may include sub-elements.

4.6.6   XML Attribute

Attributes are used in XML to add information to the start-tag of an element to describe some aspect of a specific element occurrence. Attribute values are written in quotes and are separated from the attribute name by an equals sign. For example, a hypertext link in HTML is shown as <A HREF = "URL">, where URL is the address of the uniform resource location (URL). Any number of attribute–value pairs may be defined for any element.

4.6.7   Entity

XML entities are named bodies of data, which can be referenced by an entity reference. Entity references always begin with "&" and end with ";". A small number of entities are used to represent single characters that have special meanings in XML, such as <(<), >(>) and & (&). Numeric character references can be used to represent Unicode characters. For example, © is used to represent the © symbol. Other entities can be defined.

4.6.8   Namespace

A Namespace mechanism is provided to eliminate confusion when combining formats. This is used in XML schema to combine two schemas, to produce a third which covers a merged document structure.

4.6.9   The XML Family

XML is a family of technologies.

- CSS and XSL are style sheet languages.
- XPath provides a way to refer to individual parts of an XML document.

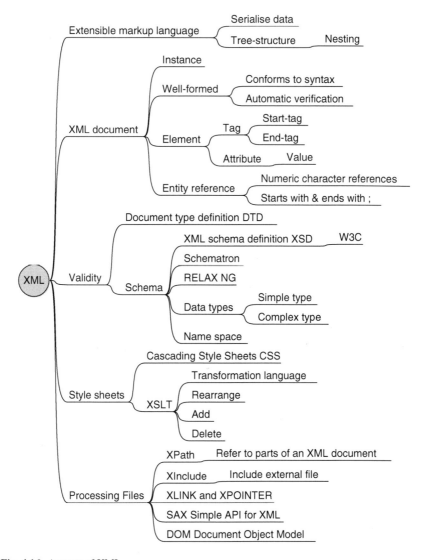

Fig. 4.16 Aspects of XML

- XSLT is a transformation language for rearranging, adding, and deleting tags and attributes.
- DOM is a standard set of function calls for manipulating XML (and HTML) files from a programming language.
- SAX is a simple API for XML.

A short introduction such as this can do no more than scratch the surface of XML (Fig. 4.16).

Chapter 5
Standards Development Organizations

Healthcare interoperability is based on the application of standards. This chapter introduces some of the major Standards Development Organizations in e-health.

A report produced for the European Union concluded:

> Despite a generally large number of conflicting e-health standards, versions and implementations, there may be a lack of the "right" standards. For particular applications and for concrete processes there may be no well-developed standards. In an expert survey, 80% of the respondents stated that there is a lack of sufficiently developed standards, and 64% said that there is a lack of standards for electronic health records (EHRs). (EU 2008)

5.1 What is a Standard?

ISO defines a standard as a document, established by consensus and approved by a recognized body, that provides, for common and repeated use, rules, guidelines, or characteristics for activities or their results, aimed at the achievement of the optimum degree of order in a given context.[1]

Two of the key terms are consensus and recognized body. Consensus is general agreement, characterized by the absence of sustained opposition to substantial issues by any important part of the concerned interests and by a process that involves seeking to take into account the views of all parties concerned and to reconcile any conflicting arguments. Consensus need not imply unanimity.

A recognized body is understood to be an internationally recognized standards development organization such as ISO, CEN, BSI, ANSI, and its accredited SDOs including HL7.

There are two main types of standard: exact specifications, which enable interworking of nuts and bolts, paint colors and computers; and minimum thresholds to ensure the safety and quality of processes, materials, and the environment. For healthcare interoperability we need stringent specifications.

---

[1] ISO/IEC Guide 2:2004, definition 3.2

T. Benson, *Principles of Health Interoperability HL7 and SNOMED*, HI,
DOI 10.1007/978-1-84882-803-2_5, © Springer-Verlag London Limited 2010

One of the limiting factors in market growth for health information systems has been the inability for different systems to interoperate, due to lack of suitable standards. Standards have a multiplier effect, the more people can interoperate, the more cost-effective is every new application and the larger the IT market becomes.

Interoperability standards have already become the foundation of whole industries.[2] This is well-illustrated by the explosive growth of the World Wide Web and mobile telephone markets, and should also be true of healthcare computing. In general, the healthcare standards development organizations have failed to provide sufficiently stringent standard specifications to enable plug and play, leaving this to local implementers.

The benefits of using standards increase exponentially with the number of different systems that need to be linked.

Purchasers of computer systems should insist on open interoperability standards to avoid supplier lock-in and give them choice and flexibility in procurement, allowing them to shop around for whatever meets their needs most closely. Open standards offer a guarantee for future migration, growth and evolution, foster competition between suppliers, drive down costs, and push up cost-effectiveness.

Suppliers also benefit; their criterion for success is return on investment. The actual return is often outside each supplier's direct control, so their priority is always to minimize investment and risk.

5.2   International Standards Development Organizations

The organization of health informatics standards development internationally is complex, changes frequently, and can easily become a fog of acronyms. The intent here is to introduce the most important players and to provide some important information, which does not readily fit into other chapters.

About 100 years ago the International Standardization Organization (ISO) was established to provide a focal point for all international standards. ISO is a membership organization, with one member in each c ountry. In the USA the member is the American National Standards Institute (ANSI) and in the UK the member is the British Standards Institute (BSI). The Vienna agreement specifies how conflicts between different standards should be handled. In particular, work done at the international level takes precedence over national standards.

When the European Union was established, it was agreed that the common market required common standards and the European Standards Organization (CEN) was established in Brussels, along the same lines as ISO as a national member organization.

---

[2] ISO Strategic plan 2005–2010: standards for a sustainable world. Geneva: ISO 2004

In 1990, CEN set up the first formal international standards organization in health informatics, CEN TC251. Each European country established its own mirror committee; for example in the UK, the mirror committee is BSI IST/35.

In the USA, ANSI acts as an umbrella organization for a number of affiliates with an interest in health informatics.

In 1999, ISO established a committee for Health Informatics (ISO TC215). The main task of this committee is to ratify existing standards, such as the HL7 RIM, as full international standards.

A number of other international organizations have also emerged, which do not fit neatly into the traditional ISO pattern. These include:

- IHTSDO The International Health Terminology Standards Development Organization, responsible for SNOMED CT
- CDISC (Clinical Data Interchange Standards Consortium) responsible for coordinating data capture for clinical trials
- IHE Integrating the Healthcare Enterprise, which develops profiles for specific use cases leveraging existing standards
- Continua, which focuses on home tele-health devices
- OpenEHR which focuses on elements of EHR architecture
- Open Health Tools a collaboration to develop tools for developing and implementing standards

In 2007, a joint initiative on SDO Global Health Informatics Standardization was established to coordinate the work done by ISO TC215, CEN TC251, HL7, IHTSDO, and CDISC. The major SDOs are shown in Fig. 5.1.

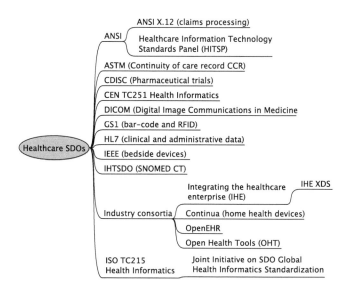

Fig. 5.1 Healthcare Standard Development Organizations

5.3   Health Level Seven

Health Level Seven (HL7) is an international standards development organization (SDO), with Affiliates in 31 countries.[3] Health Level Seven produces the world's most widely used standards for healthcare interoperability. Most of the leading suppliers use and support the development of HL7 standards across six continents.

HL7's vision statement is "to create the best and most widely used standards in healthcare." Its mission reads:

> HL7 provides standards for interoperability that improve care delivery, optimize workflow, reduce ambiguity and enhance knowledge transfer among all of our stakeholders, including healthcare providers, government agencies, the vendor community, fellow SDOs and patients. In all of our processes we exhibit timeliness, scientific rigor and technical expertise without compromising transparency, accountability, practicality, or our willingness to put the needs of our stakeholders first.

HL7 creates standards for the exchange, management, and integration of electronic healthcare information for clinical and administrative purposes. HL7 does not develop software, but simply provides healthcare organizations with specifications for making their systems interoperable. It develops coherent extensible standards using a formal methodology. It collaborates with and provides a meeting place for healthcare information experts from the healthcare IT industry and healthcare providers to work together and with other standards development organizations. And, it promotes its own standards and provides education for the healthcare industry and policy makers.

HL7 is accredited with the American National Standards Institute (ANSI). It is one of several SDOs operating in the healthcare IT domain. HL7 focuses on the domain of clinical and administrative data. Other ANSI-accredited SDOs have responsibility for pharmacy (NCPDC), medical devices (IEEE), imaging (ACR/NEMA), insurance (claims processing) transactions (X12), and dentistry (ADA). These SDOs are all working with the Health Information Technology Standards Panel (HITSP), which was established in 2005 under contract to the US Department of Health and Human Services (HSS) to:

> achieve a widely accepted and useful set of standards specifically to enable and support widespread interoperability among healthcare software applications, as they will interact in a local, regional and national health information network for the United States.

HL7 also collaborates with international (ISO TC215) and European (CEN TC251) standards development organizations, and with other specialized SDOs such as IHTSDO (SNOMED terminology) and CDISC (clinical trials) through the Joint Initiative on SDO Global Health Informatics Standardization.

HL7 is a voluntary standards organization; most of the work in developing the standards is performed by volunteers, working over many years. Much of the work is done in small committee meetings and is then presented to a much larger group to achieve a consensus. HL7 volunteers meet together three times a year in

---

[3] More information about HL7 is available on the HL7 web site www.hl7.org.

week-long working group meetings at which more than 30 specialized committees meet face-to-face. Work continues throughout the rest of the year coordinated by regular telephone conferences.

Hammond and Cimino have described the process as follows:

> The writing of the draft standard is usually the work of a few dedicated individuals – typically people who represent the vendors in the field. Other people then review the draft; controversial points are discussed in detail and solutions are proposed and finally accepted. Writing and refining the standard is further complicated by the introduction of people new to the process who have not been privy to the original discussions and want to revisit points which have been resolved earlier. The balance between moving forward and being open is a delicate one. Most standards-writing groups have adopted an open policy; anyone can join the process and be heard. (Hammond and Cimino 2006)

5.3.1 What Does the Name HL7 Mean?

The name Health Level Seven is derived from the seventh level of the ISO's Open Systems Interconnect (OSI) model: the application layer, which provides a framework for communication between disparate computer systems. The OSI model has seven layers; the top three layers are concerned with applications (interworking); the lower four layers are concerned with the transmission of data (interconnection):

Layer 7 – Application: addresses definition of the data to be exchanged, the timing of the interchange, and the communication of certain errors to the application.

Layer 6 – Presentation: is concerned with the syntax of information transfer between end systems.

Layer 5 – Session: provides mapping between physical and logical sessions, including checkpoint recovery and restart.

Layer 4 – Transport: provides end-to-end transmission of data to the required quality of service (e.g., error-free).

Layer 3 – Network: is concerned with routing and relaying between multiple sub-networks.

Layer 2 – Data-link: transmit a stream of bits from one network node to another with indication of errors and limited error correction.

Layer 1 – Physical: provide the interface to the physical communications medium.

Enveloping is a key concept in the OSI model. Data from a source system enters the OSI stack at layer 7 (application) and is encapsulated by another envelope at each layer, so that by the time it reaches the communication medium (the wire) at Layer 1, it has collected seven envelopes. At the destination, each envelope is checked and removed, one by one, so that the data exiting from layer 7 at the destination is exactly what the source system sent.

Layers 1 to 6 of the OSI model deal with various aspects of technical interoperability. The only domain-specific aspect is the application layer – Layer 7, which deals with the semantics or meaning of what is exchanged. This is why the founders of HL7 chose the name Health Level Seven.

5.3.2 HL7 Products

HL7 produces four types of document:

- Normative Standard: content is balloted by the general membership and is considered a structural component of the HL7 Standard. Negative ballots must be resolved.
- Draft Standard for Trial Use (DSTU): content is balloted by the general membership as the draft of a future standard which will, following a prespecified period of evaluation and comment (usually 2 years), be expeditiously incorporated into normative standard.
- Reference: content is harmonized during HL7 meetings or approved by the HL7 Board. It is not subject to ballot acceptance.
- Informative: content is balloted by the general membership. However, it is not considered to be a structural part of the Standard but only supporting information.

All HL7 Balloted Standards are introduced first as a DSTU and must show some successful implementation before being advanced as a Normative Standard.

5.3.3 Ballot Process

Ballots normally progress through two or more cycles of ballots. The ballot pool is limited to declared interested members. Negative votes must be accompanied with a specific reason justifying the negative vote. Work Groups must resolve negative votes either by accepting the voters comment and recommended solution, negotiating with the voter and getting them to agree to withdraw their negative or declare the vote nonpersuasive.

Voters may appeal to the TSC and Board. They can also revote their same negative vote on the next round of balloting. Substantive changes to a ballot (either to fix a negative or add new material) merit another ballot round. When 75% (for normative documents) of the responses are registered as affirmatives and (hopefully) all negatives withdrawn, a document is ready for publication as a HL7 Standard.

5.3.4 Language

HL7 has produced a "Version 3 Publishing Facilitator's Guide," which is a style guide for v3 documentation.

The stringency of conformance statements is specified by use of SHALL, SHOULD, and other modal verbs. For example, the word SHALL conveys the sense of being mandatory or required; SHOULD implies best practice or a recommendation, and MAY implies acceptable or permitted.

5.3.5 Membership

HL7 offers two main types of membership:

- Individual for those with a personal interest in the standards.
- Organizational include benefits crucial to those who rely on the standard as part of their business plan – the most critical of these being the right to distribute excerpts of the standard to clients (as part of technical documentation or proposals) – or distribute the standard within your organization. Organizational members may also elect to be Supporters or Benefactors.

Members of HL7 who meet together electronically or in person are collectively known as the Working Group and are self-organized into a number of different technical committees. There are usually 3-week-long working group meetings each year.

5.3.6 International Affiliates

Internationally, HL7 is organized into a set of International Affiliates in 32 countries, in addition to the USA, where HL7 HQ performs the affiliate role (Fig. 5.2).

5.3.7 The Technical Steering Committee

The HL7 Technical Steering Committee oversees and coordinates the technical effort contributed by the HL7 volunteers who make up the HL7 Working Group. Its mission is to assure that the efforts of the Working Group are focused on the overall HL7 mission. There are four steering divisions:

Foundation and Technology work groups provide the fundamental tools and building blocks for all HL7 activities.

Structure and semantic design focuses on creation of basic patterns and common messages that could exist on their own, but are mostly used by others.

Domain Experts committees and projects in this space focus on creation of messages, services, documents using many of the common structures in place, yet expanding it in key areas as well.

Technical & Support Services committees support to the Technical Steering Committee and Committees of the Working Group (Fig. 5.3).

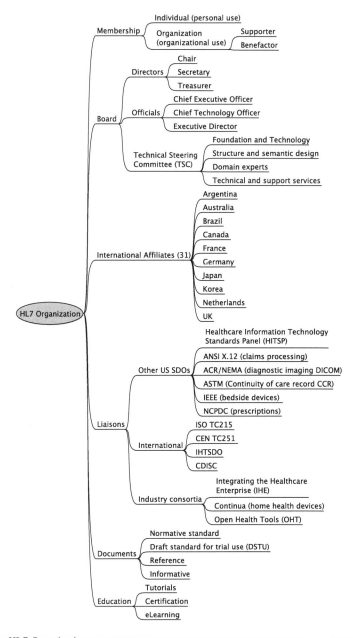

Fig. 5.2 HL7 Organization

Fig. 5.3 HL7 Technical Steering Committee

5.4 Other SDOs and Consortia

5.4.1 IHTSDO

IHTSDO (International Health Terminology Standards Development Organization) is an international not-for-profit organization, based in Copenhagen. IHTSDO was established in 2007, when it acquired the IP of SNOMED CT from the College of

American Pathologists (CAP). CAP-STS (SNOMED Terminology Services) still provide an important support service for IHTSDO and provides support in the USA.

The IHTSDO vision is to enhance the health of humankind by facilitating better health information management; to contribute to improved delivery of care by clinical and social care professions and to facilitate the accurate sharing of clinical and related health information, and the semantic interoperability of health records.

The achievement of this vision for broad, demonstrable, and successful use of SNOMED CT requires a globally coordinated effort to gain agreement on a core terminology for recording and sharing health information, pooling resources to share costs and benefits relating to the development of terminology products and consistent promotion of the uptake and correct use of the terminology.

An important strand is active harmonization activity with other SDOs, including HL7 and the Open Health Tools consortium.

Current (2009) members include Australia, Canada, Cyprus, Denmark, Lithuania, The Netherlands, New Zealand, Singapore, Sweden, United Kingdom and United States. IHTSDO is responsible for the core content of SNOMED CT, while each member country has a National Release Centre, which distributes SNOMED CT and has responsibility within its territory for liaison with IHTSDO, licensing and distribution of SNOMED CT, quality assurance and conformance with IHTSDO standards, issues tracking, change control and monitoring IP (products, trademarks, etc.).

5.4.2 IHE

IHE (Integrating the Healthcare Enterprise) was established in 1999 by the Healthcare Information Systems and Management Society (HIMSS) and the radiological Society of North America (RSNA) to help improve the way healthcare computer systems in share information, initially in the imaging domain where there was clear overlap between the HL7 and DICOM set of standards. IHE's initial focus was interoperability between equipment in clinical departments with hospital information systems. The starting point was radiology, where it developed profiles which specify how to use DICOM and HL7 together and it has moved on to cardiology, clinical laboratories, and other specialties.

The second dimension to IHE's work has been the development of IT infrastructure standards for use across departmental and institutional boundaries. The XDS (Cross-enterprise Document Sharing) profile, described below, is one example of this.

The next stage was to develop a set of integration profiles for healthcare IT infrastructure.

Systems developed in accordance with IHE profiles can communicate with one another better, and may be easier to implement.

IHE has established a four-stage approach:

- Identify Interoperability Problems. Clinicians and IT experts work to identify common interoperability problems with information access, clinical workflow, administration, and the underlying infrastructure.

- Specify Integration Profiles. Experienced healthcare IT professionals identify relevant standards and define how to apply them to address the problems, documenting them in the form of IHE integration profiles.
- Test Systems at the Connectathon. Vendors implement IHE integration profiles in their products and test their systems for interoperability at an annual IHE Connectathon. This allows them to assess the maturity of their implementation and resolve issues of interoperability in a supervised testing environment.
- Publish Integration Statements for use in RFPs. Vendors publish IHE integration statements to document the IHE integration profiles their products support. Users can reference the IHE integration profiles in requests for proposals, simplifying the systems acquisition process.

5.4.3   Continua Alliance

The Continua Health Alliance[4] is a nonprofit, open industry coalition of healthcare and technology companies working to establish a system of interoperable personal health solutions. The driver is that use of tele-health solutions in the home can foster independence, empower individuals, and provide the opportunity for personalized health and wellness management.

Continua has set out to develop an ecosystem of connected technologies, devices, and services that will enable the more efficient exchange of fitness, health, and wellness information. The foundation of this ecosystem is a set of interoperability guidelines which specify how systems and devices made by different companies can work together. Such products are expected to become common over the next few years. The first set of Continua standards includes specifications for using existing standards such as Bluetooth, USB, medical devices (IEEE 1173), and HL7 to enable people to use home-based devices to monitor their weight, blood pressure, glucose, and blood oxygen levels and share this with their healthcare professionals.

Continua has developed a product certification program with a recognizable logo signifying interoperability with other certified products, intended to build trust and confidence among customers.

5.4.4   OpenEHR

OpenEHR is a not-for-profit foundation, which has developed a technology-independent architecture, including a Reference Model, Archetypes, and Templates. The main activities are to promote the uptake of openEHR technologies globally;

---

[4] See www.continuaalliance.org/

to maintain the openEHR specifications and control the change management process for the openEHR model; to protect the copyright of open source software components based on openEHR; and to act as a forum for discussion and contribution on openEHR and related technologies.

5.4.5 Open Health Tools

A new generation of tools is being developed by the Open Health Tools collaborative (OHT), which uses the Eclipse framework and OMG standards.[5]

Eclipse is an open source community, which builds tools for building, deploying, and managing software across the life cycle. Licensing uses the Eclipse Public License (EPL). The EPL allows organizations to include EPL-licensed software in their commercial products, while at the same time requiring those who modify derivative works of EPL code to contribute the modifications (but not the derivative works) back to the community.

The vision of the Open Health Tools collaboration is to produce machine-processable artifacts, spanning through all stages of the message design cycle (requirements, design, implementation, and testing) along with a framework for publishing documentation about the artifacts generated throughout the process.

It will standardize the type and quality of the information conveyed between each stage and between communicating organizations. It will also produce coherent, traceable, and versioned concepts from analysis to implementation and facilitate consistent workflows and project management /oversight.

This will reduce message development time and allow the automatic translation of message designs to supplier-specific formats and support end-to-end automated testing of interoperability solutions. It will facilitate direct involvement /feedback in international standards and tools development, ensuring ongoing alignment of implementation specifications with industry standards, including HL7 V3.

A number of projects are already underway in OHT, but this number is expected to grow, if only because the needs of those involved in developing and authoring standards are quite different from those who implement and test them.

The OHT HL7 Tooling Project is an open software development project which aims to provide second generation tools to support the HL7 version 3 message modeling methodology. The toolset is based on the Eclipse Platform and Tools. The HL7 tools supporting the v3 message modeling methodology will be designed to be an integral part of a wider suite of tools covering conformance/testing, clinical modeling, and terminology maintenance.

Deliverables from this project are expected to include:

- Static model designer, to replace the V3 Visio RMIM editor
- XML schema generator with tight vocabulary binding, data type specializations, and cross-references for vocabulary, CMETs, data types and templates

---

[5] See www.openhealthtools.org

- Instance editor
- Vocabulary tooling to edit and maintain value sets for HL7 V3 message specifications

The OHT Conformance Services project set out to develop a set of tools and services to support the implementation of applications, which conform to standards such as HL7 in a consistent way with reduced effort and cost. Conformance testing is just one of a set of tests that includes testing the implementation, interface, integration, user acceptance, nonfunctional aspects (e.g., security), and unit.

Conformance services cover test authoring, tools and test execution related to test data, vocabulary, business rules, message structure, and the conformance profile. A conformance profile is a constrained set of standards, based on expected product functionality, grouped into testable units.

A repository is needed to hold the structured conformance profiles, test cases, test data, business rules, etc.

The OHT SNOMED CT Tooling Project is an open software development project, which aims to provide second generation tools which can be used to develop, maintain, promote, and enable the uptake and correct use of SNOMED CT in health systems around the world.

5.4.6 CDISC

The Clinical Data Interchange Standards Consortium (CDISC) has been founded by the pharmaceutical industry to develop worldwide industry standards to support the electronic acquisition, exchange, submission, and archiving of clinical trials data and metadata for medical and biopharmaceutical product development. The CDISC mission is to lead the development of global, vendor-neutral, platform-independent standards to improve data quality and accelerate product development.

Part II
HL7 – Health Level Seven

Chapter 6
HL7 Version 2

HL7 Version 2 is the most widely used healthcare interoperability standard in the world. It is used in over 90% of all hospitals in the USA and is widely supported by healthcare IT suppliers worldwide.

At first sight, the HL7 V2 documentation may appear to be large and formidable, but it is based on a few basic principles, which are quite easy to grasp.

To understand some of the features of HL7, we need to go back to its origins in 1987. The initial focus of HL7 was on exchanging information about admissions, discharges, and transfers (ADT) within hospitals. The first version, HL7 V1.0 was issued a few months later. In the following year, 1988, HL7 V2.0 was published, and this included a major extension to add in messages for exchanging orders and reports for tests and treatment, based closely on the ASTM (American Society of Testing and Materials) E.1238.88 standard. Version 2.1, which was the first widely used version, was published in 1991.

The HL7 V2 standard has been in continuous development for over 20 years. At the time of writing, the latest version is Version 2.6, which was approved as an ANSI standard in October 2007. Version 2.6 is organized as a set of chapters and appendices as shown in Fig. 6.1:

During its long development period the scope of HL7 Version 2 has increased enormously, but the basic principles have hardly changed. The Version 2.6 standard now has 1,965 pages and 717,000 words. It contains an enormous amount of knowledge and experience about health informatics.

One of the basic principles of HL7 V2 has been the preservation of backward compatibility, while the standard has evolved by addition. The idea being that a system, which can understand a new message in a new version, should also be able to understand a previous version. Ideas, which have been superseded, are flagged as being deprecated, but not replaced.

Older versions are still widely used, because there is minimal return on investment achieved by replacing a working interface with a later version and a significant risk of hitting unexpected problems. However, interface engineers may need to work with several different versions and recognize the differences between them. It is always important to know what version is being used.

T. Benson, *Principles of Health Interoperability HL7 and SNOMED*, HI,
DOI 10.1007/978-1-84882-803-2_6, © Springer-Verlag London Limited 2010

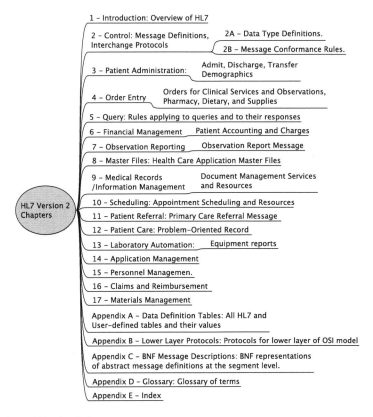

Fig. 6.1 HL7 Version 2 chapters

To understand the HL7 V2 documentation, you need to know about the message syntax and data types.

Message syntax describes the overall structure of messages and how the different parts are recognized. Each message is composed of segments in specified sequence, each of which contains fields also in a specified sequence; these fields have specified data types.

Data types are the building blocks of the fields and may be simple, with a single value, or complex, with multiple components. These components themselves have data types, which can be simple or complex, leading to subcomponents (Fig. 6.2).

6.1 Message Syntax

HL7 V2 messages are sent in response to trigger events. The message name is derived from the message type and a trigger event. The message type is the general category into which a message fits. For example, patient administration

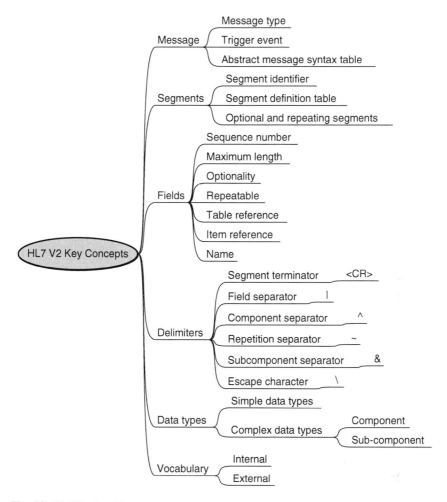

Fig. 6.2 HL7 Version 2 key concepts

messages are ADT. Examples of message types are shown in the following table, which also shows the HL7 V2 Chapter where they are described in detail:

Value	Description	V2 Chapter
ACK	General acknowledgment message	2
ADT	ADT message	3
ORM	Order message	4
ORU	Observation result – unsolicited	7

The trigger event indicates what happened to cause a message to be generated. Trigger events are specific to a message type. For example some of the ADT trigger events are:

Value	Description
A01	Admit/visit notification
A02	Transfer a patient
A03	Discharge/end visit
A04	Register a patient

The full message name is ADT^A01 (the "^" is the HL7 field component separator). The message name is always entered in the ninth field of the message header segment (MSH-9).

Each HL7 V2 message comprises a set of segments. The overall structure and allowable content of each message is defined in an abstract message syntax table, which lists segments in the order in which they occur. For example, a simple message, noting that a patient has been admitted to the hospital contains the following segments in the order shown:

MSH Message Header
EVN Event Type
PID Patient Identification
PV1 Patient Visit

The abstract message syntax also shows which segments are optional and which can be repeated. A segment listed on its own is mandatory and may not repeat. Optional segments are surrounded by square brackets [. . .]. Segments that are allowed to repeat are indicated using curly braces { . . . }. If a segment is both optional and repeatable, it has both brackets and braces [{ . . . }]. Note that the order is not important: [{...}] and {[...]} are equivalent.

The abstract message syntax table also shows which chapter of the HL7 V2.x standard contains the segment definition. Part of the abstract message syntax table for the ADT^A01 message is shown below:

ADT^A01	ADT Message	Chapter
MSH	Message Header	2
EVN	Event Type	3
PID	Patient Identification	3
[PD1]	Additional Demographics	3
[{ NK1 }]	Next of Kin/Associated Parties	3
PV1	Patient Visit	3

This shows that segments MSH, EVN, PID, and PV1 are mandatory. PD1 is optional. It is also indented, which indicates that it is nested under the PID segment, creating a group. NK1 is both optional and repeatable.

Each segment has a three-character identifier, the segment ID (e.g., MSH). In a message this segment ID is always the first three characters of the line.

Segments contain fields and fields contain components; components may contain subcomponents.

6.1.1 *Delimiters*

Delimiters (such as field separators, component separators, and subcomponent separators) are used to indicate the boundaries between these elements. The term element is used to refer to a field, a component, or a subcomponent.

Within the HL7 syntax, the size of messages transmitted is reduced by truncation. If fields at the end of a segment or component are not needed, the appropriate terminator or separator character truncates them. The segment terminator (carriage return) truncates segments. In the same way, field separators truncate components and component separators truncate subcomponents.

Most HL7 V2 implementations use default encoding with the delimiters to terminate segments and to separate components and subcomponents. The delimiters are defined in the first two fields of the MSH segment (MSH-1 and MSH-2). There is also an XML representation (not described here).

Symbol	Usage
|	Field separator
^	Component separator
~	Repetition separator
\\	Escape character
&	Subcomponent separator
<CR>	Segment terminator

The field separator (|) is always the fourth character of each segment. Fields are named according to their sequential position within a segment. For example, MSH-9 is the ninth field in the MSH segment and is preceded by nine field delimiters. Two adjacent field separators (||) indicate an empty field. If an application wishes to state that a field contains null and expects the receiving system to act on this, then an explicit null is represented as |""|.

The component separator (^) separates the components of a field. Components are referred to by the segment, field, and position in the field (e.g., MSH-9.1). For example, the MSH-9 field contains two components: MSH-9.1 (message type) and MSH-9.2 (trigger event) and might be represented as ADT^A01. The field separator truncates any components, not needed at the end of a field. For example, the following two data fields are equivalent: |ABC^DEF^^| and |ABC^DEF|.

The repetition separator (~) is used to separate the first occurrence or repetition of a field from the second occurrence and so on.

The escape character (\\) is used mainly in text elements to bracket text for special processing. The escape character can be used to send delimiters within a message.

Symbol	Escape sequence
|	\\F\\
^	\\S\\
~	\\R\\
\\	\\E\\
&	\\T\\ e.g., |Marks \\T\\ Spencer|

The escape character may also be used to indicate certain formatting commands, such as \.br\ to indicate line break, or \.sp 3\ to skip 3 spaces in the formatted text (FX) data type.

The subcomponent separator (&) is used to separate subcomponents within components, providing an additional level of granularity.

Each segment is ended with an ASCII carriage return <CR> character.

6.2   Segment Definition

Each segment is defined in a table such as that shown below for the MSH Message Header segment. All HL7 V2 messages begin with a single MSH segment and this provides an example of how segments are defined.

SEQ	LEN	DT	OPT	RP/#	TBL#	ITEM #	ELEMENT NAME
1	1	ST	R			00001	Field Separator
2	4	ST	R			00002	Encoding Characters
3	180	HD	O			00003	Sending Application
4	180	HD	O			00004	Sending Facility
5	180	HD	O			00005	Receiving Application
6	180	HD	O			00006	Receiving Facility
7	26	TS	O			00007	Date/Time Of Message
8	40	ST	O			00008	Security
9	7	CM	R			00009	Message Type
10	20	ST	R			00010	Message Control ID
11	3	PT	R			00011	Processing ID
12	8	ID	R		0104	00012	Version ID
13	15	NM	O			00013	Sequence Number
14	180	ST	O			00014	Continuation Pointer
15	2	ID	O		0155	00015	Accept Acknowledgment Type
16	2	ID	O		0155	00016	Application Ack Type
17	2	ID	O			00017	Country Code
18	6	ID	O	Y/3	0211	00692	Character Set
19	60	CE	O			00693	Principal Language Of Message

The columns of this table show:

SEQ: Field sequence number

LEN: Maximum field length

DT: Data type

OPT: Optionality: R (required), O (optional), C (conditional), B (deprecated but retained for backward compatibility)

RP/#: Repeatable field. If "y" can repeat any number of times; a number indicates the maximum number of repeats

TBL#: The reference number of the HL7 table which contains a controlled vocabulary from which values can be taken

ITEM#: HL7's internal database item number

ELEMENT NAME: Human readable name of the field

Other required fields in addition to the Field Separator and Encoding Characters are:

- HL7V2 Message Type is entered in MSH-9.1, which is the first component of field MSH-9.
- Trigger Event is entered in MSH-9.2, which is the second component of field MSH-9.

We now describe some of the commonly used segments (Fig. 6.3). It might be an idea to bring Fig. 6.3 forward.

6.2.1 Message Header MSH

The report header (MSH) contains common metadata found in most messages, irrespective of subject. The first two fields of the MSH segment specify the delimiters used (see above).

SenderID is a unique identifier for the sender, expressed as the combination of an identification code for the sender and a code for the naming authority that controls the assignment of these identification codes. The only constraint is that the combination of MSH-4.2 and MSH-4.3 is unique.

For example: |^123457^Labs|.

DateTime of message is the exact date/time, that the sending system created the message. It is held in field MSH-7. For example |20080805183015 + 0000| indicates Aug 5, 2008 6.30 pm and 15 s GMT.

MessageType is the HL7 V2 message type and trigger event, transmitted in field MSH-9. Laboratory report messages all have the content |ORU^R01|.

MessageID is used to uniquely identify the message. This is transmitted in field MSH-10. The sending system must assign an identifier, which is unique to the extent in combination with the SenderID it is globally unique. One way of ensuring uniqueness is to use a globally unique identifier such as a GUID, which is produced on the fly by software. However, GUIDs are longer than the 20 characters prescribed by HL7.

ProcessingStatus shows whether the message is production (P) or for some other use such as debugging (D) or training (T). Production messages have the code P in field MSH-11, |P|.

SyntaxVersion indicates the HL7 version with which this message claims compliance. Compliance with HL7 V2.4 is shown by entering 2.4 in field MSH-12, |2.4|.

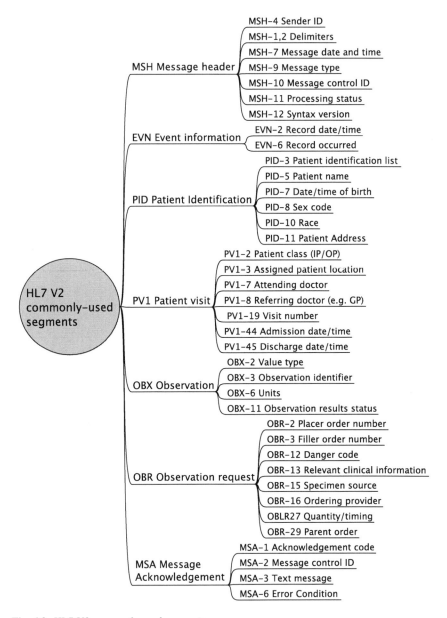

Fig. 6.3 HL7 V2 commonly used segments

6.2.2 Patient Identification Details (PID)

PatientID refers to the patient identifiers (one or more), which are used by the healthcare facility to uniquely identify a patient (e.g., hospital number, NHS number). In HL7 V2 these identifiers are sent in field PID-3, with the identifier in the first component (PID-3.1), an optional identifier for the issuing authority in the fourth component (PID-3.4), and an identifier type code (required) in the fifth component (PID-3.5).

For example, a patient with hospital number 123456 at St Mary's Hospital (SMH) may be entered as |123456^^^SMH^PI|, where PI indicates that this is a Patient internal identifier.

If the sender only uses the NHS number, e.g., 9999999904, this could be exchanged as |9999999904^^^NHS^NH|.

The repetition separator, ~, separates the combination of both hospital number and NHS number, together:

|123456^^^SMH^PI ~ 9999999904^^^NHS^NH|

PatientName includes the first (given) and last (family) name of the patient. These are provided in fields PID-5.1 and PID-5.2 respectively.

Mary Smith would become |Smith^Mary|.

DateOfBirth is recorded as a date in field PID-7 in format YYYYMMDD. e.g., |19620114| for 14 January 1962.

SexCode is in field PID-8, using an agreed coding system, such as M = Male and F = Female, e.g., |M|.

Patient address is transmitted in field PID-11, using the following components:

Street address	PID-11.1
Second line of address	PID-11.2
City	PID-11.3
State, province or county	PID-11.4
Zip or postal code	PID-11.5
Country	PID-11.6

For example |14 Pinewood Crescent^Hermitage^^^RG18 9WL| shows two lines of address and a postcode.

6.2.3   Patent Visit (PV1)

The PV1 (patient visit) segment is used in this example for both the patient's GP and the patient location at which the sample was taken.

Patient Location is the location at which the sample was taken. This information is mandatory for infection control. It is exchanged using the PV1-3 field (assigned patient location), using a mutually agreed code.

General Practitioner (person responsible for the Patients Health in the Community). The patient's GP identifier is shown in the PV1 segment, field PV1-8. In most cases only an agreed identifier is sent in component PV1-8.1. This data is desirable but not mandatory.

6.2.4   Request and Specimen Details (OBR)

The laboratory allocates each specimen an accession number, which is used to identify that specimen and any derivatives. In HL7 this is referred to as the Filler Order Number and is provided in field OBR-3.1.

Lab Test Code records what was requested to be done. An agreed code system, such as LOINC should be used. It is provided in field OBR-4, component OBR-4.1 with the text name in component OBR-4.2 and the name of coding system in OBR-4.3.

The date and time that the specimen was collected from the patient is provided in field OBR-7, using format YYYYMMDDHHMM. The time is optional.

The specimen source is provided using an agreed code or controlled vocabulary in field OBR-15.1 (e.g., WOUND SWAB).

Body Site (desirable) states the part of the body from which the specimen is taken. This is provided as a string in field OBR-15.4 (e.g., FOOT).

Site Modifier (optional) is sometimes reported, to provide additional information about the body site. If used it is provided in field OBR-15.5 (e.g., Right).

The doctor who ordered the test is recorded in field OBR-16, using an agreed identifier in OBR-16.1.

6.2.5   Result Details (OBX)

Each separate result is entered as a separate OBX segment, which relates to a single observation or observation fragment. It represents the smallest indivisible unit of a report.

Each result is represented as an attribute–value pair.

The *data type* of the value is specified in OBX-2. In HL7 terminology the attribute being measured is specified in OBX-3 (Observation Identifier) and the value is in OBX-5 (Observation Value). Internal references are specified in OBX-4.

In Microbiology, organisms, or the presence of an organism, are identified by either isolating the organism on a medium, or testing for the presence of an organism using a variety of tests. Isolates generally have associated antibiotic susceptibilities.

Observation Identifier (OBX-3) is the test that is being done (the attribute being measured) and typically uses LOINC or locally defined codes. Field OBX-3.1 contains the code; OBX-3.2 contains the human-readable display text; OBX-3.3 contains the coding scheme identifier if used.

For example: |9999-9^Test name^LN|.

(OBX-5) is the value of the result and typically uses SNOMED or SNOMED CT coding system.

The value type – the data type of the observation value – is specified in the Value Type (OBX-2).

The code value is OBX-5.1, display text is OBX-5.2, and code system identifier is OBX-5.3. Text strings can be transmitted in OBX-5.2 (e.g., |^This is a result|). Numeric values are represented as strings to allow non-numeric characters to be used (such as ">").

OBX|1|CE|5182-1^Hepatitis A Virus IgM Serum Antibody EIA^LN||G-A200^ Positive^SNM|

Some microbiology results have an extra complication. The first stage is to identify the various isolates (such as bacteria), which are present in the specimen. The second stage is to test each of these isolates for susceptibility to treatment by various antibiotics. The solution is to use internal references to link all of the results for the same isolate together using the Observation Sub-ID (OBX-4). Each OBX segment for the same isolate contains the same integer value in OBX-4.

The Abnormal Flag (OBX-8). If the observation is an antimicrobial susceptibility, the interpretation codes are: S = susceptible; R = resistant; I = intermediate; MS = moderately susceptible; VS = very susceptible.

The observation result status is required to indicate whether the result is Final, Preliminary, or otherwise and should be present in OBX-11.

6.2.6 Z-Segments

HL7 V2 provides a facility for any users to develop their own segments, message types, and trigger events using names beginning with Z. Z-segments are widely used and are one of the main reasons why there are so many different variants of HL7 V2 messages.

Z-segments can be placed anywhere in a message. Some message designers place all Z-segments at the end of a message, whilst others place them adjacent to related information.

6.3 Data Types

Data types are the basic building blocks used to construct or constrain the contents of each element. Every field, component, and subcomponent in HL7 V2 has a defined data type, which governs the information format in the element, what sub-elements it can contain and any vocabulary constraints. Some data types are Simple others are Complex.

HL7 V2 has 89 data types in all, but most applications use only a small number of common data types.

Simple data types contain just a single value, while complex data types may contain more than one sub-element, each of which has its own data type. The data type of a component can also be a complex data type. In this case, that component's components are subcomponents of the original data type. No further recursion is allowed.

Complex data types reflect associations of data that belong together, such as the parts of a person's name, address, or telephone number, or linking identifiers with their issuing authority (Fig. 6.4).

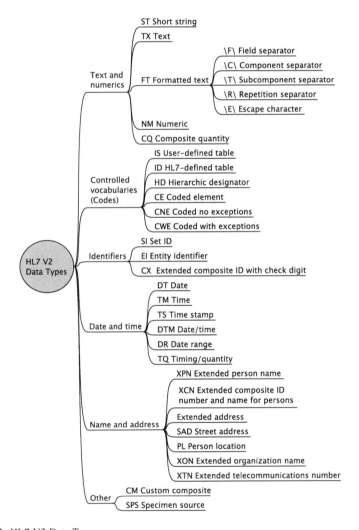

Fig. 6.4 HL7 V2 Data Types

6.3.1 Simple Data Types

Simple data types include:

- DT (date) represents a date in format: YYYY[MM[DD]]. For example, 2 August 2008 is represented as 20080802.
- DTM (date/time) is used to represent an event date and time including time zone if required. YYYY[MM[DD[HHMM[SS[.S[S[S[S]]]]]]]][+/–ZZZZ] where +/–ZZZZ indicates the time zone.
- FT (formatted text) allows embedded formatting commands, bracketed by the escape character.
- ID represents a value from a HL7-defined table. Users are not allowed to add their own values.
- IS represents a value from a user-defined table.
- NM (numeric) is used for numeric values. It may be preceded by a sign and may contain a decimal point.
- SI (set ID) gives the order of a segment instance within a message that may contain more than one segment with the same segment ID.
- ST (string) is used for short strings up to 200 characters.
- TX (text) is used for longer texts up to 64 K characters. In the TX data type the repetition separator (~) is used to indicate a hard carriage return (line break).

6.3.2 Complex Data Types

HL7 V2 supports a variety of complex data types to handle items such as coded values, identifiers, names, addresses, and so on. The most commonly used complex data types fall into three broad categories: Codes and Identifiers; Names and Addresses; and Other Complex Data Types.

6.3.3 Codes and Identifiers

Codes and identifiers are particularly important in interoperability and HL7 V2 supports both internally defined (by HL7) and externally defined coding schemes.

Coded values need to be uniquely identified, but there is always the problem that two different coding schemes use the same code value. The solution is to explicitly identify both the coding scheme and the code value. HL7 V2 enables this in two ways.

The first method is to populate the code values from a table, which is explicitly named in the data type definition. This method is used for the ID and IS data types. The second more general method is to transmit an agreed coding scheme identifier with each code value.

Coding schemes are either internal, which means defined by HL7, or external, which means defined by some other party. There are two main data types, CNE and CWE, which are very similar and replace the CE data type used in early versions of HL7 V2.

CNE (Coded with No Exceptions) is used when a required or mandatory coded field using a specified internal or external coding system must be used and may not be extended with local values. In CNE, the identifier component (CNE.1) is required.

CWE (Coded With Exceptions) is used when the set of allowable code values may vary on a site-specific basis or no code value is available for transmission, just a text string (CWE.2). CWE is very similar to CNE, but the identifier component (CWE.1) is optional.

The CNE and CWE data types have a similar structure:

Seq	Name	Data Type	Use
1	Identifier	ST	Code for the concept being represented
2	Text	ST	Name of the concept being represented
3	Name of Coding System	ID	Coding system identifier from which code value (in component 1) is selected
4	Alternate Identifier	ST	
5	Alternate Text	ST	
6	Name of Alternate Coding System	ID	Identifies coding system used for Alternate Identifier
7	Coding System Version ID	ST	
8	Alternate Coding System Version ID	ST	
9	Original Text	ST	Original text before coding

In most applications only the first three components of coded element are used. However, both CNE and CWE allow the expression of a single concept in two different coding schemes. This may be useful when a sending system holds data using a different coding system than that required by the destination. The original text may also be transmitted.

The commonly found complex data types for names and identifiers include:

- CE (coded element) can be used to represent an external code set or a non-coded text value.
- CNE (coded with no exceptions) strictly constrains an element to the values in a specified coding system.
- CWE (coded with exceptions) allows local codes or text to be used to supplement the specified coding system.
- CX (extended composite ID with check digit) is used for identifiers, including context and optional check digit information.
- EI (entity identifier) is used to specify identifiers.
- HD (hierarchic designator) is used to represent a code value or an identifier. It is useful for elements that some systems may treat as a code and other systems may treat as an identifier.

6.3.4 Names and Addresses

- FN (family name) surname.
- PL (patient location) within an institution; may include bed, room, ward, floor, building, facility, status, and type.
- SAD (street address), house number, and street.
- XAD (extended address) the full location address. Street address (SAD), city, state, postal code, country; also allows start and end dates.
- XCN (extended composite ID number and name for persons) is used for clinical staff. This is the largest data type with 23 components, combining the features of both CX and XPN into a single field.
- XON (extended organization name) is used for healthcare organizations.
- XPN (extended person name) is used for patients and their relatives. Includes family name (FN), given name(s), title, suffix, type, and date range.
- XTN (extended telecommunication number) is for electronic addresses including telephone and email. It includes optional codes for use (e.g., home or work) and type (e.g., direct line or mobile).

6.3.5 Other Complex Data Types

- CQ (composite quantity) has subcomponents quantity and units.
- SPS (specimen source) covers information about specimen type, body site, collection method, additives, etc.
- TQ (timing/quantity) allows the specification of the number, frequency, priority, etc. of a service, treatment, or test.

6.4 A Simple Example

The following example is from a simple feed of laboratory test reports from a microbiology laboratory to an infection control monitoring system. Each report includes:

- A header stating the type, origin, and date time of the message
- A single patient with ID number, name, sex, date of birth, address, and General Practitioner identifier
- Specimen details of the laboratory accession number (ID), source, body site, time of collection, and requester
- A set of test results, including the test name and result and abnormality flag

The abstract syntax of the HL7 V2 message is:

MSH Message header
PID Patient Identification Details
PV1 Patient Visit

OBR Results header
{OBX} Results detail (repeats)

All segments are required.
    The structure of an HL7 V2 message which meets these requirements is:

```
MSH|delimiters||sender|||dateTime||messageType|messageID
   |processingStatus|syntaxVersion
PID|||patientID^^^source^IDtype||familyName^givenName||d
   ateOfBirth|sex|||streetAddress^addressLine2^^^postCode
PV1|||patientLocation|||||patientsGP
OBR|||accessionNumber|testCode^testName^codeType|||speci
   menDate||||||||specimenSource^^^bodySite^siteModifier
   |requester
OBX||valueType|observableCode^observableName|observatio
   nSubID|valueCode^valueText^valueCodeType|||abnormalFl
   ag|||result status
OBX ...
```

A populated example is:

```
MSH|^~\&||^123457^Labs|||200808141530||ORU^R01|12345678
   9|P|2.4
PID|||123456^^^SMH^PI||MOUSE^MICKEY||19620114|
   M|||14 Disney Rd^Disneyland^^^MM1 9DL
PV1|||5N|||||G123456^DR SMITH
OBR|||54321|666777^CULTURE^LN||20080802|||||||||SW^^^FO
   OT^RT|C987654
OBX||CE|0^ORG|01|STAU||||||F
OBX||CE|500152^AMP|01||||R|||F
OBX||CE|500155^SXT|01||||S|||F
OBX||CE|500162^CIP|01||||S|||F
```

This could be rendered as:

> Report from Lab123457, 15:30 14-Aug-2008, Ref 123456789
> Patient: MICKEY MOUSE, DoB: 14-Jan-1962, M
> Address: 14 Disney Rd, Disneyland, MM1 9DL
> Specimen: Swab, FOOT, Right, Requested By: C987654,
> Location: 5N
> Patients GP: Dr Smith (G123456)
> Organism: STAU
> Susceptibility: AMP R
> SXT S
> CIP S

Note that the OBX segment repeats. Information about the susceptibilities of organism detected (STAU – staphylococcus aureus) is linked to that organism finding by using the OBX-4 Observation Sub-ID field.

Chapter 7
The HL7 V3 RIM

7.1 Origins

Even its supporters accept that HL7 V2 was developed in an ad hoc and unplanned way. For example, when an additional element is needed, it is added in the next available spot. Perhaps more importantly, V2 provides multiple ways of doing the same thing, leading to the well-founded jibe: "when you have seen one implementation of V2, you have seen one implementation; every one is different."

Work on HL7 Version 3 began in 1992 with the establishment of the HL7 Version 3 Task Force. As with many things, many of its characteristics are best understood by considering its origins as the planned successor to Version 2. The HL7 web-site explains the rationale for V3 as follows:

> Offering lots of optionality and thus flexibility, the V2.x series of messages are widely implemented and very successful. These messages evolved over several years using a "bottom-up" approach that has addressed individual needs through an evolving ad hoc methodology. There is neither a consistent view of that data that HL7 moves nor that data's relationship to other data.

HL7 Version 2's success is also largely attributable to its flexibility. It contains many optional data elements and data segments, making it adaptable to almost any site. While providing great flexibility, its optionality also makes it impossible to have reliable conformance tests of any vendor's implementation and also forces implementers to spend more time analyzing and planning their interfaces to ensure that both parties are using the same optional features.

Version 3 addresses these and other issues by using a well-defined methodology based on a reference information (data) model. Using rigorous analytic and message building techniques and incorporating more trigger events and message formats with very little optionality, HL7's primary goal for Version 3 was to offer a standard that would be definite and testable and provide the ability to certify vendors' conformance.

Version 3 uses an object-oriented development methodology and a Reference Information Model (RIM) to create messages. The RIM is an essential part of the HL7 Version 3 development methodology, as it provides an explicit representation

T. Benson, *Principles of Health Interoperability HL7 and SNOMED*, HI,
DOI 10.1007/978-1-84882-803-2_7, © Springer-Verlag London Limited 2010

of the semantic and lexical connections that exist between the information carried in the fields of HL7 messages.[1]

In summary, HL7 V3 is designed to be comprehensive in scope, complete in detail, extensible as requirements change, up-to-date and model-based, conformance testable, and technology-independent. It is based on the RIM (Reference Information Model). The RIM was conceived as a universal reference model for healthcare interoperability, covering the entire healthcare domain. Each message specification would be a view into this model. The RIM is at the core of HL7 Version 3; you cannot understand V3 without understanding the RIM.

The effort to develop the RIM took place in two distinct phases.

During the first phase, from about 1992 to 1999, a large complex class model with more was developed comprising more than a hundred classes and several hundred attributes and associations, supported by extensive documentation. In many ways, this was just a rationalized super-set of the content of HL7 V2. However, many people considered this model to be just too large to learn and use.

During 1998–1999, a radical approach, known as the Unified Service Action Model (USAM), was proposed to simplify the problem (Schadow et al. 2000). After a heated debate, HL7 resolved to adopt USAM with effect from January 2000. USAM is based on two key ideas, which lead directly to the structure of the RIM as we know it today.

The first idea is that most healthcare documentation is concerned with "happenings" and things (human or other) participate in these happenings in various ways. Furthermore, happenings have a natural life cycle such as the concept itself, an intent for it to happen, the happening, and the consequences of its happening. These are like the moods of a verb.

The second idea is to recognize that the same people and things can perform different roles when participating in different types of happening. For example, a person can be either a care provider or the subject of care.

7.2 Overview

HL7 Version 3 is a lingua franca used by healthcare computers to talk to other computers, to help provide information when and where needed. Healthcare communication is complex and any language needs to accommodate this complexity and also handle future needs. HL7 Version 3 is designed to handle most if not all healthcare communications in an unambiguous way, using a relatively small set of constructs, which can be learnt relatively easily.

The HL7 RIM (Reference Information Model) specifies the grammar of V3 messages and, specifically, the basic building blocks of the language (nouns, verbs, etc.), their permitted relationships, and Data Types. The RIM is not a model of health care, although it is healthcare-specific, nor is it a model of any message, although it is used in messages.

---

[1] HL7. *HL7 Standards – HL7 Version 3*. www.hl7.org

At first sight, the RIM is quite simple. The RIM backbone has just five core classes and a number of permitted relationships between them. However, it presents quite a steep learning curve. The good news is that once you reached the plateau the ground becomes much less steep.

The RIM defines a set predefined Attributes for each class and these are the only ones allowed in HL7 messages. Each attribute has a specified Data Type. These Attributes and Data Types become tags in HL7 XML messages. Message specifications, to do a particular task, use a subset of the available RIM Attributes, listing each element used and how many repeats are allowed. This is known as refinement. Each Data Type is constrained to the simplest structure that meets the requirements of the task.

HL7 V3 uses a graphical representation, called Refined Message Information Model (RMIM) to display the structure of a message as a color-coded diagram. Most RMIMs can be shown on a single sheet of paper or PowerPoint slide and these RMIM diagrams are used to design messages and to explain what each HL7 message consists of. The actual interchange (the wire format) is usually XML.

All of the XML tags and attributes used in V3 messages are derived from the HL7 Reference Information Model (RIM) and the HL7 V3 Data Types. The structure of each HL7 message is set out in an XML schema, which specifies which tags and attributes are needed or allowed in the message, their order, and the number of times each may occur, together with annotations describing how each tag shall be used. HL7 message schema are lengthy, detailed, and verbose.

The RIM itself is shown in Fig. 7.1. The next part of this chapter sets out to explain how it works.

7.3 The RIM Backbone

The V3 RIM is based on a simple backbone structure, involving three main classes, Act, Role, and Entity, linked together using three association classes: ActRelationship, Participation, and RoleLink.

In HL7 V3, every happening is an Act, which is analogous to a verb in English. Each Act may have any number of Participations, which are Roles, played by Entities. These are analogous to nouns.

Each Act may also be related to other Acts, via Act-Relationships.

Act, Role, and Entity classes have a number of specializations. For example, Entity has a specialization called Living Subject, which itself has a specialization called Person. Person inherits the attributes of both Entity and Living Subject (Fig. 7.2).

7.3.1 Structural Attributes

Structural Attributes are a device, which is used to reduce the size of the original RIM from over 100 classes to a simple backbone of six main classes. Structural attributes are used to specify what each RIM class means when used in a message.

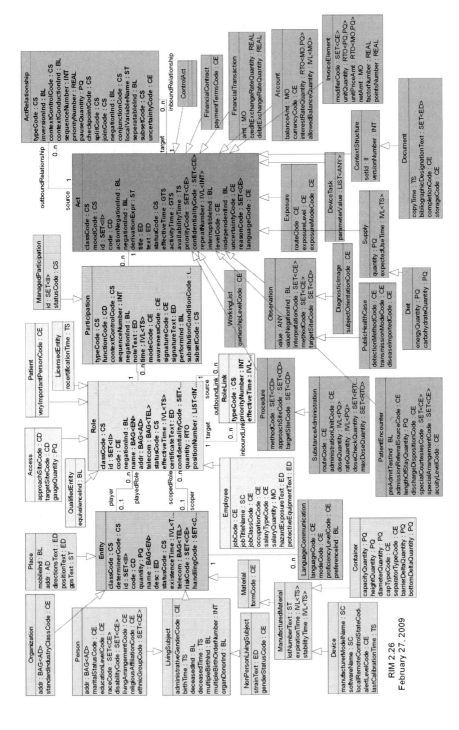

Fig. 7.1 HL7 V3 RIM normative content

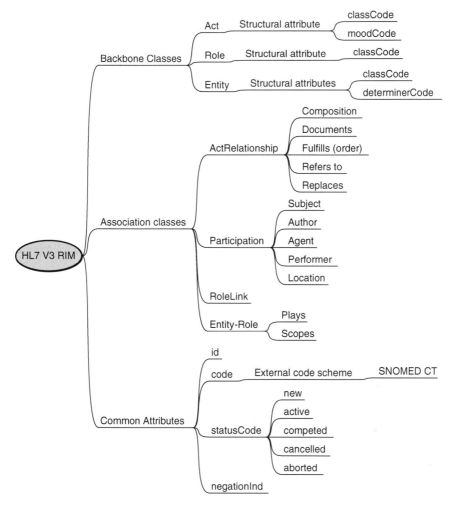

Fig. 7.2 HL7 V3 Reference information model backbone

For example, every Act has a *classCode* and a *moodCode*. The *classCode* states what sort of Act this is, such as observation, encounter, or administration of a drug.

The primary use of structural attributes is in the design of messages or other services, which are then implemented in computer applications. Message designers select the values of structural attributes when designing messages, or groups of related messages. These values are then frozen and may not be changed by application programmers or anyone else downstream.

In a very real sense, each class is named by its structural attributes. The semantic meaning of every class in an HL7 V3 message specification is specified by its structural attributes. The actual name of the class does not really matter; what matters is the meaning of its structural attributes.

The full set of structural attributes for each of the backbone RIM classes is:

- Act: classCode, moodCode, negationInd, levelCode
- Entity: classCode, determinerCode
- Role: classCode, negationInd
- ActRelationship: typeCode, inversionInd, contextControlCode, contextConduction Ind, negationInd
- Participation: typeCode, contextControlCode
- RoleLink: typeCode

7.3.2 Specializations

Each of the main backbone classes (Act, Role, and Entity) has a number other classes linked to it, using a line with an open triangle arrowhead at the backbone-class end. This is the UML symbol for specialization. The class that is pointing is a specialization of the class that is being pointed toward, which is a generalization.

The specialization inherits all of the properties of the generalization, while adding any specific attributes of its own. For example, the class Patient, at the top center of the RIM, is a specialization of Role with the addition of the optional attribute veryImportantPersonCode. The convention is that only a class, which has one or more additional attributes specific to itself, is shown on the RIM.

A number of frequently used attributes are found in more than one class. These include: *id, code,* and *status code.*

The conventional way to denote each attribute is to prefix it with its class name, so *Act.id* is the attribute *id* in Act, and *Role.id* is an *id* in Role.

id is used to identify classes and has the II (Instance Identifier) Data Type, which may be a universally unique identifier (UUID) or/and object identifier (OID).

Codes and identifiers avoid ambiguity in messages. The *id* attribute is used to give unique identity to people, persons, organizations, things, and information objects. There are also two main types of code. The first type covers the specialized codes used for structural attributes and are defined by HL7 itself. The second covers externally defined terms and codes such as SNOMED CT (Clinical Terms).

While *classCode* is a structural attribute used to indicate the name of an Act, Role, or Entity, the *code* attribute, is used to specify precisely what the class means at a leaf level of granularity. Unlike *classCode*, the code attribute is not a mandatory nor is it a structural attribute.

The *classCode* and *code* attributes are related in so far as *code* should always be a specialization of *classCode*. For example, if *Act.classCode* is a procedure, the *Act. code* must be a type of procedure and may not be anything else.

The *code* attribute is usually populated from an external coding scheme. External coding schemes are identified using an OID. The combination of the OID and *code* value is unique.

Each class may only contain a single *code*. If it is necessary to apply several attributes to a class, which are best done with *code*, then each code has to be in a separate class, which must be linked to the parent class using an ActRelationship.

The *negationInd* can be used to reverse the meaning of a class.

We now discuss the three core classes, Act, Entity, and Role in more detail.

7.4   Act

Act is a record of something that has happened or may happen.

Full representation of an Act identifies the kind of act (what happens), the actor who performs the deed, and the objects or subjects (e.g., patients) that the act affects. Additional information may be provided to indicate location (where), time (when), manner (how), together with reasons (why), or motives (what for).

Acts can be related to many other Acts using the ActRelationship class. For example, one Act may contain, cause, lead to, update, revise, or view information about other Acts.

Information in a document is treated as an Act – the act being the creation of the document content. Each transaction is a kind of act. An account is a record of a set of transactions.

7.4.1   Act classCode

Acts include an enormous range of happenings: events, such as encounter, visits, and appointments; observations such as tests, diagnoses, and examination findings; notifications such as alerts, confirmation, and consent; the supply and administration of medicines and other consumables; clinical, administrative, and financial procedures. The *classCode* field determines whether an Act is an observation, an encounter, or a procedure.

7.4.2   moodCode

Act has another important structural attribute called *moodCode*, which is similar to the tense of a verb. The term mood is a grammatical term representing a category of verb use typically expressing: fact (indicative mood), command (imperative mood), question (interrogative mood), wish (optative mood), or conditionality (subjunctive mood). *moodCode* indicates whether an Act has happened (an event), is a request for something to happen, a goal, or a criterion. For example, "weight = 100kg" is an observation event; "measure weight daily" is a request; "reduce weight to 80Kg" is a goal and "if weight is greater than 80Kg" is a criterion.

EVN	Event (occurrence)	A service that actually happens, may be an ongoing service or a documentation of a past service
RQO	Request	A request or order for a service is an intent directed from a placer (request author) to a fulfiller (service performer)
PRMS	Promise	An intent to perform a service that has the strength of a commitment. Other parties may rely on the originator of such promise that said originator will see to it that the promised act will be fulfilled
PRP	Proposal	A nonmandated intent to perform an act. Used to record intents that are explicitly not Orders
DEF	Definition	Definition of a service

moodCode is used to distinguish between an order (RQO), which is something you want to happen, and a report (EVN), which is something that has happened.

In clinical guidelines, *moodCode* can be used to distinguish between the definition of the guideline as originally authored (DEF), the intent that it should be followed for a particular patient (PRP) and the actual compliance (EVN).

7.4.3   StatusCode

statusCode specifies the state of an Act, such as:

New	Act is in preparatory stages and may not yet be acted upon
Active	The Act can be performed or is being performed
Completed	An Act that has terminated normally after all its constituents have been performed
Canceled	The act has been abandoned before activation
Aborted	The act has been terminated prior to the originally intended completion

The full state-machine diagram for the Act class is shown in Fig. 7.3.

7.4.4   Times

The Act class has two important time attributes: *activityTime* and *effectiveTime*, which have rather different meanings. The *activityTime* states when the Act itself occurs, but *effectiveTime* states the clinically relevant time of the Act. The difference is best explained by examples.

- The *activityTime* for an appointment booking is the time of making the appointment, while the *effectiveTime* is the appointment date/time.
- For a laboratory request, the *activityTime* is the time the request is made, while the *effectiveTime* is the time that the sample is requested to be taken (in

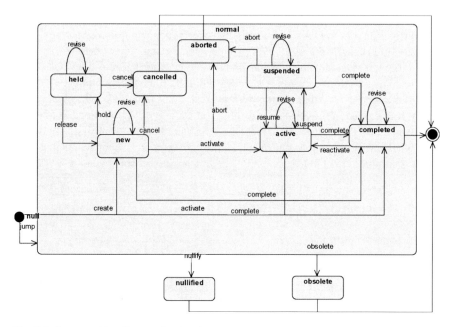

Fig. 7.3 State-machine diagram for Act class

hospitals, doctors often order blood tests with instructions for the sample to be taken at some future time).

- For a laboratory test result, the *activityTime* is the time the test was performed, but the *effectiveTime* is the time the sample is taken from the patient.
- For a contract, the *activityTime* is the date of the contract itself, while the *effectiveTime* is the time that the contract holds good.
- The activity time for a prescription is the date of the prescription, while the *effectiveTime* is how long the medication is to be taken.

7.4.5   Act Specializations

The most important Act specializations are Observation, Procedure, Substance Administration, Supply, and *PatientEncounter*.

7.4.5.1   Observation

Observation is defined as an Act of recognizing and noting information about the subject, and whose immediate and primary outcome (postcondition) is new data about a subject. Observations often involve measurement or other elaborate methods of investigation, but may also be simply assertive statements, such as a diagnosis.

Many observations are structured as name-value pairs, where the Observation. code (inherited from Act) is the name and the Observation.value is the value of the property. The Observation class is always used to hold name-value pairs.

Observation.value contains the information determined by the observation action. It is unique in the RIM in that it has the Data Type ANY, which is to say it can be any Data Type, although in messages, the Data Type is usually constrained to a specific Data Type, such as physical quantity (PQ) or a code. This works in a way, which is similar to the OBX segment in V2, which can also contain any Data Type.

7.4.5.2   Procedure

A Procedure is defined as an Act whose immediate and primary outcome (postcondition) is the alteration of the physical condition of the subject.

Note that this definition of procedure is more limited than the definition of procedure used in SNOMED CT (see Chapter 12), although it includes most surgical procedures and physical treatment such as physiotherapy. It does not cover imaging or laboratory investigations, administrative procedures, counseling, or medication.

7.4.5.3   Substance Administration

Substance Administration is defined as the act of introducing or otherwise applying a substance to the subject. This class is used when prescribing a medicine, with a mood code of Intent, because the intent of a prescription is to administer medication.

Substance Administration is also used in Event mood to record that a medication has been administered to a patient.

7.4.5.4   Supply

Supply is defined as an act that involves provision of a material by one entity to another.

For example, dispensing a medicine is a Supply Act, while prescribing and administration are both *SubstanceAdministration* Acts.

Supply and *SubstanceAdministration* Acts require a participation link to identify the material or medicine involved.

7.4.5.5   *PatientEncounter*

PatientEncounter is defined as an interaction between a patient and a care provider for the purpose of providing healthcare-related services. Examples of *PatientEncounter* include inpatient and outpatient visits, home visits, and even telephone calls.

Appointments, which have been booked, are *PatientEncounters* in the mood Promise, until they have taken place, when the mood is changed to Event.

Details of the HL7 V3 Act Class are summarized in Fig. 7.4.

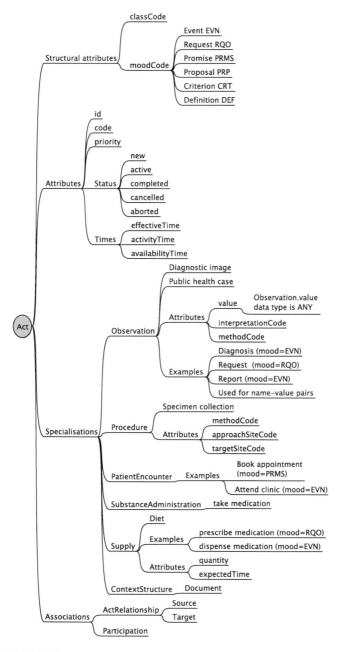

Fig. 7.4 HL7 V3 RIM – Act

7.5   Entity

Entity is the second main backbone class in the RIM. Entity is any living or nonliving thing, such as a person, animal, organization, or thing, which has or will have existence. It can also represent a group of things. An Entity can also be a group of things or a category or kind of thing.

Entities cover the whole universe of

- Living things, such as people, animals, plants, and microorganisms
- Nonliving things such as places, manufactured items, and chemical substances
- Abstract things such as organizations

Entity has a *classCode*, which states whty type of thing it represents. It also has a second structural attribute, *determinerCode*, Which is used to help distinguish between an individual instance of an Entity, such as a person, a collection of instances, such as a herd or the generic class of that entity, such as a particular type of micro-organism.

Entities may either play a Role directly, or may provide the "scope" for a Role. For example, Dr Smith plays the Role of Doctor, but this Role may be scoped by the organization she works for, such as St Mary's Hospital. Similarly, the scope link may also be used to note the manufacturer of a medicine. An Entity may perform any number of Roles, but every instance of Role is only played by a single Entity.

7.5.1   Entity Specializations

Entity has four main specializations, *LivingSubject* (incuding Person), Material, Place, and Organization (Fig. 7.5).

Person is a specialization of Living Subject, which is a specialization of Entity. Person has the attributes inherited from Entity and Living Subject as well as its own.

For example, *name* is an attribute of Entity, while sex (*administrativeGender-Code*), date of birth (*birthTime*), and date of death (*deceasedTime*) is each an attribute of LivingSubject.

LivingSubject has a second specialization, *NonPersonLivingSubject*, which is mainly used for veterinary subjects (animals, birds, fishes, etc.), but also includes bacteria, plants, fungi, etc.

Some attributes of an Entity, are also found in the Role class. These include *id, code, name, addr* (address), *telecom, statusCode, and quantity*. The primary rule for determining whether to use an Entity attribute or a Role attribute is whether or not an attribute value is permanent. If it is permanent, then use Entity, if it is not permanent, and in particular, if it is related to how a thing is used or what a person does, then it is a Role attribute.

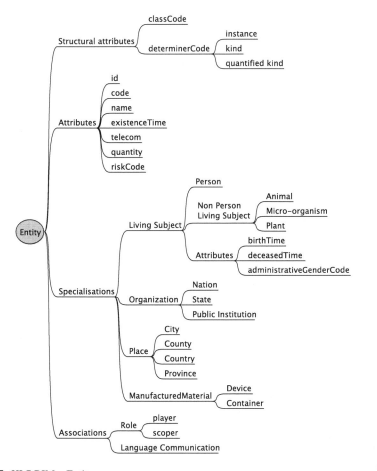

Fig. 7.5 HL7 RIM – Entity

7.6 Role

Role is the third main backbone class. A Role is defined as a competency of an Entity playing the Role. Roles for people are usually positions, jobs, or "hats," which they are qualified to do. Roles for inanimate objects such as places and machines are what they are normally used for.

There is also a wide variety of Roles, which can be played by:

- People, such as patient, practitioner, or employee
- Places, such as hospital, home, clinic, or place of birth
- Organizations, such as care provider, employer, or supplier

- Things, such as drug, instrument, or computer system
- Responsible entities, such as parent, employer, or manufacturer

7.6.1 Role Specializations

The most important Role specialization is Patient. However, it is important to remember that specializations are only shown explicitly in the RIM when they add additional attributes to the general class (Fig. 7.6).

Patient is defined as a Role of a person (player) as a recipient of healthcare services from a an Organization (scoper).

7.7 Association Classes

This simple backbone structure of Act, Role, and Entity is sufficiently flexible to cover almost anything you may want to say. However, we also need explicit connectors between each of these classes.

The *contextControlCode* specifies how the source contributes to the context of a target Act, and whether it may be propagated to descendent Acts whose association allows such propagation.

7.7.1 ActRelationship

ActRelationship is a relationship between two Acts, used to link Acts together, from a source Act to a target Act. There are various types of link, including composition, documentation, fulfillment, etc. Every ActRelationship has a source and a target to which it points. An Act can have any number of ActRelationships, which may be organized as a hierarchy.

ActRelationship *typeCode* describes the type of association between Acts:

- Composition *comprises* entries
- Discharge summary *documents* a hospital visit
- Test report *fulfills* a test request
- Discharge summary *refers* to a referral
- Final report *replaces* a preliminary report

7.7.2 Participation

Participation defines the involvement of a Role in an Act. It shows how an Entity, in a particular Role, functions during the scope of an Act. Participants take part in Acts as either actors or targets in the Act. Actors do things, while targets are

Fig. 7.6 HL7 RIM – Role

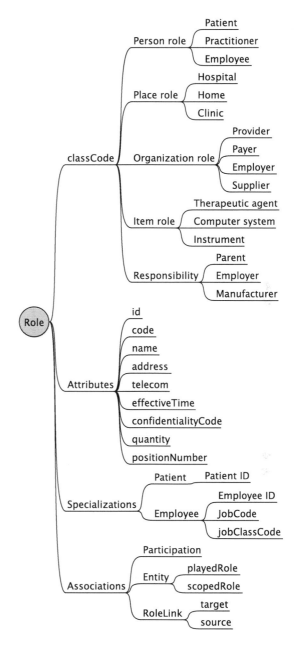

essentially passive. Participation is specific to a single Act. When the Act stops, the Participation ceases.

A particular Entity in a particular Role can participate in an Act in many ways. Thus, a person in the role of surgeon may participate in an act as primary surgeon or as assistant surgeon.

Participation Type Code describes the type of association between an Act and each participating Role:

- Performer of act (surgeons, observers, practitioners)
- Subject of act, such as the patient
- Location of act
- Author, informant, addressee, or information recipient

7.7.3   Role Link

Role Link is a relationship between two Roles. It provides a simple way of linking Roles together such as between jobs in an organization chart, family members, or between members of a medical team.

7.8   HL7 Version 3 Data Types

In Version 3, Data Types have a similar role as in Version 2, providing fine detail.

7.8.1   Basic Data Types

Basic Data Types include:

BL Boolean – true or false
BIN Binary
ST Character String – unformatted text string
ED Encapsulated Data – text data that is primarily intended to be read by a human. ED can include format information
INT Integer number – any positive or negative integer
REAL Real number
PQ Physical Quantity – a measure quantity with units
MO Money – a currency amount

7.8.2   Codes and Identifiers

7.8.2.1   Instance Identifier (II)

The II (Instance Identifier) data type has two main flavors: UUIDs and OID-based identifier.

Universally Unique Identifiers (UUID) are software-generated identifiers, created on the fly to identify information artefacts uniquely. UUIDs are 16-byte (128 bit) numbers. The number of theoretically possible is large (more than ten followed by 37 zeroes).

The standard way of displaying a UUID is as 32 hexadecimal digits, displayed in five groups separated by hyphens in the form 8-4-4-4-12, such as:

550e8400-e29b-41d4-a716-446655440000

UUIDs are usually used when the identifier in question is generated by a software application without human assistance.

The second type of identifier is that held in some type of register. Here we use an identifier for the register itself and each item which is registered is allocated an identifier that is unique within that register. The convention is HL7 to use an OID (object identifier) to identify the register itself.

An OID is a node in a hierarchical tree structure, with the left-most number representing the root and the right-most number representing a leaf. Each branch under the root corresponds to an assigning authority. Each of these assigning authorities may, in turn, designate its own set of assigning authorities that work under its auspices, and so on down the line. Eventually, one of these authorities assigns a unique (to it as an assigning authority) number that corresponds to a leaf node on the tree. The leaf may represent an assigning authority (in which case the root OID identifies the authority), or an instance of an object. An assigning authority owns a namespace, consisting of its sub-tree.

While most owners of an OID will "design" their namespace sub-tree in some meaningful way, there is no generally applicable way to infer any meaning on the parts of an OID.

HL7 has its own OID 2.16.840.1.113883 (iso.country.us.organization.hl7) and maintains an OID registry with around 3,000 nodes.

The combination of an OID and a value is intended to be globally unique.

One way to obtain an OID in the UK is to use the company registration number. All companies registered in England and Wales may append their company registration number to the 1.2.826.0 root to obtain an OID that is unique to the company without further formality or charge. The hierarchy is:

- Top of OID tree
- 1 – ISO assigned OIDs
- 1.2 – ISO member body
- 1.2.826 – Great Britain (GB/UK)
- 1.2.826.0 – UK National registration

For example, 1.2.826.0.1.4224538 means Abies Ltd.

7.8.2.2 Code Data Types

HL7 Version 3 has four code Data Types (CS, CV, CE and CD) listed in increasing order of complexity:

CS is just a simple code value, optionally accompanied by a display name. CS does not include any coding system identifier, which means that the meaning is determined by the context in which it occurs. CS is only used only for codes such as structural attributes, which are defined by HL7 itself and are always required.

CV includes a code value, an optional *displayName*, a *coding system*, identifier, enabling externally defined coding schemes to be used, and original text used. CV can be qualified as being CNE (coded no exceptions) or CWE (coded with exceptions).

CE is an extension of CV, which allows a term to be coded in more than one way. It includes the original code (such as a local code used in the sending system) to be sent along with a translation into a code required by the receiving system, which may have courser granularity.

CD is the most complex code Data Type, providing the functionality of CE as well as qualifiers to enabling complex postcoordinated expressions to be exchanged. For example the term "compression fracture of neck of femur" can be represented as a postcoordinated SNOMED CT expression using compositional grammar as follows:

71620000|fracture of femur|: 116676008|associatcd morphology|=21947006|compression fracture|,363698007|finding site|=29627003|structure of neck of femur|

This expression can be represented in HL7 using the CD Data Type as:
```
<code code="71620000" codeSystem="2.16.840.1.113883.6.96"
displayName="fracture of femur">
<qualifier>
<name code="363698007" displayName="finding site"/>
<value code="29627003" displayName="structure of neck of femur"/>
</qualifier>
<qualifier>
<name code="116676008" displayName="associated morphology"/>
<value code="21947006" displayName="compression fracture"/>
</qualifier>
</code>
```

7.8.3 Date/Time

Dates and times are represented by a hierarchy of Data Types:

TS Point in time
IVL <TS> Interval of time
PIVL Periodic interval of time
EIVL Event-related periodic interval of time
GTS General Timing Specification

The time format is similar to that used in Version 2, based on ISO 8601 (e.g., YYYY MMDDhhmmss).

Most, practical needs are met by TS, which may specify either a date or date/ time. Interval of Time may be expressed with start and end dates/times, or as a duration or as an open range, with only the start or end date specified.

The more complex specifications were developed to meet the potential requirements of complex medication regimes.

7.8.4 Name and Address

The Data Types used in V3 for names and addresses are similar to those used in Version 2. Each name or address can be structured or unstructured and may include codes to specify its type and use and a date range for validity dates.

Types of name and address include:

TN Trivial name (unstructured)

ON Organization name

EN Entity name (any thing)

PN Person name in a sequence of name parts such as family given name(s), family and given, together with name use (legal, maiden name, former name, alias)

AD Postal Address as a sequence of address parts, such as house, street, city, postal code, country, and the address use (home, temporary, etc.)

TEL Telecommunication Address is specified as a Universal Resource Locator (URL), which covers telephone numbers (voice, fax, or mobile), e-mail addresses, and web pages.

7.8.5 Generic Collections

Multiple repeats can be specified in four ways:

SET is an unordered collection of values without any repeats

LIST is a sequence, containing values in a defined sequence (repeats not allowed)

BAG is an unordered collection of values, which are allowed to repeat

IVL is a set of consecutive values of an ordered base type such as time or physical quantity

7.9 Communication Infrastructure

The communication infrastructure is a collection of subject areas that define the technical infrastructure of HL7, including messaging and structured documents such as CDA. Structured documents are discussed in Chapter 9, Clinical Document Architecture; Messaging is discussed further in Chapter 10, HL7 Dynamic Model.

7.9.1 Infrastructure Root

All classes in the RIM are regarded as being specializations of the Infrastructure Root, which has four optional fields, which can be used in any RIM class or clone to support special communications needs. For example, the *templateId* field is used to specify the identity of the template being applied to any class. These special fields are:

- *nullFlavor* – When valued in an instance, this attribute signals that the class instance is null, and that the remainder of the information for this class and its properties will not be communicated. The value of this attribute specifies the flavor of null that is intended. Flavors of null include: no information (default), unknown, asked but unknown.
- *realmCode* – signals the imposition of realm-specific constraints. The value of this attribute identifies the realm in question.
- *TypeId* – When valued in an instance, this attribute signals the imposition of constraints defined in an HL7-specified message type. This might be a common type (also known as CMET in the messaging communication environment), or content included within a wrapper. The value of this attribute provides a unique identifier for the type in question.
- *templateID* – When valued in an instance, this attribute signals the imposition of a set of template-defined constraints. The value of this attribute provides a unique identifier for the templates in question (Fig. 7.7).

7.10 Use of the RIM

The Health Level Seven (HL7) Reference Information Model (RIM) is a static model of health and healthcare information as viewed within the scope of HL7 standards development activities. It is the combined consensus view of information from the perspective of the HL7 working group and the HL7 international affiliates. The RIM is the ultimate source from which all HL7 version 3.0 protocol specification standards draw their information-related content.

The classes, attributes, state-machines, and relationships in the RIM are used to derive domain-specific information models that are then transformed through a series of constraining refinement processes to eventually yield a static model of the information content of an HL7 standard. The HL7 V3 standard development process defines the rules governing the derivation of domain information models from the RIM and the refinement of those models into HL7 standard specifications. The rules require that all information structures in derived models be traceable back to the RIM and that their semantic and related business rules not conflict with those specified in the RIM.

The RIM is only one model of healthcare information needs. The abstract style of the RIM and the ability to extend the RIM through vocabulary specifications

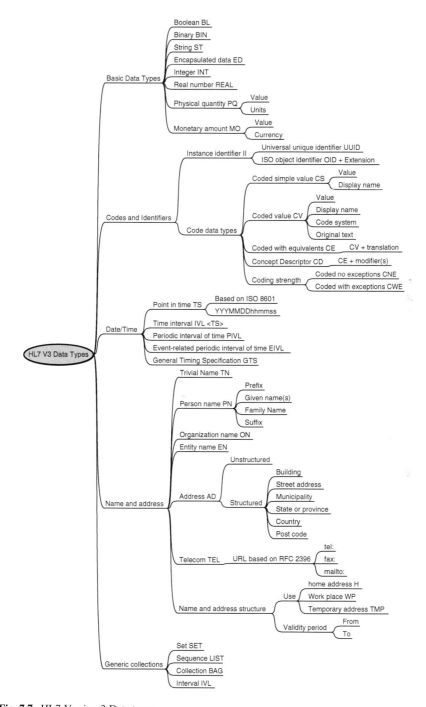

Fig. 7.7 HL7 Version 3 Data types

make the RIM applicable to any conceivable healthcare system information interchange scenario. In fact, it is conceptually applicable to any information domain involving entities playing roles and participating in acts.

The universal applicability of the RIM makes it particularly useful for an organization like HL7 that has to consider the needs of a large and diverse membership. The style of the RIM makes it extremely stable, which is another important characteristic for HL7.

The HL7 standards development process calls for the creation of domain-specific models derived from the RIM and the incremental refinement of those models into design models that are specific to the problem area. These problem-area-specific design models narrow the abstractness of the RIM and include constraints on attribute values and class relationships that are use-case-specific. External organizations considering using the HL7 RIM are advised to adopt a similar process of deriving design models as a transformation of the RIM.

In summary, the RIM has six backbone classes: Act, *ActRelationship*, Participation, Role, *RoleLink*, and Entity. The meaning of each class is determined by one or more structural attributes, such as classCode and moodCode. Each class has a predefined set of possible attributes and may have specializations, which provide additional attributes for specialized classes. Each attribute has a *Data Type*.

Chapter 8
Constrained Information Models

A central idea of the HL7 V3 approach is that of constraining or refining a general model, for the specific use case being considered, by limiting optionality. This idea of constraining a general model to create an agreed subset and interpretation of the specification is widespread in the standards world. Such constrained specifications are called profiles.

Many standards have a large number of optional aspects, and if different suppliers do not implement the same subset, they will fail to interoperate. The use of profiles is a way to enforce a particular interpretation to ensure interoperability.

The idea of constrained information models creates a tree-like hierarchy of possible models. At the root lies the RIM. Everything else is a constraint on the RIM.

8.1 Types of Constrained Information Model

The following types of constrained model are recognized within HL7 V3, starting with the broadest, proceeding to the narrowest.

DMIM   Domain Message Information Model
RMIM   Refined Message Information Model
HMD   Hierarchical Message Description
MT   Message Type

8.1.1 Domain Message Information Model

Domain Message Information Models (DMIM) have been defined for many subject areas.

A DMIM is a general model of a domain, in HL7 notation, from which a related family of message specifications can be derived. A DMIM may be created top-down from domain experience or bottom-up as a superset of messages in a domain. Once created, a DMIM can be used as reference from which further messages may be defined.

T. Benson, *Principles of Health Interoperability HL7 and SNOMED*, HI,
DOI 10.1007/978-1-84882-803-2_8, © Springer-Verlag London Limited 2010

A DMIM does not have a hierarchical structure and cannot be serialized, which means that it cannot be implemented as it is but needs to be further constrained as RMIMs. Not all projects use DMIMs, but their purpose is to provide a common point of reference to ensure compatibility between all RMIMs in the same domain.

8.1.2 Refined Message Information Model

The most widely used constrained information model is the RMIM (Refined Message Information Model), which is a diagram of a message specification. RMIMs and DMIMs use the same notation. One important difference is that an RMIM can only have one point of entry and can be expressed in a serialized format, which is essential if a message has to be transmitted as a string of bits over a wire.

8.1.3 Hierarchical Message Description

An RMIM can also be expressed in a tabular format, known as a hierarchical message description (HMD). HMDs and RMIMs can contain the same information, but most people find that RMIMs are easier to use and understand.

8.1.4 Message Type

A message type (MT) is a particular specification of a message which can be used in a data interchange. Any one RMIM or HMD can be further constrained in various ways to create a set of closely related message types, which are then exchanged as a linear string of XML and validated using an XML schema.

8.2 Types of Constraint

The RIM, DMIMs, and RMIMs can be constrained in several different ways.

8.2.1 Omission and Cloning

The simplest form of constraint is by omission. Classes or attributes with classes are simply left out. All classes and all attributes (apart from structural attributes) in the RIM are optional, so you only use the ones you need.

8.2.2   Cloning

The same RIM class can be used many times in different ways in DMIMs and RMIMs. This process is referred to as cloning and the classes selected for use in constrained models are referred to as clones.

The metaphor being that you take a clone of a class from the RIM and then constrain that clone in the constrained information model. Cloning limits the number of classes that need to be defined in the RIM, leading to a small stable RIM.

8.2.3   Multiplicity and Optionality

The next form of constraint is to constrain multiplicities in terms of repeatability and optionality. Most associations and attributes in the RIM are optional and allow any number of repeats.

These can be constrained by making such multiplicities nonrepeatable mandatory $(1..1)$ – you need to have one, but only one; or nonrepeatable optional $(0..1)$ – if you have any, you can only have one.

In HL7 Version 3 specifications, the correct verb form for indicating a require-ment is "SHALL." The correct verb form for indicating a recommendation is "SHOULD." The correct verb form for an option is "MAY." Universally accepted standardization terminology does not recognize "must." "SHALL" is used to indi-cate a mandatory aspect or an aspect on which there is no option. The negatives are SHALL NOT, SHOULD NOT, MAY NOT.

8.2.4   Data Types Constraint

The third type of constraint involves constraining data types. The HL7 V3 data types have been designed with a hierarchical structure. For example, there are four code data types: CS (code simple), CV (coded value), CE (code with equivalents), and CD(concept descriptor) in increasing order of complexity. A more complex data type, such as CD can be constrained to a simple data type such as CV. Similarly, the data type GTS (General Time Specification) can be constrained to IVL<TS> (Time Interval) or to TS (Timestamp).

8.2.5   Code Binding

The final type of constraint involves code binding – specifying what code value sets shall be used. The coding strength of a code may also be restricted to CNE (Coded No Exceptions) or may be specified as CWE (Coded With Exceptions).

This may all sound quite complex but is a lot simpler than it sounds. The simple rule is that you only specify what you need, leave out everything else, or make it as simple as possible.

8.3   Vocabulary and Value sets

The HL7 V3 standards talk about vocabulary domains and value sets and it is important to understand the difference between them.

A value set is the set of codes that may be used to populate a specific attribute in a message instance, and is usually specified by the message designer. A value set may be a single code only, for example to specify a structural attribute, a subset of an HL7 defined code, or all or part of an externally defined coding system.

A vocabulary domain is the set of codes available to the message designer for a specific attribute. For example, the vocabulary domain for the *Act.moodCode* is the set of all *mood code* values defined and maintained by HL7.

Message users are concerned with value sets, message designers need to think about vocabulary domains and select their value sets from these.

The concept of vocabulary domains is most applicable to HL7's own internally defined vocabulary tables, which are quite extensive. These must be used for structural attributes and are widely used within Data Types.

Each concept normally has a mnemonic code, which is the code value used; a print name which explains its meaning; a concept ID, used for internal reference; a level; and type. Mnemonic codes are unique for a particular coding scheme. These tables have a hierarchical structure, with each concept being allocated a level, so a level 2 concept is the child of the preceding level 1 concept and so on. The code type may be

- Abstract (A) does not have a code, but does contain child concepts
- Specialized (S) has a code and contains child concepts
- Leaf (L) has a code, but no child concepts

8.4   Artifact Naming

HL7 V3 artifacts are identified using a common naming scheme, which is at first sight a bit complex. The format is SSDD_AAnnnnnnRRVV.

The first four characters identify the subsections and domains.

COCT   Common Message Elements
COMT   Common Message Content
FIAB   Accounting & Billing
FICR   Claims & Reimbursement
MCAI   Message Act Infrastructure

MCCI	Message Control Infrastructure
MFMI	Master File Management Infrastructure
POLB	Laboratory
PORX	Pharmacy
PRPA	Patient Administration
PRPM	Personnel Management
PRSC	Scheduling
QUQI	Query Infrastructure
RCMR	Medical Records

The first four characters are followed by an underscore character "_" and then the artifact type, identified with a two-character acronym.

AR	Application Role
DM	D-MIM (Domain Message Information Model)
DO	Domain
EX	Example
HD	HMD (Hierarchical Message Descriptor)
IN	Interaction
MT	Message Type
NC	Narrative Content
RM	R-MIM (Refined Message Implementation Model)
ST	Storyboard
ST	Storyboard Narrative
TE	Trigger Event

The artifact type is followed by a six-digit identifier allocated by the committer responsible. The final characters are a 2-character Realm Code, identifying which international affiliate of HL7 is responsible for this. The default is UV (Universal) followed by a version number in the range (00–99).

For example: PRPA_RM001234UV00 may be recognized as an RMIM in the Patient Administration, used universally, revision 00. This artifact-naming convention is a bit awkward, but it is worth taking the trouble to memorize the main acronyms.

The name of each cloned class in an RMIM is derived from its structural attributes (Fig. 8.1).

8.5   A Simple Example

The entry point or focal class is an ObservationEvent. This is the default name for any Act with *classCode* = OBS (observation) and *moodCode* = EVN (event). This has three other attributes: a unique identifier *id* (such as a UUID), a *code*, which states the type of report, and an *effectiveTime*, which refers to the date/time of the observation (Fig. 8.2).

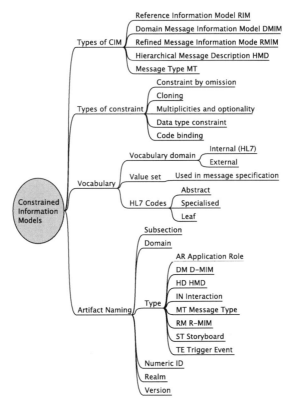

Fig. 8.1 Constrained information models

This report contains one or more InvestigationEvents (*classCode* = INVSTG, *moodCode* = EVN), each of which has an *id* (such as a UUID or a line number), a *code* (in this case a CPT4 code to indicate what it is) and a *value*, which is a simple text string (ST).

The report has two Participations: Subject and Author. The way to read the Participations is that the ObservationEvent has subject Patient and has author Agent.

The subject is a Patient, with an *id*, such as a hospital number. The Patient is scoped by an Organization, which has an agreed identifier (*id*). The combination of the Organization *id* and the Patient *id* should be globally unique.

The patient has an optional *name*, in the Person class (Entity). The playing association (patientPerson) between Person and Patient is indicated as [0..1], and is not in bold font, indicating that this is not mandatory. Similarly the *name* attribute in Person is not in bold font and is annotated as [0..1].

The author is an Agent, which could be a clinician, technician, or a machine. The Agent has a unique identifier.

In this RMIM all elements are mandatory (and therefore required), which is why they are all written in bold font and suffixed with the "*" indicator.

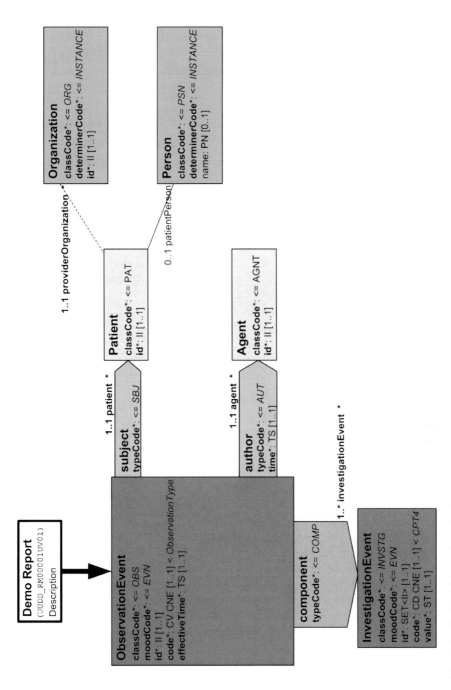

Fig. 8.2 A simple RMIM for an investigation report

8.6   Diagram Notation

8.6.1   Classes

HL7 uses a special graphical notation for specifying RMIMs and DMIMs (Fig. 8.3).

- Each Act is represented as a red rectangle
- Role as a yellow rectangle
- Entity as a green rectangle
- ActRelationship is usually shown as pink (salmon), arrow-shaped pentagon
- Participation as a cyan (light blue) pentagon
- RoleLink as a light yellow pentagon.

Each of the arrow-shaped pentagons has a source for the relationship and a target. The direction of the arrow indicates the meaning of the association, but this is not always the way that the diagram should be navigated.

The direction of navigation (the way you read the diagram) is indicated by the location of the multiplicity shown just outside the class. This may sound confusing, but the important thing to remember is that the direction of the arrows is not always the way that the diagram should be read.

ActRelationship and RoleLink may be recursive, that is, point back to itself. This is indicated by a "pig's ear" box with a notched out corner which fits around one corner the Act or Role.

8.6.2   Attributes

Each attribute uses exactly the same attribute name as is in the RIM. The attributes selected for use in RMIMs are formed by constraining or limiting the attributes as defined in the RIM. This allows checking and validation and is the key reason why the RIM may not be changed.

- The attribute name in an RMIM diagram may be in bold print. This indicates that this attribute is mandatory, it must always be present, null values are not allowed. This is a responsibility of the sender Application Role.
- The attribute name may have a star "*" next to it. This indicates that this attribute is required to be present in messages. If data is not available a "null" value may be sent.
- The multiplicity or cardinality of the attribute is denoted within square brackets [ ] to indicate how many times this attribute may be repeated. [0..1] indicates zero or one; [1..1] indicates exactly one. "*" indicates no upper limit, so [0..*] indicates zero to many.
- The attribute's Data Type is specified after the attribute name, separated by a colon ":". The specified Data Type must be either the same as or a valid constraint on the RIM Data Type for that attribute.

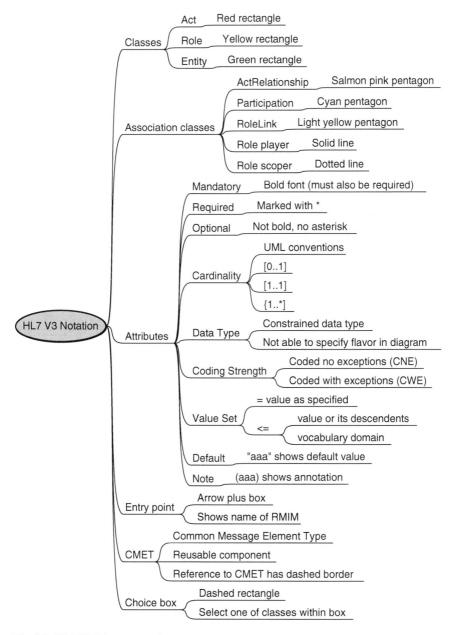

Fig. 8.3 HL7 V3 Diagram notation

- If the data type is a code, then the coding strength may be denoted by adding either CNE (coded no exceptions) or CWE (coded with exceptions) after the data type designator.
- The value set or vocabulary domain to be used with this attribute is specified after either an "<=" or "="; "<=" indicates that the value may be taken from a vocabulary domain or the code specified or any of its descendants in a hierarchy. The equals sign indicates that the value should be as specified. The domain specification must be either a domain name defined in the vocabulary tables, or a single code value from the appropriate domain.
- A string in quotes (e.g., "string") indicates a default value for this attribute.
- Finally, a brief description of attributes may be included, enclosed within parentheses (..).

If the attribute information extends beyond one line, then second and subsequent lines are indented.

8.6.3   Entry Point

Every RMIM has an entry point, which points to the focal class. This also states its name, identifier, and any descriptive notes the author has provided.

8.6.4   CMET

Common Message Element Types (CMET) is a reusable module, which can be used in multiple messages, rather like a program subroutine. Using CMETs can speed up the process of developing messages and increase consistency between different specifications.

Each CMET has two parts. The CMET reference is a special class, which can be added to an RMIM. When a CMET is referenced, or used in another diagram, it is shown with a special notation, a box with dashed edges. It contains the name of the CMET, its artifact *id*, its *class code*, and its level of attribution. It is color-coded in a manner consistent with its root class. Each CMET has a unique artifact identifier (beginning with COCT_), which is the primary link between each CMET reference and its content.

The CMET content itself is defined as a small RMIM, which is stored in a CMET library. This is included automatically in messages when they are constructed.

Each CMET has a single entry point, which is the point at which it is attached to any containing message, which references it. CMETs do not have exit points, which means they have to be at the terminal or leaf point in the hierarchical structure of a message.

Because CMETs are designed for common use by any HL7 committee they are kept in a separate common components library.

8.6.5   *Choice Box*

HL7 RMIMs show choices or options by using a "choice box." Each of the options is shown in a box with a dashed line border, from which a single choice is made.

Associations may be made to a specific class within the choice box, or to any of the classes, irrespective of which is selected.

8.7   Tooling

RMIMs are built using a special tool set developed by HL7. The original tools, based on Microsoft Access and Visio are in the process of being replaced by a new generation of tools, which use a slightly modified notation.

The basis of these tools is a set of interrelated XML schema, known as Model Interchange Format (MIF). MIF defines the primary artifacts that can be developed or exchanged as a result of HL7 V3 standards development and implementation.

8.8   Templates

In HL7, templates are used to constrain and verify conformance to profiled HL7 Version 3 Refined Message Information Models (RMIMs). A template is an expression of a set of constraints on the RIM, which is used to apply additional constraints to a portion of an instance of data expressed in terms of some other Static Model. Templates are used to further define and refine these existing models within a narrower and more focused scope.

Each template is identified with a *templateId*, a globally unique identifier.

8.9   HL7 Development Framework

HL7's standard development methodology is documented in the HL7 Development Framework (HDF)[1]. The HDF is written for HL7 members who are developing standards within HL7 committees. However, much of what it says is of universal relevance. The HDF adopts a project-oriented approach, based on a Product Life Cycle for Product Development.

---

[1] HL7 Development Framework. Version 1.3, 2009

The HDF identifies the following major stages (Fig. 8.4):

- Project Initiation Process
- Domain Analysis Process
- Specification Design Process
- Standard Profiling Process
- Technology Specification Process

8.9.1 Project Initiation

The Project Initiation Process (PIP) includes initiation, planning, and approval substages, including the development of a detailed Project Scope Statement (PSS) and plan. The project plan identifies the business case and objectives,

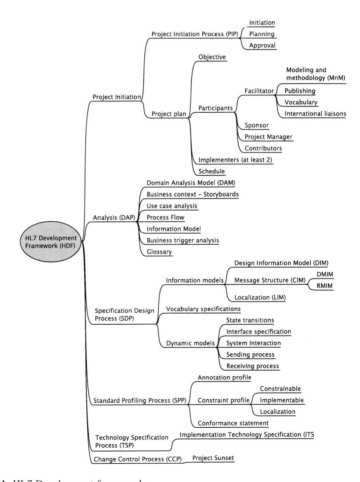

Fig. 8.4 HL7 Development framework

participants including sponsor committee, project leader, contributors and early implementers, and a time schedule.

8.9.2   Domain Analysis

Domain Analysis Process (DAP) includes analysis and requirements documentation, including the development of a Domain Analysis Model (DAM), which includes:

- Business context including documentation using storyboards and identification of relevant actors and interactions
- Use case analysis documenting use cases and actors
- Process model, documented using activity diagrams
- Information model, documented using classes and attributes
- Business rules including trigger events
- Glossary

8.9.3   Specification Design

Specification Design Process (SDP) is the core of the process. It involves mapping the requirements as set out in the Domain Analysis Model to the HL7 RIM, data types and vocabulary to specify the message structures, value sets, and dynamic processes.

8.9.4   Standard Profiles

A profile is a set of information used to document system requirements or capabilities from an information-exchange perspective and is expressed in terms of constraints, extensions, or other alterations to a referenced standard or another profile. Profiles of HL7 Version 3 are derived from a Version 3 specification, as balloted either by HL7 or by one of its affiliates.

The categories and use of profiles include annotation, constraint, localization implementable, and conformance profiles.

Annotation profiles document the standard exactly but with more information to further explain the base document to educate prospective users and/or implementers.

Constraint profiles may contain unchanged and constrained elements, reducing the optionality and cardinality of the base specification (i.e., the HL7 V3 standard) in order to make the specification more exact.

Localization profiles meet the same objectives as a constraint profile, with the addition of some additional elements (extensions). HL7 Version 3 allows localization of some parts of the standard but not others. In particular, HL7 does not allow anyone, apart from HL7 itself through a formal process, to change or modify the RIM or any of the Data Types. Localization can make full use of the constraint mechanisms and make certain changes to RMIMs, Data Types, Message Types, CMETs, and Vocabularies.

Implementable profiles are the most constrained constraint profiles and eliminate all optionality in the base specification (the HL7 V3 standard) in order to make the specification exact and approach "plug-and-play" interoperability. Optionality for a profile is eliminated when the conformance indicator for every attribute and association is either Required or Not Permitted and every vocabulary domain is bound to a value set.

Conformance statements set out a computer system's conformance claim to a set of interactions. A conformance profile indicates the set of interactions that a computer system (or application role) supports. It implies a commitment to fulfill all of the responsibilities of the interactions specified and to implement faithfully the artifacts that constitute the interactions and any further constraints or extensions.

8.10   Implementation Technology Specification (ITS)

The XML implementation technology specification describes how individual instances of message types shall be rendered in XML for serial transmission over the network and the structure of schemas used to validate each instance. Note that the HL7 generated XML schemas are not able to test all of the constraints defined in a HL7 message definition.

The generation of the schemas and message representation is done automatically. Those not directly involved in that process do not need to understand the technical details. The key points are as follows:

One XML element is defined to correspond to each row in the HMD grid, with the exception of structural attributes which are expressed as XML attributes.

Each Data Type has a defined XML representation. The "restriction base" feature in an XML schema is used extensively to define how data types are implemented.

The schema files for CMETs are supplied separately and then used by each message schema as required.

The XML schemas defined support V3 Data Types, and Data Type refinement, through the use of the W3C Schema restriction element. Additional standard schema sections support RIM classes and the HL7-defined vocabulary definitions. These schema sections can be selectively combined with a specific message schema through the "include" function in the XML schema standard.

HL7 messages all share the same XML namespace.

Message version information is conveyed as attributes within the message rather than by changes to the namespace identifier.

8.11   Documentation

HL7 V3 documentation is voluminous. The full set of HL7 V3 standards is published annually and can be downloaded from the HL7 web-site (www.hl7.org).

Foundation documents are the basis of the standard. The Foundation documents
in 2008 contain 359,000 words (about 30 h reading at 200 words per minute. In
addition there are 30 or more domain-specific standards (Fig. 8.5):

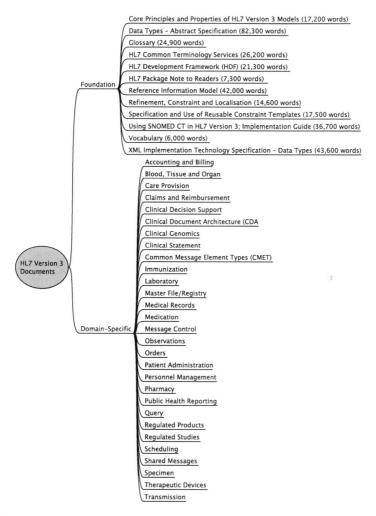

Fig. 8.5 HL7 Version 3 documentation

Chapter 9
Clinical Document Architecture

9.1 Documents and Databases

Worldwide, Clinical Document Architecture (CDA) is the most widely adopted application of HL7 V3. The CDA paradigm takes the document metaphor seriously.

It is illuminating to compare the differences between the database transaction and document metaphors (Benson 1997; Spronk 2007).

Databases are organized for rapid search and retrieval and are updated by transactions. The database structure is designed by a computer professional, updated by various people, who may or may not know each other, and is accessed by others using queries. The person who updates the database is seldom able to control who, if anyone, will read the data, or for what purpose. The person who uses the data may not know who entered them and lack of context makes it difficult to evaluate whether or not they can be relied on.

In contrast, a document, electronic or paper, is organized as a stand-alone artifact mainly to convey human understanding. Each document has a clearly identified set of meta-data stating who created it, for whom, when, where, and about what subject. The author determines the entire content and is responsible for it. If there is any doubt about how to interpret a message, the receiver can contact the author requesting elaboration.

We are all familiar with documents such as letters and invoices, but we seldom notice how much information is contained in each. Some data are fixed and are always present; other data are variable, changing with each document instance.

Consider a typical letter from a company. Fixed data include the company name, logo, address, phone, fax, e-mail, and web addresses; the company's registered name and address, registration number, and place of registration, and may also include tax identifiers (e.g., VAT number), bank information, and lists of directors or partners.

Variable data fall into two types; first, data that are always present on a particular type of document but may vary in every instance, such as the date, reference, recipient name, and address, and the author, including name, job title, and signature. Finally, we have the variable content of the letter, which contains the core of the message.

Even a simple letter contains quite a lot of data that have little to do with the actual message content, but serve to provide context and verification data, allow us

T. Benson, *Principles of Health Interoperability HL7 and SNOMED*, HI,
DOI 10.1007/978-1-84882-803-2_9, © Springer-Verlag London Limited 2010

to trust that it really is what it says it appears to be, and let us check their validity if we have any suspicions.

Documents have a number of properties, which are not shared with databases or transactions used to update database records. These properties include: persistence, stewardship, authentication, wholeness, and human readability.

Persistence is a feature of documents. Every document has a life cycle; it is created, then used, and eventually destroyed (perhaps many years later). While it exists, it remains a single coherent whole. On the other hand, information in a relational database is distributed across the rows of many tables. Different people may be authorized to update the different tables. After numerous updates, it may be impossible to recreate the information as it was originally, without the use of sophisticated roll-back processes.

Stewardship is another document property. At any time, some body or organization is responsible for looking after it. It should always be clear who is responsible for filing, copying, forwarding, or destroying a document. Organizations invariably keep copies of documents they send out. Again, this is not true of a database, where different rules may apply to different types of data.

Authentication is simpler with documents than database records. It is relatively easy to maintain an audit trail for the whole life cycle. Each document may be signed, physically or electronically. Validity can be attested in ways that are difficult to replicate with database records. Only authenticated documents are likely to be of value in medico-legal disputes.

Each document is complete and whole in itself, including context information, such as who created it, when, where, and for what purpose. This makes it easier for others to use it outside the immediate purpose for which it was created. Without strong evidence on the original context, it can be hazardous to place meaning on any statement.

Finally, documents are human-readable. Meaning, as perceived by the human reader, is paramount, even when there is coded machine-readable information within the same statement. Human-readable messages have a long-term value (medical records may have to be preserved for 100 years or more), whereas machine-readable data depend on specific technology, which may not be available many years in the future. For example, few modern computers can read floppy disks or magnetic tapes that were ubiquitous a couple of decades ago.

The need for long-term human-readable persistence was one of the motivations behind the development of XML and its predecessor SGML (Fig. 9.1).

9.2   CDA History

CDA's naming structure can be best understood in reference to its history.

In 1997, XML was the new kid on the block and attracted a lot of interest. Every instance of an XML file is referred to as a document, which is one of the reasons

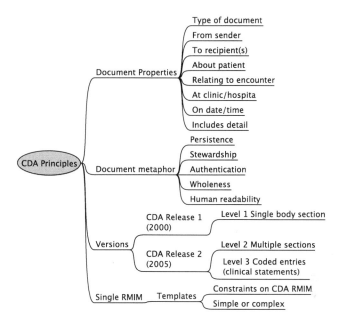

Fig. 9.1 CDA principles

why people began to think seriously about the document metaphor. XML is a simplification of an earlier standard, SGML, which was mainly used for complex documents such as technical specifications and manuals for aircraft and military equipment, which need to be rendered in a variety of different formats. The analogy between complex instruction manuals and medical records was not lost. Both are voluminous and difficult to navigate.

In 1997, a group of people with an interest in both HL7 and SGML/XML met at the Kona Mansion in New Hampshire, where they agreed a three-level plan for using XML in medical documents, along with the emerging HL7 Version 3 reference model. This plan has been largely followed in two main releases.

Release 1, published in 2000, is a simple standard, describing a header and body. Only the header is based on the HL7 V3 RIM, while the body uses a variety of human-readable non-XML formats such as text or images.

Release 2, published in 2005, is more complex and both the header and the body are based on the HL7 V3 RIM, allowing fine granularity of structured data. The body may be non-XML (providing backward compatibility to Release 1) or it may be organized into one or more sections, which may have structured entries.

The development of CDA is continuing, with CDA Release 3 expected in 2010 and the development of a Structured Document Architecture (SDA) with increased flexibility (Spronk 2009).

9.3   CDA Levels

The three levels are:

CDA Level 1 has a header and a human-readable body. The header contains basic meta-data, primarily intended to enable information retrieval, while the body is human-readable text or image. For example, the body can be a PDF document, a jpeg image, or a text document, possibly containing simple formatting markup.

CDA Level 2 allows the body to be either an unstructured blob (enabling compatibility with Level 1) or one or more structured sections. Each section contains a single narrative block, which contains XML markup that can be rendered in human-readable form. The general structure of CDA Levels 1 and 2 was agreed in 2000 and published as CDA Release 1 (ANSI/HL7 CDA R1.0–2000).

CDA Level 3 allows each section to include machine-processed entries at almost any level of granularity. Thus, it offers the benefits of both human-readable and machine-processed documents. Machine-processed data are encoded using the HL7 V3 Clinical Statement pattern.

The relationships between these are shown below:

Release	CDA Release One (R1)	CDA Release Two (R2)
Date	2000	2005
Level 1	CDA R1 Level 1	CDA R2 Level 1
Level 2	CDA R1 Level 2	CDA R2 Level 2
Level 3	Not available	CDA R2 Level 3

Naturally, prior to 2005, all use of CDA used Release 1. Since its release, CDA Release 2 Level 3 has become popular, although it is more complex than Levels 1 and 2.

All levels validate against the generic CDA schema. Additional validation is provided by templates and constraints on the generic CDA schema.

One of the attractive features of CDA is that it lets you start simply, with Level 1 or 2, and then evolve over time. Health care is a long-term business and it is vital that records and documents are kept safely and can be accessed many years into the future. The lower levels of CDA provide rather low technical barriers to adoption, while providing a migration route toward structured coded records.

CDA can be deployed easily to enable web-based access to patient data.

CDA is at the core of almost every standards-based health information exchange architecture, worldwide. Countries that adopted simple CDA level 1 architecture several years ago are now meeting substantial portions of their information exchange requirements with CDA. Resource-strapped countries have adopted CDA because it allows them to immediately share information at the point of care without sacrificing scalability or reuse in the future.

For example CDA is a core component of the National Health Service strategy for interoperability in England. In the USA, institutions like Mayo Clinic that place a high value on information as an asset have committed to CDA because it provides a single architectural foundation for their clinical information requirements that can be sustained over generations of application development.

A key to this acceptance is the "A" for architecture in CDA, which promotes reusability across a sufficiently wide range of documents to cover clinical information sharing, public health, quality reporting, and clinical trials (Fig. 9.2).

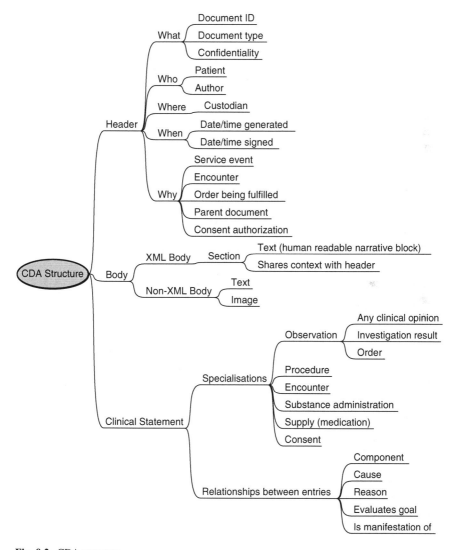

Fig. 9.2 CDA structure

9.4   CDA Header

The CDA header is common to all three levels of CDA.

The primary purpose of the header is to provide unambiguous, structured meta-data about the document itself, which can be used in document registers and databases to classify, find, and retrieve documents. These meta-data include information about what the document is, who created it, when, where, and for what purpose.

The root class of all CDA documents is an Act called Clinical Document.

9.4.1   What?

Identification of the document itself is done at three levels: first, there is a pair of codes which state that this is a CDA document, then there is another code which indicates the type of CDA document (e.g., discharge summary), and finally a unique identifier for the document instance. These are mandatory in all CDA documents.

We state that this is a CDA document using two structural attributes: *ClinicalDocument.classCode* and *ClinicalDocument.moodCode* and these have been allocated predefined values, DOCCLIN and EVN respectively.

The type of document being exchanged is specified using *ClinicalDocument. code*, which is usually an externally specified coding scheme. Use of externally specified coding schemes places no limit on the potential number of different types of CDA document that could be used.

Each specific instance of a CDA document is identified using the *ClinicalDocument. id* attribute. This may be any unique identifier, but is often a UUID (Universally Unique ID).

ClinicalDocument.confidentialityCode is another mandatory attribute in the root class. It defines the overall confidentiality status of the document and has a default value of N for normal.

9.4.2   Times

The time of generation of a CDA document is always recorded in *ClinicalDocument. effectiveTime*.

As well as the time of creation, each document must also include the *author.time*, which is the data and time that the original author is considered to have signed or approved the document. This may be the same as the *ClinicalDocument.effectiveTime*.

9.4.3   Participations

Every clinical document has at least three participations, which are links to specific roles.

- RecordTarget represents the medical record that this document belongs to. In most healthcare organizations this is effectively an identifier of patient.
- The Author responsible for the content of the clinical document.
- The Custodian, which is usually the originating organization which keeps the medical record.

The intended recipient(s) may also be specified.

Other participations, including dataEnterer, Informant, Participant, and Authenticator may be specified, but are rare in practice.

9.4.4 Relationships

A clinical document may have relationships with other documents or events including:

- ServiceEvent represents the main Act, e.g., a colonoscopy or discharge from hospital, which is being documented
- Reference to a parent document, which may be being changed or replaced by the present document
- Fulfillment of an order, for example when a test report references a request
- Authorization of consent
- Reference to an encompassing encounter

9.5 CDA Body

Every CDA document has one header and one body part. The body is either a NonXMLBody or a StructuredBody. NonXMLBody is present to provide upward compatibility with CDA Level 1, and may contain any type of human-readable data including text (txt, rtf, html, or pdf) or image (gif, jpeg, png, tiff, or g3fax). Data encoded using XML may not be put in the NonXMLBody.

StructuredBody is used for XML-encoded data. It is the root node for one or more Sections.

9.5.1 Section

Each Section contains a human-readable narrative block, called *Section.text*. This narrative block is one of the key components of CDA and contains the human-readable content of the Section. One of the responsibilities of the originator of any CDA document is to ensure that the narrative block of each Section accurately conveys the meaning of that Section in a way that can be rendered appropriately for human readability.

Section.text can include special XML markup, which is similar to but simpler than XHTML. However, relatively few documents use markup within narrative blocks other than < paragraph > and < br > (line break), although this might change.

The original vision of CDA was for each Section to comprise either a whole document content or at least a significant chunk, such as a composition or section as defined in EN 13606. However, many implementations of CDA, such as the NHS Care Record Service have chosen to implement Sections with rather fine granularity, so each Section is no more than a single line or entry.

Fine-grained sections allow Sections to be filtered, sorted, and rendered in different ways, chronologically, or by author, or by record type, for example, to display all allergies, diagnoses or medication records.

Sections may contain subsections within them, although this is not common, because it adds to the processing complexity.

Sections usually share the same context data as that found in the header, although this can be overridden for each specific Section, although this is not common.

9.5.2   Clinical Statement (Entry)

Each section can contain any number of entries, which are clinical statements, in a structured computer-processable form.

The HL7 Version 3 Clinical Statement is as a common pattern for the development of all types of clinical messages, used for the exchange of information between different computer systems. The same pattern is used in CDA, for complex messages such as the exchange of complete electronic patient records between GPs, and for simpler messages such as prescriptions. HL7 defines a Clinical Statement as:

> an expression of a discrete item of clinical (or clinically related) information that is recorded because of its relevance to the care of a patient. Clinical information is fractal in nature and therefore the extent and detail conveyed in a single statement may vary.

Any clinical statement may have a number of participants, including subject, author, location, performer, participant, and informer.

Each clinical statement is one of the following specializations:

- Observation, which may refer to specimen(s) and reference ranges. Observations cover a very broad range of statements relating to history, examination, tests, diagnosis, and prognosis. It is important to remember that, depending on the mood, an observation can be an actual observation (Event), a requested observation (Request), or a goal set for a future observation (Goal). Also that Observation Events are usually reported using code–value pairs, where the code represents what is being observed and value represents the result. The Observation class may be linked to a specimen and normal range values.
- Procedure, which may refer to a specimen(s) or images and is used for all invasive procedures including surgical procedures and imaging.

- Encounter, which covers most administrative procedures including appointment scheduling and waiting list management.
- Substance Administration or Supply, which may refer to products such as medication and are mainly used for prescribing, dispensing, and administration of drugs.
- Consent.

Several types of associations between clinical statements are provided such as containment, cause and effect, problem linkage, etc.

9.5.3 Relationships Between Entries

The Clinical Statement pattern allows for a rich set of relationships between entries, to reflect the structure of clinical information and links between different items.

CAUS Used to show that the source caused the target, such as substance administration (e.g., penicillin) caused an observation (e.g., a rash), or observation (e.g., diabetes mellitus is the cause of kidney disease).

COMP Used to show that the target is a component of the source (e.g., hemoglobin measurement is a component of a full blood count).

GEVL (evaluates (goal)) Used to link an observation (intent or actual) to a goal to indicate that the observation evaluates the goal (for instance, a source observation of "walking distance" evaluates a target goal of "adequate walking distance").

MFST (is manifestation of) Used to say that the source is a manifestation of the target (for instance, source "hives" is a manifestation of target "penicillin allergy").

RSON (has reason) Used to show the reason or rationale for a service (for instance, source "treadmill test" has reason "chest pain").

SAS (starts after start) The source Act starts after the start of the target Act (for instance, source "diaphoresis" starts after the start of target "chest pain").

SPRT (has support) Used to show that the target provides supporting evidence of the source (for instance, source "possible lung tumor" has support target "mass seen on chest X-ray").

Any clinical statement may inherit context information from the CDA header or context information may be defined within the clinical statement, in which case it overrides the default inherited data. Examples of participations, which can be applied to any clinical statement, are Subject, Author, Performer, Informant, Location, and Participant.

9.6 CDA Templates

CDA Templates are used to specify how CDA is to be used for particular purposes and specific use cases. The development of templates is relatively new and there are likely to be significant changes in this area over the next few years.

A CDA Template is an expression of a set of constraints on the CDA RMIM, which apply additional constraints to a portion of an instance of data. Templates are used in a variety of different ways.

- Narrative – this can be used to reference an implementation guide or pattern "A valid legal authenticator must be provided"
- Schematron assertions "legalAuthenticator and not legalAuthenticator [@nullFlavor]"
- Static Model (RMIM) Publish a new static model making legalAuthenticator mandatory

The CCD specification provides one exemplar of how the *templateId* can be used to reference a template or implementation guide that has been assigned a unique identifier. The following example shows how to formally assert the use of this implementation guide. Use of the *templateId* indicates that the CDA instance not only conforms to the CDA specification, but in addition, conforms to constraints specified in this implementation guide.

```
<ClinicalDocument xmlns = 'urn:hl7-org:v3'>
<typeId extension = 'POCD_HD000040' root = '2.16.840.1.1
13883.1.3'/>
<templateId root = '2.16.840.1.113883.10.20.1'/>
</ClinicalDocument>
```

In addition to assigning a template identifier to the overall implementation guide, template identifiers can be assigned to other patterns, such as document sections and specific clinical statements within document sections. Using the *templateId* to reference one of these patterns indicates that the CDA instance conforms to the constraints specified in that pattern.

```
<Section>
<templateId root = '2.16.840.1.113883.10.20.1.14'/>
<Observation classCode="OBS" moodCode="EVN">
<templateId root = '2.16.840.1.113883.10.20.1.32'/>
</Observation>
</Section>
```

Templates allow constraints to be applied to all or any part of a CDA document including the roles (e.g., author or patient details), sections (such as business headings), and entries (such as clinical statements), to say exactly how each is to be specified with a narrower and more focused scope. CDA Templates may be simple, or quite complex.

Multiple CDA Templates can constrain the same portion of a CDA document specification.

A CDA Profile is a set of Templates that correspond to a particular document type.

A Template list provides a set of Templates which provide choices for the user.

The NHS Connecting for Health program has defined a large set of templates, specified using RMIMs, and Schematron schemas for EHR components to be used in CDA messages.

CDA Templates have a *templateId* and may be stored in a repository. The *templateId* is one of the hidden attributes of the HL7 RIM, which can be used in all RIM classes. The *templateId* is used to indicate which template is being used; it is useful in document validation, software, and human-readable specifications. Validators use *templateId* to check that a document complies with the rules specified in the template; computer software uses *templateId* to indicate how this part of a document should be used. Humans use the *templateId* to reference how each part of the specification is to be used. A *templateId* may be a UUID or a locally specified identifier.

Each template has a set of meta-data to describe the purpose and use of the template. The meta-data include a globally unique identifier, a name, description, version, an identifier of the model from which it is derived, the RIM version, and publication details. The use of standard meta-data allows templates to be stored in repositories, which can be queried and the templates shared.

Currently, most CDA Template constraints have been implemented in Schematron, and are used primarily for validating CDA document instances.

9.7 The Continuity of Care Record (CCR)

The ASTM Continuity of Care Record (CCR), also referred to as ASTM E2369-05,[1] has been developed by ASTM to provide a common XML format for a patient health record (PHR) summary of clinical, administrative, and demographic patient data to be sent to the next healthcare provider when a patient is referred or transferred to another hospital, clinic, or other care provider. It can reference one or more healthcare encounters.

The CCR is a core data set of the most relevant administrative, demographic, and clinical information facts about a patient's health care, covering one or more healthcare encounters. It provides a means for one healthcare practitioner, system, or setting to aggregate all of the pertinent data about a patient and forward them to another practitioner, system, or setting to support the continuity of care. The primary use case for the CCR is to provide a snapshot in time containing the pertinent clinical, demographic, and administrative data for a specific patient. It supports a variety of coding schemes including SNOMED CT.

The key motivation was to allow data from multiple sources to be brought together in a single format, to enable portable PHRs, needed when more than one care provider is treating a patient. Each data element is data/time and source stamped.

The CCR has a header, a footer, and 17 optional sections, which cover a wide range of functions including detailed insurance and payment-related administrative data that are highly specific to the USA.

The CCR Header defines the document parameters, including its unique identifier, language, version, date/time, the patient whose data it contains, who or what has generated the CCR, to whom or what the CCR is directed, and the CCR's purpose.

---

[1]ASTM. Specification for Continuity of Care Record, E2369-05, 2006

The CCR Footer contains data defining all of the actors, as well as information about external references, all text comments, and signatures associated with any data within the CCR.

The CCR Body contains the core-patient-specific data, such as current and past medications, problems, and procedures. Data are aggregated into sections based on common clinical conventions. In a typical scenario, pulling in existing data from a variety of sources dynamically creates the body, and no new content is specifically created for the summary. In some cases, the source data will be narrative; in other cases there may be coded data supporting some aspects of the narrative; and in some cases the source data will be fully coded.

Google Health has adopted a pragmatic profile of the CCR for the Google Health PHR.[2] The items supported in the Google Profile (2008) include:

- Patient demographics (e.g., date of birth and sex)
- Problems/diagnoses (e.g., condition or symptom)
- Allergies and alerts
- Medication list
- Immunizations
- Social history (e.g., race)
- Vital signs
- Results
- Procedures
- Functional status (e.g., pregnant or breast-feeding)

The XML structure described in the CCR standard is a simple ad hoc structure, which has the advantage of being simple to use, but lacks some of the flexibility of CDA.

9.8   Continuity of Care Document (CCD)

CCD (Continuity of Care Document) maps the CCR functionality into HL7 V3 CDA format, setting out a set of constraints on CDA, using templates. Although the stated purpose of CCD is to communicate clinical summaries, it is increasingly being used as a framework for developing other types of message (Fig. 9.3).

One way of looking at CCD is to consider it as a set of templates, because all parts are optional and it is practical to mix and match the ones you need. This is the direction of travel for future versions of CCD.

A CCD is the semantic equivalent of a CCR – both are in XML and both adhere to ANSI-based specifications. Implementers must choose either one or the other standard as the primary data format.

CCD has been endorsed by HIMSS and HITSP as the recommended standard for exchange of electronic exchange of components of health information.[3]

---

[2]See http://code.google.com/apis/health/

[3]HL7 Implementation Guide: CDA Release 2 – Continuity of Care Document (CCD)

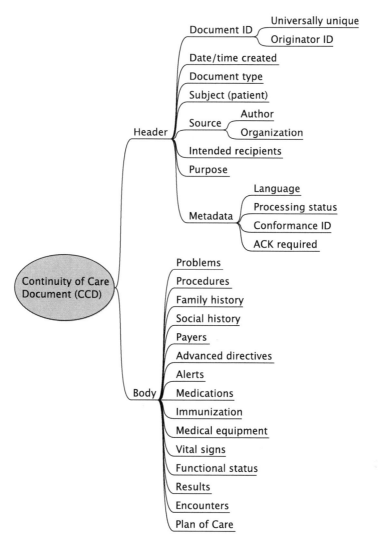

Fig. 9.3 Continuity of Care Document

9.9 CCD Header

9.9.1 Document Identification

Each instance of a CCD document is identified by a universally unique identifier (UUID) generated by the originating system. The use of UUID is mandated as the simplest way to ensure that each document generated is unique and will be understood to be unique by any receiving system.

A separate originator document ID may be provided, which is a human readable identifier for a document, used by the originator. It is not guaranteed to be universally unique, although no such identifier should be used which is known to contain any duplicates. It should be used only in combination with an identified patient and a specific date and time of document creation.

The date/time created represents the exact clock time that the document is created and must include a time zone offset. It is not the time that the document is sent.

The document type is the type or title of the document, e.g., Cardiology Follow-up. Ideally coded, but may be just text.

9.9.2 Document Meta-data

Each CCD document contains several items of meta-data. Meta-data are information about the document which is used to support electronic processing and information retrieval.

languageCode in the form nn, or nn-CC (e.g., en or en-US). The nn portion shall be a legal ISO-639-1 language code in lower case. The CC portion, if present, shall be an ISO-3166 country code in upper case.

processingStatus indicates whether a document is being used in production, testing or training.

ConformanceId is a unique identifier, which identifies the specific version of the clinical document to which conformance is claimed, such as an XML Schema or Schematron.

ACK required specifies the circumstances under which acknowledgment of receipt and or processing is required (always, on success or on error).

9.9.3 Subject

Each CCD refers to a single patient or subject, who is the person seeking to receive, receiving, or having received health care. It can only refer to one patient. Examples: A treated patient, a client of a physiotherapist, each particular member of a target population for screening, each particular member of a group of diabetic persons attending a session of medical education.

Each patient has one or more identifiers. For example, patients may have different identifiers in different units. Patients may also have a full set of demographic details (name, date of birth, sex, address, etc.)

9.9.4 Other Parties

A CCD always has at least one source. Multiple sources may be specified when it is useful to specify the person(s), organization, and or system responsible for generating the document.

There may be any number of intended recipients (and copy recipients) of any document. This is optional, because some documents do not have an explicit recipient. The recipient may be any party (person or organization), including the patient.

9.9.5   Document Purpose

Each CCD document may have one primary purpose, which is the reason that a clinical document is generated, such as patient admission, transfer, consult/referral, or inpatient discharge. It may be associated with an indication (text or code) and a relevant date/time. Each document may also reference any number of other prior documents.

9.10   CCD Body

The CCD Body contains sections corresponding to the main sections of the CCR.

- The Problems section provides a problem list of current and historical clinical problems.
- The Procedures section includes surgical, diagnostic, or therapeutic procedures or treatments pertinent to the patient.
- Family history.
- Social history includes administrative data such as marital status, race, ethnicity, and religious affiliation as well as information about the patient's occupation, lifestyle, social, environmental history, and health risk factors.
- For each payer, all the pertinent data needed to contact, bill to, and collect from that payer should be included as well as authorization details.
- Advance directives such as the existence of living wills, healthcare proxies, and resuscitation status.
- Alerts describe allergies, adverse reactions, and alerts related to current or past medical history.
- The Medications section lists the patient's current medications and medication history.
- Immunization lists current immunization status and immunization history.
- Medical equipment includes both durable medical equipment and implanted devices.
- Vital signs may include the most recent, maximum, and/or minimum, or both, baseline, or relevant trends.
- Functional status contains information on the "normal functioning" of the patient at the time the record is created and provides an extensive list of examples. Deviation from normal and limitations and improvements should be included here.
- The Results section contains the results of observations, including abnormal values or relevant trends, generated by laboratories, imaging procedures, and other procedures.

- Encounter lists healthcare encounters pertinent to the patient's current health status or historical health history.
- Plan of Care contains active, incomplete, or pending orders, appointments, referrals, procedures, services, or any other pending event of clinical significance to the current and ongoing care of the patient. The plan of care section also contains information regarding goals and clinical reminders.

All sections of a CCD document are optional and may be combined together in any way.

Chapter 10
HL7 Dynamic Model and IHE XDS

This chapter is primarily devoted to the HL7 Dynamic Model, which describes a set of related interactions, which together perform one or more use cases. It also includes a short section on the IHE cross-enterprise document sharing (XDS) profile.

Safety is paramount in health care. Examples of safety procedures include:

- Acknowledgements sent at both transport level (message received) and application level (message processed).
- Explicit validation by both sender and receiver systems.
- Use of automatic patient matching, with fallback of manual matching if not entirely unambiguous.
- Routing messages to alternative recipient if not actioned within a specified time (e.g., if a named recipient is on leave).
- Messages are not removed from a task list until all actions specified have been performed.
- If any user edits a message the original is kept unchanged (deletionless messages).
- A full audit trail is maintained.

10.1 HL7 Dynamic Model

The following aspects of the Dynamic Model have to be specified (Fig. 10.1):

- Trigger events
- Application roles (sender and receiver) and their responsibilities
- Interactions (defined as a one-way transfer of information)
- Message type(s)
- Interaction sequence
- Message wrappers
- Acknowledgments

T. Benson, *Principles of Health Interoperability HL7 and SNOMED*, HI,
DOI 10.1007/978-1-84882-803-2_10, © Springer-Verlag London Limited 2010

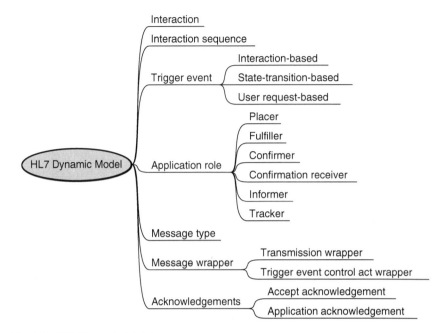

Fig. 10.1 HL7 Dynamic Model

10.2   Trigger Event

A trigger event is an explicit set of stated conditions, which can be recognized by a computer system that initiates an interaction. It may be the result of human action, such as a mouse click, a state transition for an information object (such as the successful completion of a business transaction), an exception condition (such as an error), or be specific to a point in time (e.g., midnight).

The context for each trigger event is specified in use cases, and storyboards, which form part of the requirements specification.

Trigger events may be classified as following:

- Interaction based: Trigger events can be based on another interaction. For example, the response to a query (which is an interaction) is an Interaction-based trigger event.
- State-transition based: Trigger events resulting from a state transition as depicted in the State Transition Model for a particular message interaction. The trigger for canceling a document, for example, may be considered a state-transition-based trigger event.
- User request based: Trigger events may be based on a user request. For example, the trigger event that prompts a system to send all accumulated data to a tracking system every 12 h is considered user based.

10.3   Application Role

An Application Role is a collection of communication responsibilities intended to be implemented as a group. Communication responsibilities are identified as the interactions that the system is able to send or receive. Application Roles may be specializations of other existing Application Roles, inheriting the responsibilities of their parent, with additional or more specialized responsibilities added, or they may be the merging together of other application roles acting as components.

From the Application Role definitions, the reader can identify the purpose of information flow between two health care applications and the roles they play in that exchange.

The Application Role description sets out what one application does, with respect to information exchange. It lists all of the interactions, sent or received, consequent to one particular trigger event. It is silent about the application functionality behind it – and how this is achieved.

Application Roles have responsibilities, which are restricted to sending messages (interactions). Any other responsibilities and actions are outside the HL7 model. The sender role has the responsibility to send a message in response to a trigger event, and the receiver role may have responsibilities to initiate further transactions such as an acknowledgment, error report, and response to query.

The Application Role is a key element in specifying conformance and for contractual arrangements between users and service providers. It is the intent of HL7 that healthcare systems should be able to declare conformance to the HL7 specification by creating an implementation profile that identifies the Application Roles supported by that implementation. Conformance to an Application Role means supporting each of the interactions specified.

Typically, one Application Role supports several interactions. For instance, a query is meaningless unless it includes a response; so the Application Role for the query questioner requires at least two interactions (query and response) to be supported, and similarly for the query answerer.

The names given to Application Roles provide one of the best ways of finding the transaction sets, already defined, which meet a particular requirement. The naming convention is to state the subject of the interaction (e.g., Residential Address) followed by the Application Role category.

HL7 uses the following generic terms for Application Roles:

- Placer: An application that is capable of notifying another application about a significant event, and expects the receiver to take action.
- Fulfiller: An application that is capable of receiving a request from a Placer application.
- Confirmer: An application that is capable of accepting a request from a Fulfiller application.
- Confirmation Receiver: A role implemented by a placer indicating what types of confirmations it accepts.

- Informer: An application that is capable of notifying another application about a significant event, but does not expect any action on the part of the receiver. Paired with "Tracker."
- Tracker: An application that is capable of receiving information about a significant event, but is not expected by the receiver to perform any action.

In theory, Application Roles should be helpful to the reader in understanding the business roles and functionality provided by a set of interactions. However, the use of abstract terms, such as manager, tracker, placer, and filler, makes this less useful than it might be.

10.4   Interaction

An interaction is the smallest unit (atomic) of communication that can stand on its own. It is a one-way transfer of information and ties together HL7's static models of payload content and the dynamic model of information flow and system behavior.

Formally, an interaction is a unique association between a specific message type, a particular trigger event that initiates or triggers the transfer, and the Application Roles that send and receive the message type.

In HL7 Version 3, each interaction is described in a table with its name and artifact ID, together with the sending and receiving Application Roles, the trigger event, the message type, the trigger event type, and the wrapper types and their artifact identifiers.

10.5   Message Type

A Message Type is the most precise specification of a message, with explicit constraints about what data elements are sent and what values each data element may have. These constraints should be as tight as possible to minimize any chance of ambiguity.

Message Types are derived by the intersection of specific interactions, application roles, and trigger events. The same Message Type may be associated with any number of Application Roles and be used in response to many different trigger events. However, an interaction can only ever have one trigger event and one Message Type.

10.6   Interaction Sequence

The precise flow of messages may be represented using a UML sequence diagram, which shows the Application Roles and the flow of Message Types between them in sequential order.

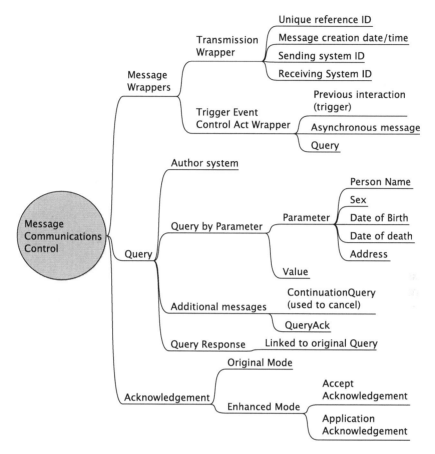

Fig. 10.2 Message communications control

10.7   Message Wrappers

Whenever domain content (as a payload) is transmitted in the form of messages they use message wrappers, analogous to a letter's envelope. HL7 defines two types of wrapper (Fig. 10.2):

- Transmission wrapper
- Trigger Event Control Act wrapper

Each HL7 Version 3 message typically consists of a Transmission wrapper, a Trigger Event Control Act wrapper and the Domain Content.

The Transmission wrapper includes a unique reference ID for each message instance sent, the precise date and time the message was created and the identity of the sending and receiving systems.

The Trigger Event Control Act wrapper sits inside the outer Transmission wrapper and may include details of a previous interaction, which has triggered this interaction. Different variants of the Trigger Event Control Act wrapper are used for asynchronous messaging and for queries, where the response needs to be coupled with the query.

10.8   Query

Queries are used to interrogate databases, such as to retrieve patient identification details from a patient master index.

The standard query message is an extension of the control act, using query by parameter. For a simple patient demographics query, the parameters could be patient name, sex, date of birth (and/or death), and address.

The query response is linked to the original query message.

10.9   Acknowledgment

Most HL7 transactions involve two or more messages: an originating message and an acknowledgement, in one of two modes: original mode or enhanced mode.

In original mode acknowledgment there are just two messages: the first, originating message comes from the sending system and the second, an acknowledgement is sent by the receiver saying whether it was able to process the originating message.

Enhanced mode is more complex, but is suited to a multi-hop environment that uses an intermediary such as an interface engine between the sender and the final recipient. In enhanced mode acknowledgement, two separate acknowledgements are sent.

The first, the "accept acknowledgment" is a message indicating whether the receiving system, which could be an interface engine, was able to take custody of the sender's message, but does not indicate whether it was able to process the information contained within it.

The second, the "application acknowledgment" indicates whether the final receiving application was able to process the sender's message successfully.

Original mode acknowledgement is more straightforward to implement, especially for simple point-to-point interfaces.

10.10   Implementation Technology Specification (ITS)

The XML implementation technology specification describes how individual instances of message types shall be rendered in XML for serial transmission over the network and the structure of schemas used to validate each instance. Note that the HL7 generated XML schemas are not able to test all of the constraints defined in a HL7 message definition.

The generation of the schemas and message representation tends to be done automatically. Those not directly involved in that process do not need to understand the technical details. Hinchley summarizes the key points as follows:

- An XML element is defined to correspond to each row in the HMD grid, with the exception of structural attributes, which are expressed as XML attributes.
- Each Data Type has a defined XML representation. The "restriction base" feature in an XML schema is used extensively to define how data types are implemented.
- The schema files for CMETs are supplied separately and then used by each message schema as required.
- The XML schemas defined support V3 Data Types, and Data Type refinement, through the use of the W3C Schema restriction element. Additional standard schema sections support RIM classes and the HL7-defined vocabulary definitions. These schema sections can be selectively combined with a specific message schema through the "include" function in the XML schema standard.
- HL7 messages all share the same XML namespace.
- Message version information is conveyed as attributes within the message rather than by changes to the namespace identifier.

10.11   IHE XDS

IHE Cross-Enterprise Document Sharing (XDS) allows health care documents to be shared over a wide area network, between hospitals, primary care providers, and social services. The idea is to build virtual patient records on the fly from a variety of clinical documents created by different healthcare organizations (Fig. 10.3).

The main innovation in XDS is the logical and physically separation of the indexing information (the metadata) used to retrieve documents from the actual content. This allows XDS to handle any type of content and simplifies the addition of an XDS export function to existing systems.

XDS enables users (document consumers) to retrieve different types of documents (letters, results, images, and folders) contained in one or more repositories in a quick and consistent way. Each document is viewed in its original form, which may include structured data. XDS provides a foundation on which to build virtual patient records on the fly from a variety of clinical documents created by different healthcare organizations.

XDS has four distinct roles or actors: document source; document repository; document registry; and the document consumer.

- The document source produces original documents, submits these to a document repository (each organization may maintain its own), and generates metadata about each, which is sent to the centralized document registry. That is all that is required.

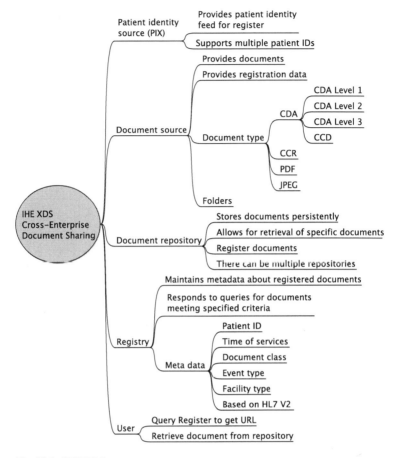

Fig. 10.3 IHE XDS

- Each document repository (there can be more than one) provides secure document storage and supports document retrieval; documents may be in folders. Documents may be stored in a number of different formats, such as CDA or PDF.
- The central document registry indexes documents, supports searches, and maintains a URI link back where the document is stored in a document repository.
- The document consumer is a user system which initiates search of the register, retrieves, and displays selected documents from their repository(ies).

To maintain security, the XDS registry has no access to the content of any document, but relies entirely on standardized metadata provided by the source to retrieve relevant items. The standardized set of metadata is the key to XDS and includes patient ID, dates/times, clinical event context, document type, author, size, format, and location.

The basic XDS has been refined to support special requirements for DICOM images (XDS-I), HL7 CDA medical summaries (XDS-MS), and structured laboratory reports (XDS-Lab).

Technically, the XDS document registry is a subset of the ebXML Registry standard (ISO 15000 parts 3 and 4). Documents are exchanged using SOAP and HTTP, while SQL is used for information retrieval. Various document formats may be used, including HL7 CDA Release 2, DICOM, and PDF. The format of the metadata is largely based on HL7 Version 2.[1]

---

[1]IHE IT Infrastructure Technical Framework Volume 1 (ITI TF-1), Chapter 10, 69–99. http://www.ihe.net/Technical_Framework/upload/ihe_iti_tf_2.0_vol1_FT_2005-08-15.pdf

Part III
SNOMED CT

Chapter 11
Clinical Terminology

11.1 Why Clinical Terminology Matters

When, in the fifteenth century, Gutenberg's invention of the movable type led to the mass production and dissemination of books and written information, language was still relatively unformalized. It took until the eighteenth century before the great dictionaries and nomenclatures such as Dr Johnson's English Dictionary and Linnaeus' biological taxonomy were produced. Medical terminology escaped formalization, leading to problems that are now recognized as significant risks to patient safety.

The lack of agreed medical terminology has been recognized as an issue for at least 250 years. There is even an old word, "nosology," to describe the development of medical terminology, but the need has increased with the use of computers. Modern nosologists call themselves terminologists.

Sciences such as biology and chemistry have an internationally agreed formal structure for their terminology. Every living organism has a generic and specific Latin name expressed within a comprehensive biological taxonomy, which in many ways anticipated the full understanding of the evolution of life. All chemical structures are expressed in internationally standardized ways. Medical terminology, in contrast, lacks any formal structure.

Scott Blois in his classic work *Information and Medicine*, showed how medical concepts can be classified into a series of connected levels. At one extreme are subatomic concepts, which are key to radiation physics and molecular biochemistry. At the other extreme are concepts relating to societies, impacting population health and wellbeing. In between are more levels relating to the structure and function of cells, organs, body systems, individuals, personal relationships and so on (Fig 11.1).

The day-to-day vocabulary of medicine relates to every level. Radio-therapists use subatomic particles, clinical chemists measure molecule concentrations, haematologists study blood cells, microbiologists grow bacteria, radiologists review images of internal structures and organs, physicians are concerned with abnormal body functions, psychiatrists with unusual behaviour and interpersonal relationships and epidemiologists and public health doctors study the spread of disease in populations (Blois 1984).

T. Benson, *Principles of Health Interoperability HL7 and SNOMED*, HI,
DOI 10.1007/978-1-84882-803-2_11, © Springer-Verlag London Limited 2010

Healthcare mixes multiple overlapping theories, each with its own sub-terminology. Any classification system is inevitably just one way of slicing up a very complex reality and is made more difficult because key medical concepts such as diseases are abstractions, defined using information from a variety of information levels; diseases are not objects which can be seen or touched.

The historical, eclectic, and ad hoc origins of medical terminology have encumbered anyone interested in healthcare with the need to learn a whole new language, replete with homonyms (where the same term means different things depending on context); synonyms (where there is more than one term for exactly the same concept); eponyms, named after people; acronyms; and abbreviations. Nobody, who has not learnt the eponym, can guess Hodgkin's disease(lymph node cancer), Bright's disease (kidney disease), and von Recklinghausen's disease (hereditary neurofibromatosis).

People use terms in the way that they and their immediate colleagues understand. Each user of a term assumes that everyone else understands precisely what he or she intends it to mean; over time, groups develop their own local dialect. Medical records staff can often identify the institution in which a doctor was trained from the way he or she uses certain terms.

Lewis Carrol expressed the same problem in an exchange between Alice and Humpty Dumpty in *Through the Looking Glass* (Carrol 1871):

> 'I don't know what you mean by "glory"' Alice said.
> Humpty Dumpty smiled contemptuously. 'Of course you don't – till I tell you. I meant "there's a nice knock-down argument for you!"'
> 'But "glory" doesn't mean "a nice knock-down argument"' Alice objected.
> 'When I use a word,' Humpty Dumpty said in a rather scornful tone, 'it means just what I chose it to mean – neither more nor less.'
> 'The question is,' said Alice, 'whether you can make words mean so many different things.'
> 'The question is,' said Humpty Dumpty, 'which is to be master – that's all.'

The representation of written information has become more and more specific over the centuries. The first way of representing information was by a picture or drawing, such as in Stone-Age cave paintings. The earliest writing was based on pictograms, such as Egyptian hieroglyphics and Chinese characters, but the need for cheap and quick writing materials led to the development of cruciform characters on wet clay blocks in Mesopotamia and the development of phonetic alphabets such as those of Greece and Rome. Modern English uses just 26 letters and 10 numerals.

11.2 Computers Need Codes

Computers hold information as sequences of binary bits and work by matching strings; they need precisely coded data. A computer can instantly check if two strings are the same, but if any difference is detected, it cannot tell whether that

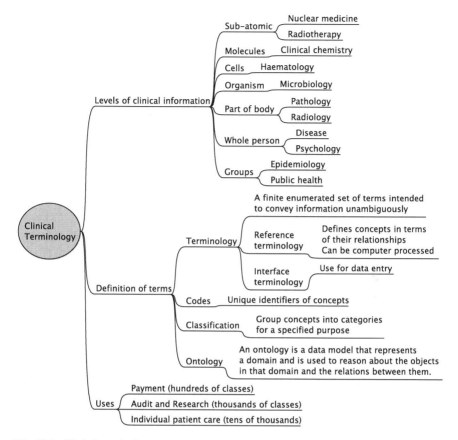

Fig. 11.1 Clinical terminology

difference is important. In spite of decades of effort, we do not yet have computers that cope well with the ambiguity inherent in natural language.

ASCII (American Standard Code for Information Interchange) was the code most widely used for representing the English alphabet in computers; it uses seven bits to provide 128 characters. ASCII was not finalized in 1967 and has since evolved into Unicode, which covers most of the world's writing systems. The ASCII coding system is important, because when lists are sorted in a computer, ASCII is the most natural order to sort them.

In ASCII (the American Standard Code for Information Interchange, which is the basis of the way that computers hold data), the numerals 0–9 precede upper case letters A–Z, which precede all of the lowercase letters a–z. Some printable characters, such as "!", "*," and ".", come ahead of the numerals; some, such as: "?" and "@," come between the numerals and uppercase letters; others, such as "\," "^," and "_," come between the upper and lower case letters; and a few, such as "|" and "~," come right at the end.

11.3   Coding and Classification

People often confuse the terms coding and classification and use them almost synonymously. This may be because the process of classification involves recording the codes used to name specific classes. However, coding schemes and classifications do different jobs. Classification allocates things into groups or classes, while coding is the allocation of identifiers, which can apply to anything (including classes in classifications).

A code is just sequence of symbols, usually digits or letters, which designate an object or concept for identification or selection purposes. It is just an alternative name for something, an identifier, designed for computer processing. Coding systems are an indispensible part of healthcare computer applications and specifications for exchanging data between computers.

The primary challenge for the designers of coding schemes is to produce something that will be widely and willingly adopted and endorsed by clinicians and managers. However, clinicians and managers have no more interest than a retail customer has in the bar code on a packet of cornflakes. Codes are needed and used by computers, not humans.

Clinicians need to record information in the form, language, and detail that is of most benefit to them when treating individual patients. Clinical records require precise and comprehensive detail about each individual patient, but statistical analysis requires patients to be classified into a relatively small number of discrete and mutually exclusive groups.

Clinicians and managers need to be interested in classification; classification is the basis for most statistical analysis, quantitative management, accountancy, and research.

Classification is the systematic placement of things or concepts into categories or classes, which share some common attribute, quality, or property. There is no limit to the number of ways that any set of objects can be classified.

The choice of what classification system to use is often determined by payment agencies, insurance companies, and national governments who control whether or not a doctor or institution gets paid or not. Such bodies usually specify the precise classification system that they require, often in collaboration with representatives from the professional and trade associations, medical colleges, and educational bodies. Once chosen it has to be accepted by users and implemented in computer software.

In *The Endangered Medical Record*, Vergil Slee and his colleagues argue that the choice of coding system used for electronic patient records represents a serious, real threat to the truthfulness and completeness of medical record content. Use of broad category codes, such as those specified by the International Classification of Diseases (ICD), rather than precise diagnoses means that we throw away detail, which should be preserved permanently. His plea is for detailed, permanent, and unambiguous codes (Slee et al. 2000).

For example, a trauma surgeon might describe a typical skiing accident as: a closed spiral fracture of the shaft of the right tibia with fractured fibula. In ICD-10, the code for fracture of shaft of tibia has the following logical structure:

Chapter XIX: Injury, poisoning, and certain other consequences of external cause (S00-T98)
Block: Injuries to the knee and lower leg (S80-S98)
S82: Fracture of lower leg, including ankle
S82.2 Fracture of shaft of tibia (with or without mention of fracture of fibula)
S82.2.1 Closed fracture of shaft of tibia

ICD-10 does not specify whether the leg is left or right, whether the fracture is simple, spiral, or compound or whether the fibula is also fractured.

Most healthcare computer systems use nationally prescribed coding systems such as the ICD, the Read Codes in UK and CPT-4. These all use a position-dependent hierarchical coding structure.

The internal structure of a position-dependent hierarchical code specifies its meaning relative to other codes. The structure of the code increases in detail from left to right, with the first character of the code specifying the chapter, the second the main subdivision, and so on until down the branches of the tree until the final leaf codes are reached.

One of the technical problems of hierarchical changes is that they cannot be modified easily without changing the meaning of codes in different versions, creating problems when, as inevitably happens, one version needs to be replaced by another.

A hierarchical classification can be thought of as an inverted tree with its trunk or root at the top. For example, biological classification places animals and plants into a hierarchical classification (a taxonomy) according to similarities in structure, origin, etc. that indicate a common relationship. The main levels in the hierarchy are Kingdom, Phylum (animals) or Division (plants), Class, Order, Family, Genus, and Species.

11.4 First Generation Clinical Coding Systems

Any coding system has various components.

- Concept: The fundamental idea is that of a concept. Each concept is identified by a concept code.
- Coding Scheme: Each concept code originates from a coding scheme. A coding scheme defines a set of concept codes, which are unique within the namespace of the coding scheme and are globally unique when coupled with the name of the coding scheme itself.
- Display Term: This is a human readable term. In some cases more than one display term may be provided for the same concept, to cover true synonyms, such as translations into different languages. One display term is usually designated as the preferred term.
- Relationship: Concepts may be related to other concept via a relationship, which allows the generation of hierarchical structures. One concept may be part of

more than one hierarchical structure. Often these relationships will be defined as part of original coding schemes, but other relationships are also possible.

- Value Set: This is a set of values that is allowed for a particular data item. Message specifications refer to value sets as the allowed values for a field.

Each concept is part of a coding scheme, but there is not a one-to-one relationship between value set and coding scheme.

The simplest code is a single code value, which needs to be unique for the field where it is used. The combination of field and concept code is unique. These codes need to be part of agreed code tables and there is no requirement to exchange the code meaning.

Simple codes are referenced using a value-set table, which has a heading which includes meta-data such as: value-set name, unique identifier, coding scheme, author, time validity, version, and other notes. Each entry in the table contains concept code value, display term, and notes about applicability.

Computer systems need unique identifiers, which have similar properties to codes. One way of achieving uniqueness is to treat each identifier as a pair, comprising a unique name for the assigner plus a value for the identification number, which is unique within assigner. It is the responsibility of the assigner to ensure that all such values are unique.

11.4.1 User Requirements

A key design requirement for any coding and classification system is to satisfy the needs of the different stakeholders.

Roger Côté views this as a pyramid with three levels of use:

1. At the tip, case-mix classifications such as DRGs, used for payment.
2. In the middle, classifications of diagnoses and procedures used to monitor and audit clinical activities.
3. At the base, clinical terminology used for individual patient care.

Healthcare managers and researchers need classified data, which enable comparisons and data exchange with existing data sources. Links between classifications must be explicit with one-to-one or many-to-one links. A many-to-one link involves loss of information, the extent of which is determined by how closely one classification is based on the other.

A multilevel classification with both course and fine granularity may allow two-way mapping from another classification. High levels of compatibility can usually be obtained only by basing a new classification directly on the target, using the same class boundaries. This requirement for cross-mapping with existing classifications inevitably drives the developers of clinical classifications to build on existing schemes, even if they are not suitable for the need in hand. For example, the ICD is organized around body systems, which is helpful in some circumstances, but not in others. Early versions of SNOMED reflected its origins as an extension of the Systematized Nomenclature of Pathology (SNOP) giving a forensic and medico-legal slant.

Doctors and nurses will not take the trouble to learn how to use any system unless it is quick and easy to use and provides information in the form and language that best helps them treat individual patients. Automatic or semi-automatic encoding software is required. Clinical records need to be as specific as possible. Hence, clinicians require a comprehensive nomenclature of medical terms covering everything that could occur within any patient's medical record. That is, all of clinical medicine and health service administration, but not the whole of biomedical science.

In 1984, the IMIA working conference on clinical terminology concluded:

> In future healthcare information systems, the user interface should be based upon natural language. The generation of numerical or alphanumeric codes should occur within the computer. Automatic encoding of natural language should be used. The morbidity and mortality statistical classification requirements of national and international groups should be the by-product of medically-based healthcare information systems.

It was not anticipated that clinical coding in hospitals would continue to be done by coding clerks.

11.4.2   Oxmis Problem Codes

Development of computing in primary care in the UK can be traced back to the formation of the Oxford Record Linkage Project in 1962, which connected birth, hospital data, and mortality data for a whole community and led directly to the Oxford Community Health Project, which maintained a central disease and encounter register for over 100 GPs. This required a coding scheme and Dr John Perry developed the Oxmis problem codes for this purpose.

The Oxmis codes were based on extending the four-digit ICD-8 classification for diseases and the OPCS classification of surgical operations. Prefixes were added to indicate F, family history; H, history from patient; K, surgical operation; L, locally defined codes; and T, items not within either ICD or OPCS classifications. Two-character alphabetic suffixes were added to provide greater specificity. Oxmis was one of the first multidimensional coding schemes, developed at around the same time as the first SNOMED.

Although no longer in use, the majority of GPs who used computers during the 1970s and 1980s in the UK used Oxmis, which also demonstrated that one person single-handedly could develop a coding system to meet the needs of many GPs.

11.4.3   The Read Codes

The Read Codes are widely used by GPs in the UK and New Zealand and are a direct predecessor of SNOMED CT.

The development of the Read Codes began in 1983, when, with colleagues James Read and David Markwell, I helped design a new computer system for use in general practice. An early design decision was to use a development tool that used fixed-length fields, requiring all codes, terms, and look-up keys to have a fixed predefined length.

The original design used alphanumeric codes with four characters (later extended to five characters) and terms up to 30 characters long. Another key requirement was that the coding scheme should be as comprehensive as possible covering everything that might be entered into a patient's computerized record. No existing coding scheme could be found which met these criteria so we chose to write one from scratch (as did many of our competitors during that period).

The motivation was commercial. We sought to commoditize GP computing, so that systems would be useful straight from the box. In earlier systems, GPs had to develop their own local coding schemes, which deterred prospective customers. It was also important to have a system that would be quick to use, so that GPs could use it themselves in the consulting room and could generate reports almost instantly.

Our idea was to take existing classifications and convert these into the appropriate format. The obvious candidates at the time were ICD-9 for diseases, the British National Formulary (BNF) for drugs, the International Classification of Procedures in Medicine (ICPM), and the national coding scheme for operations OPCS-4.

Dr James Read, a GP in Loughborough and one of my early customers, undertook the editing task and developed new sections for examination findings, preventive care, administrative procedures, and other subjects for which no suitable model could be found. Dr David Markwell developed the software. What was originally planned to take 3 months took almost 3 years and the scheme was finally launched as the Read Codes in 1986 (Read and Benson 1986). In the meantime, our customers continued to use homegrown codes.

As the work evolved, we found that we had improved on earlier classification and coding systems in several respects.

They were designed primarily for use by GPs in their surgery, not for epidemiology and international comparisons.

No paper version was ever published, facilitating regular updates and extensions.

The simple position-dependent, unidimensional hierarchy was easy to implement in software.

Each code has a uniform alphanumeric structure with five levels and 60 possible child codes at each node, by using numerals 0 to 9, upper and lowercase letters A–Z, with a couple of exceptions such as O and I that are easily confused with numeric digits, and a few printable characters such as "." (dot). This provides a large potential code space – 777 Million possible codes (60^5).

The first character of any code shows the chapter heading, the second the main subdivision, and so on. The following example shows the five-byte version (Version 2).

```
A.... Infectious and parasitic diseases
A1... Tuberculosis
A13.. Tuberculosis of the meninges and CNS
A130. Tuberculosis meningitis
```

Diseases were allocated codes with the first character in the range A–Z, so infectious diseases have codes starting with A, corresponding to the first chapter in ICD-9. The scheme was cross-mapped to ICD-9 and later to ICD-10.

Drugs were given codes starting with lower-case letters a–z, corresponding to the chapters in the first edition of the BNF.

Other concepts including occupations, history, and symptoms, examination findings, diagnostic and laboratory procedures, prevention, radiology/imaging, surgical operations, and administrative procedures were allocated first digits in the range 0–9.

The system included an index to enable quick semiautomated encoding by typing the first few letters of any term; the system responds with a list of terms to choose from, which may be context-specific.

The Read Codes combine the features of a classification and a coding scheme. However, hierarchical coding schemes can never be truly multipurpose, because they are built around a single hierarchical axis and each code is classified in one way only.

The Read Codes proved successful in General Practice, for which they were designed. However, attempts to use the original versions in hospitals proved impracticable, primarily because the simple hierarchical scheme could reflect only one view, namely the general practice perspective. Hospital doctors did not understand why information retrieval in one dimension was easy, but in another dimension was difficult and slow.

Once a concept has been placed in the classification, it is not practicable to move it, even if it has been placed in a location that is later regarded as wrong.

Another problem is the inherent multidimensionality of medicine. Tuberculosis meningitis is a type of tuberculosis, which is an infectious disease and is given code A130., but it is also an inflammatory disease of the central nervous system and has another code F004. It has two separate Read codes, creating code redundancy, which can cause inaccuracies in hierarchy-based analysis of clinical data, stored using the codes.

Being restricted to only four levels (later extended to five levels) in the hierarchy causes another problem. Consider the following hierarchy:

```
7.... Operations, procedures, sites
71... Endocrine system and breast operations
713.. Breast operations
7130. Total mastectomy operations
71304 Subcutaneous mastectomy
```

It is not possible to add a more detailed variant of this operation, such as subcutaneous mastectomy for gynecomastia in the appropriate position because there is no sixth level. A possible solution is to add it as a sibling alongside subcutaneous mastectomy in the fifth level with a code such as 71307. However, this creates the danger that when retrieving cases of subcutaneous mastectomy (71304), those recorded using 71307 would be missed.

The Read Codes were purchased by the Department of Health in April 1990, leading to the establishment of the NHS Centre for Coding and Classification (Chisholm 1990).

The NHS Clinical Terms project was started in 1992, as a major attempt to address these issues. The resulting scheme, which is known as Clinical Terms Version 3 (ctv3), was merged with the College of American Pathologist's SNOMED RT during 1999–2002 to create SNOMED CT (see the next Chapter). First we consider the history of SNOMED (Fig. 11.2).

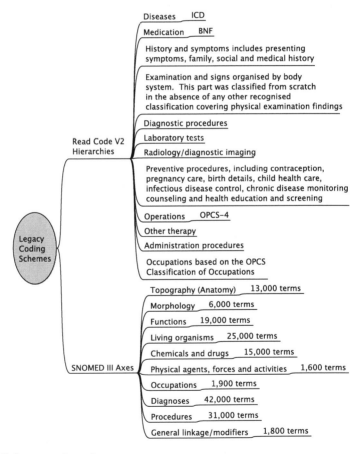

Fig. 11.2 Legacy coding schemes

11.4.4 SNOMED

SNOMED has a long history.

Back in 1955 the College of American Pathologists (CAP) established a committee to develop a nomenclature for anatomic pathology. In 1965, they published the *Systematized Nomenclature of Pathology* (SNOP), which describes pathology findings using four axes:

- Topography (anatomic site affected)
- Morphology (structural changes associated with disease)
- Etiology (the cause of disease) including organisms
- Function (physiologic alterations associated with disease).

SNOP was the first multi-axial coding system used in healthcare. By 1975 Roger Côté and colleagues had extended SNOP by adding additional dimensions covering diseases and procedures to give it a broader scope with the name *Systematised Nomenclature of Medicine* (SNOMED).

SNOMED was developed around a model of illness that started with normal structure (topography) and function. Sickness typically involves some abnormal function and abnormal structure (morphology). This has some cause (aetiology), which may be internal or external. Medicine seeks to reverse the process from the sick state to the healthy state by using administrative, diagnostic, and therapeutic procedures, which act on function or body structure. Disease was added to give easy mapping to ICD.

Occupations and organisms were added later. SNOMED III, published in 1993 had ten axes and 156,000 terms.

In 1999 the NHS and the College of American Pathologists (CAP) agreed to merge SNOMED with the NHS Clinical Terms Version 3 (also known as CTV3 and the Read Codes Version 3) to produce a single joint clinical terminology – SNOMED CT (Clinical Terminology). The merger was completed in 2002 with the first release of SNOMED CT.

While SNOMED has its origins in North American pathology laboratories, the Clinical Terms Version 3, formerly known as the Read Codes Version 3, was developed from the earlier versions of the Read Codes (see Chapter 11). SNOMED CT is a true merger. Every Read Code and previous SNOMED code ever released is present in SNOMED CT so migration to SNOMED CT should not result in loss of information.

In 2007, the International Health Terminology Standards Development Organization (IHTSDO) acquired all of the IPR of SNOMED (See Chapter 5).

Over a period of 40 years SNOMED has evolved from a pathology-centric terminology distributed and used in print format to a comprehensive clinical terminology, which is only available in electronic format and needs to be integrated with clinical applications software.

11.5   Desiderata

In 1997, Jim Cimino produced a paper, *Desiderata for Controlled Medical Vocabularies in the Twenty-First Century,* which brought together a number of common requirements for clinical terminologies, which had been developed in leading terminology projects such as GALEN (Rector et al. 1994), UMLS (Unified Medical Language System) (Lindberg et al. 1993), SNOMED RT (Reference Terminology) (Spackman et al. 1997), and the NHS Clinical Terms Project (O'Neil et al. 1995). This paper was particularly influential in influencing the design of SNOMED CT (Cimino 1998).

The desiderata are (Fig. 11.3):

- Vocabulary Content
- Concept Orientation
- Concept Permanence
- Non-Semantic Concept Identifiers

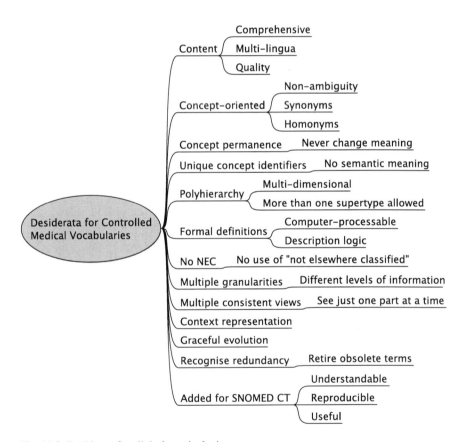

Fig. 11.3 Desiderata for clinical terminologies

- Polyhierarchy
- Formal Definitions
- Rejection of "Not Elsewhere Classified" Terms
- Multiple Granularities
- Multiple Consistent Views
- Context Representation
- Graceful Evolution
- Recognize Redundancy (Fig. 11.3)

Content, in terms of scope and quality, is paramount. Any practical clinical terminology needs to be comprehensive in terms of both domain coverage (concepts) and human readable terms (descriptions and synonyms). A methodology is required to allow the content to be expanded as and when required, including translation into other languages and dialects, while retaining high quality.

Concept orientation means that each concept term has one meaning (non-vagueness) and only one meaning (nonambiguity). A concept can be described by several terms (synonyms) in the same language and different terms in each language or dialect. Note also that one term can have several meanings (homonyms) each relating to a different concept.

Once a concept is created its meaning is persistent. It must not be changed or deleted by updates. However, a concept may be marked as retired where its meaning is found to be ambiguous, redundant, or otherwise incorrect.

Each concept should have a unique identifier, which should be meaningless. Semantic information should be handled as attributes of the concept, not as part of its identifier. Some of the problems with position-dependent hierarchical coding schemes have been reviewed above.

It is widely accepted that it is useful to organize medical concepts in a hierarchical way, but many clinical concepts are naturally multidimensional, with more than one super-type (parent) concept. For example, a fractured tibia is both a type of fracture and a type of leg injury.

The means of classifying a concept is independent of the means of identifying it. The development of formal, descriptive logic to define and classify clinical concepts is a major development away from the traditional position-dependent coding schemes and dictionary type of definition. For example, *pneumococcal pneumonia* may be defined using a hierarchical (*is a*) link to the concept *pneumonia* and a *caused by* link to the concept *streptococcus pneumoniae*.

Many existing classifications include one or more catch-all categories for concepts not covered. The problem with such *not elsewhere classified* or *NEC* categories is that they tend to change their meaning over time, as and when a new category is added which covers some of the NEC scope. The meaning is not permanent, which was a previous criterion.

Different users require different levels of granularity. Different levels of granularity are needed for defining concepts, navigation, decision support, and reporting. For example, a manager may only need to know that a patient has a broken leg; the finance department that it is a fractured tibia, but the clinician needs to know that it is a spiral fracture of the shaft of the right tibia. In principle, there should be no limitations on the number of levels in the display tree hierarchy.

When a concept has multiple hierarchical parents, the view of that concept should not depend on whether it was reached by following the hierarchy from a particular parent. Different requirements need different views on the terminology. The complete structure of a terminology, including all hierarchies and relationships can be complex and perhaps unusable. Each user needs to be able to see one or more views that reflect his or her own needs and understanding, but each of these views needs to be consistent with the underlying model.

Part of the problem of medical terminology is that information is usually recorded in a particular context and cannot be interpreted without that under-standing. The context needs to be computer-processable. One approach to this problem is to provide a means of recording context explicitly within the terminology.

Terminologies change over time, which can create major problems for users if the meanings of aggregated time series data change in an uncontrolled manner. Care is needed to design the whole structure to support graceful evolution of con-cepts, terms, and relationships.

When terminologies change, some components will become redundant and so it is important to recognize explicitly that this has happened.

Three other criteria were added for SNOMED CT:

- Understandable: definitions should be understandable by average clinicians, given brief explanations.
- Reproducible: retrieval and representation of the same item should not vary according to the nature of the interface, user preferences, or the time of entry.
- Usable: we can ignore distinctions for which there is no use in healthcare.

11.5.1 The Meaning of Meaning

The Guidelines for Translation of SNOMED CT (Høy 2009) provide a short intro-duction to terminological principles, on which the following section is closely based.

The basic idea in the science of terminology is an onomasiological approach (concept-based approach) as opposed to a semasiological approach (term/word-based approach) that is applied in lexicography. With an onomasiological approach, the starting point is the concept; with a semasiological approach, the starting point is the linguistic expression, i.e., the word/term. A lexicographer would ask the ques-tion: "How many meanings could this term have/how many different concepts could be reflected by this term?" But a terminologist will ask: "Which terms could reflect this particular concept?"

The semasiological (term-based) approach will reveal the existence of hom-onyms and/or polysemes: homonyms are identical designations representing different concepts (e.g., *race* = taxonomic distinction of human beings and *race* = competition of speed). If the designations have the same origin they are referred to as polysemes (e.g., *bed* = piece of furniture and *bed* = the ground under a body of water).

The onomasiological (concept-based) approach will reveal the existence of synonymy: synonyms are different designations representing the same concept. The recommended approach to use is that applied within terminology, i.e., the onomasiological approach.

A concept is a "unit of knowledge created by a unique combination of characteristics." In other words, the concept corresponds to the image or idea created in our brains when we are presented with an object in our surroundings. The object may be physical, such as a car, or abstract, such as speed.

Any concept may be represented by a designation, which, in this context, would be a term. In other contexts, the designation could be a drawing or a photograph. The concept, i.e., the unit of knowledge/idea/thought, forms the connection between the object and the designation. This designation is defined as a "representation of a concept by a sign, which denotes it," and a term is the "verbal designation of a general concept in a specific subject field." The term will denote a concept, and a concept will refer to a particular object.

Traditionally, these principles are represented in the Ogden-Richards "Semiotic Triangle," which differentiates between three separate dimensions: the conceptual domain - thoughts that are in our minds; the symbolic domain - words and symbols that we use to communicate with others; and the real world - things in the real world that we refer to in our thoughts and with symbols (Ogden and Richards).

Whenever we are presented with an object, we automatically perceive its position in some kind of organized system – provided, of course, that experience tells us where it belongs. In the case of an abstract concept such as *democracy*, it would automatically be placed in our mind as a "type of government" – i.e., we would conceive it as belonging to the level below the concept *government*. Therefore, utilizing concept systems is useful in many contexts.

Concept systems allow us to place an unknown concept in a semantic context and give us a good idea of the importance, or, the "size" (magnitude) of specific concepts in relation to other concepts. Therefore, for didactic purposes, in connection with translation work as well as for storing and retrieving information in a systematic way, concept systems are extremely useful.

There are various principles that may be used when establishing a concept system: typology, partition, chronology, to name a few. The most common systems are based on generic relationships (IS-A -relationships) and partitive relationships (PART OF - relationships). In these systems, each concept belonging to the hierarchy is a TYPE OF and respectively a PART OF the immediate superordinate concept. In a generic system, a *metacarpal bone* could be considered as "a type of bone of hand," whereas in a partitive system, a *metacarpal bone* could be considered as a "part of the bone structure of hand."

In a generic system, the subordinate concept will be differentiated from its superordinate concept by means of at least one particular, distinguishing characteristic.

In a representation of a concept system, one will always find the generic concepts at the top levels and the more specific or "granular" concepts further down.

It is possible to establish "combined" concept systems that contain both generic and partitive relationships.

A definition is a "representation of a concept by a descriptive statement which serves to differentiate it from related concepts." To define a concept may take just a few words or it may entail a long phrase. Ideally, the definition will be based on the immediate superordinate concept in the concept system.

For example, a sedan could be defined as a "closed car having two or four doors and front and rear seats" (i.e., a type of *car*), and the *transmission* could be defined as a "set of mechanical parts in a car that transmits power from the engine to the wheels" (i.e., a part of *car*). In both cases, there is a reference to the immediate superordinate concept, and in the case of the generic definition, the particular, distinguishing characteristic(s) is/are added.

Instead of such narrative definitions, the "descriptive statements" which serve to differentiate concepts from one another may be expressed in description logic. This principle is applied in SNOMED CT where the concepts are defined by their hierarchical and defining attribute relationships.

Chapter 12
SNOMED CT

SNOMED CT is the most comprehensive, multilingual clinical healthcare terminology in the world. It is used in electronic health record systems for clinical documentation and reporting. It can be used to retrieve, and analyze clinical data.

When considering SNOMED CT and its use, we need to remember that on its own SNOMED CT does very little. The value of SNOMED CT can only be realized when it is built into software and systems that are designed around it.

Kent Spackman, the leader of the team that developed SNOMED CT, has postulated two golden rules (Spackman 2005):

- The first rule of data quality is that the quality of data collected is directly proportional to the care with which options are presented to the user.
- The first rule of coding is that yesterday's data should be usable today.

The rule of data quality recognizes the heterogeneity of medical care and implies that we cannot adopt a one-size-fits-all approach to the detailed design of clinical applications.

The rule of coding recognizes that clinical data need to be treated as being permanent. We have to be able to use yesterday's data today and today's data tomorrow and for the indefinite future.

SNOMED CT has been designed and built for this. SNOMED CT is a comprehensive clinical terminology for recording the health and care of individual patients in a way that the information can be indexed and retrieved for reuse both at the point of care and subsequently for management, surveillance, and research. It is able to provide the clinical content and expressivity required for precise clinical documentation.

SNOMED CT was founded on four basic principles that have guided development activities and will continue to guide the future directions of SNOMED.

1. Development efforts must encompass broad, inclusive involvement of diverse clinical groups and medical informatics experts.
2. The clinical content must be quality-focused and adhere to strict editorial policies.

T. Benson, *Principles of Health Interoperability HL7 and SNOMED*, HI,
DOI 10.1007/978-1-84882-803-2_12, © Springer-Verlag London Limited 2010

3. The quality improvement process must be open to public scrutiny and vendor input to ensure that the terminology is truly useful within healthcare applications.
4. There must be minimal barriers to adoption and use.

SNOMED CT is the most comprehensive, multilingual clinical terminology in the world. In January 2009, it contained over 310,000 active concepts, 990,000 English descriptions, and 1.38 million relationships. There is no paper version. The sheer size of SNOMED CT is a significant issue in developing, using, and maintaining it.

In comparison, ICD-10 has 10,760 classes (excluding Chapter XX, external causes) and comes in three large volumes.

SNOMED CT is both a coding scheme, identifying concepts and terms, and a multidimensional classification, enabling concepts to be related to each other, grouped, and analyzed according to different criteria.

Numeric codes (the SNOMED CT identifier – SCTID) identify every instance of the three core building blocks: concepts, descriptions, and relationships. Each *concept* represents a single specific meaning; each *description* associates a single term with a concept (any concept may have any number of descriptions or names); and each *relationship* represents a logical relationship between two concepts.

SNOMED CT is used only in computer systems – it cannot be used manually, partly because it is so large, and more importantly because it works in a different way than earlier coding schemes such as ICD or the Read Codes. The relationship structure in SNOMED CT relies on a large number (well over a million) of explicitly defined relationships to work. The mechanism used is more complex than a code-dependant hierarchy used in earlier schemes, but is enormously more powerful, flexible, and future-proof. It allows any concept to be classified or qualified in any number of ways.

SNOMED CT provides an extensible foundation for expressing clinical data in local systems, for interoperability, and for use in data warehouses.

SNOMED CT is designed for clinical documentation and reporting. The terminology is made up from concepts, terms, and relationships to provide a way of representing clinical information across the broad scope of health care to support analysis and clinical decision support.

The content of SNOMED CT is organized into a number of hierarchies, including clinical finding, procedure, observable entity, body structure, organism, substance, pharmaceutical/biological product, specimen, physical force, event, environment/geographical locations, social context, staging and scales, etc.

12.1 SNOMED CT Documentation

The SNOMED CT User Guide, Technical Reference Guide, and Technical Implementation Guide are three key documents describing SNOMED CT in detail.

12.1.1 SNOMED CT User Guide

The User Guide is intended for clinical personnel, business directors, software product managers, and project leaders; information technology experience, though not necessary, can be helpful (IHTSDO 2009a). The User Guide is intended to explain SNOMED CT's capabilities and uses from a content perspective. It explains the content and the principles used to model the terminology.

12.1.2 SNOMED CT Technical Reference Guide (TRG)

The TRG is intended for SNOMED CT implementers, such as software developers (IHTSDO 2009b). The TRG assumes an information technology background. Clinical knowledge is not a prerequisite. The TRG contains reference material related to the current release of SNOMED CT and includes file layouts, field sizes, required values and their meanings, and high-level data diagrams. It can be used to install and use SNOMED.

12.1.3 SNOMED CT Technical Implementation Guide (TIG)

The TIG is intended for SNOMED CT implementers, such as software designers (IHTSDO 2009c). The TIG assumes information technology and software development experience. Clinical knowledge is not required, although some background is helpful to understand the application context and needs. The TIG contains guidelines and advice about the design of applications using SNOMED CT and covers topics such as terminology services, entering and storing information, and migration of legacy information.

12.2 Commom Aspects

SNOMED CT is composed of components, which include concepts, relationships, descriptions, subsets, and cross maps, each of which is identified by a SNOMED CT Identifier (SCTID) and has a validity status (Fig. 12.1).

12.2.1 The SCTID

All components are identified using a special SNOMED Clinical Terms Identifier (SCTID). The SCTID is an integer between 6 and 18 digits long. One way of thinking of the SCTID is as a 64-bit integer, although it does have an internal structure.

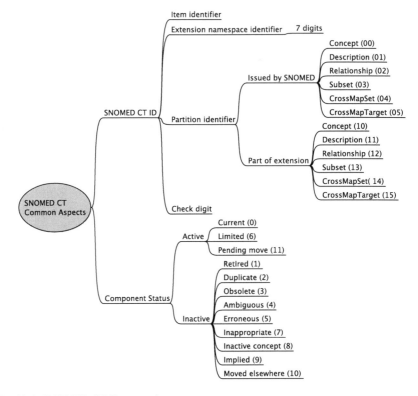

Fig. 12.1 SNOMED CT Common Aspects

The internal structure of the SCTID includes a meaningless item identifier, a check digit at the end and a partition identifier just in front of the check digit (the check digit algorithm is Verhoeff's Dihedral Group D5 Check).

The partition identifier indicates the type of component referred to by that SCTID. The SCTID may also contain a namespace-identifier, which is used in local extensions.

The partition identifier is a two-digit number. If the first digit of the partition identifier is a zero (0) then this component is part of the International Release; if it is a 1, then the component is part of an extension set. The second of the two digits in the partition identifier indicates which of the partitions of SNOMED CT the SCTID is identifying, where:

- Concept (0)
- Description (1)
- Relationship (2)
- Subset (3)
- Cross Map Set (4)
- Cross Map Target (5)

Extensions are additions to SNOMED CT, usually specific to one country or organization, and are identified using a seven-digit namespace-identifier.

12.2.2 Status

An important principle of SNOMED CT is that of permanence. Once a component such as a concept or description has been created it is never deleted, but may be given an inactive status, which also indicates the reason why it is inactive. The status field has the following values, with code values in parenthesis:

- Active: Current (0), Limited (6), Pending move (11)
- Inactive: Retired (1), Duplicate (2), Obsolete (3), Ambiguous (4), Erroneous (5), Inappropriate (7), Inactive concept (8), Implied (9), Moved elsewhere (10)

12.3 Concept

SNOMED CT is concept-oriented (Fig. 12.2). A concept is just a clinical idea to which a unique ConceptID (which is a SCTID) has been assigned in SNOMED CT. Concepts are in people's heads; codes (ConceptIDs) are in the terminology and they refer to real things in the real world. A concept is a clinical meaning that never changes.

In addition to the ConceptID, each concept has a unique fully specified name (FSN), which is human-readable. Each concept is also linked to a set of terms (descriptions), which name the concept in a human-readable way.

Concepts are formally defined in terms of their relationships with other concepts, based on the principles of reference terminology. These defining relationships may be either subtype relationships (also called IS_A) or attribute relationships. For example, the concept "appendicectomy" IS_A "procedure" and also has attributes "method" = "excision" and "procedure site" = "appendix."

SNOMED CT is organized into a set of hierarchies in which concepts are related by IS_A relationships to their more general parent concepts directly above them in a hierarchy. General concepts are at the top of the hierarchy; at each level down the hierarchy, concepts become increasingly specialized. Unlike a pure tree-structure, any SNOMED CT concept can be the subtype of more than one concept in the same hierarchy – concepts can have more than one parent.

SNOMED CT has 19 Top-level hierarchies (the number changes from time to time as the system evolves), which descend from a single Root concept (the SNOMED CT Concept). Some of the hierarchies also have well-defined sub-hierarchies. For example, the Clinical Finding top-level hierarchy has a sub-hierarchy for Disease (or disorder); the Organism hierarchy has sub-hierarchies for Animals, Plants, and Microorganisms (Fig. 12.3).

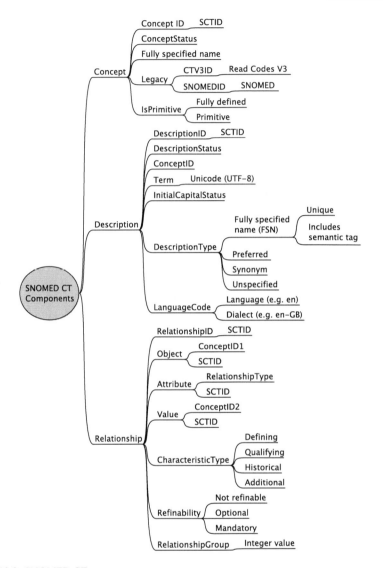

Fig. 12.2 SNOMED CT components

The SNOMED CT hierarchies fall in three main groups: object hierarchies, which mainly comprise concepts which are likely to be qualified; value hierarchies, which are mainly concepts which act as values, when qualifying or defining an object concept in a relationship as an object-attribute-value triple; and finally a miscellaneous group.

Legacy references are provided to the primary sources of SNOMED CT, the NHS Clinical Terms Version 3 (CTV3) and the original version of SNOMED.

Fig. 12.3 SNOMED CT hierarchies

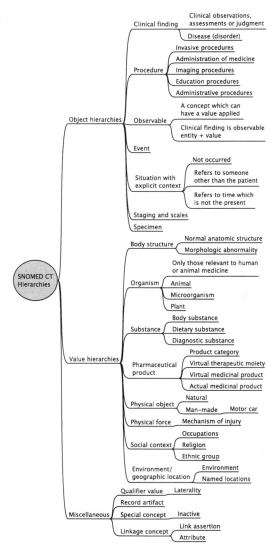

An indicator is also provided to indicate whether the concept is fully defined (using relationships) or is a primitive concept. A concept is "primitive" if it is not "fully defined," which is to say that its modeling (attributes and parents) does not fully express its meaning. Fully defined concepts are differentiated from their parent and sibling concepts by virtue of their attribute relationships.

12.4 Description

Each description links a human-readable term (a sequence of readable characters) with a concept. It has an associated unique numeric DescriptionID, which is a SCTID.

Every concept has at least two descriptions: the fully specified name (FSN) for that concept and a preferred term, sometimes called the display term, for that concept in the language or dialect being used.

Terms are encoded using Unicode (UTF-8), which supports all languages.

SNOMED CT supports multiple dialects and languages. For example, British English (en-GB) and US English (en-US) are different dialects of English in which many medical terms have different spellings; English, French, and Spanish are different languages.

The fully specified name (FSN) is a phrase that names a concept in a way that is both unique and unambiguous. Each FSN contains a suffix (hierarchy tag) that indicates its primary hierarchy, e.g., myocardial infarction (disorder).

The preferred term is the common phrase or word used by clinicians to name a concept and is used as default display term for that concept. Each concept has one preferred term in any dialect. The preferred term is often the FSN without its suffix (hierarchy tag), e.g., myocardial infarction.

Each concept may have multiple synonyms and translations e.g., heart attack or cardiac infarct. A synonym in SNOMED CT must be a clinically acceptable alternative to the preferred term as a way of expressing a concept. A list of synonyms for a concept shows the various ways a concept may be described, rather like a thesaurus.

SNOMED CT terms can also be homonyms in which the same term is used for different concepts. The preferred terms and synonyms are not necessarily unique within a language or dialect. For example, the FSN "cold sensation quality (qualifier value)" has a preferred term of "cold," but "cold" is also a synonym of "common cold (disorder)."

The case of the first letter of the term can be marked as significant as in pH or Alzheimer's.

12.5   Relationship

Relationships are at the heart of SNOMED CT and are the distinguishing feature of any reference terminology. More than 1.3 million relationships have been defined in SNOMED CT and this number is likely to continue to grow.

Each relationship is defined as an object-attribute-value triple. The object is the source concept – the one that has the relationship, identified by a concept identifier (ConceptID1). The attribute specified the type of relationship (RelationshipType) and is also a SNOMED CT concept. The value is the target (ConceptID2).

All relationships may be written using a notation known as description logic, such as:

Concept: attribute = value

The attributes and values which may be used to define or qualify concepts are set out in the SNOMED CT Concept Model (see below).

There are four categories of relationship (CharacteristicType).

(1) Defining relationships define the meaning of concepts. These are pre-coordinated concepts.
(2) Qualifying relationships do not define concepts but may be used in clinical systems to modify the meaning of terms using post-coordination.
(3) Historical relationships provide a link from retired or inactive concepts to the current replacement concept.
(4) Additional relationships allow nondefinitional information to be distributed.

12.5.1 Defining Relationships

Defining relationships are used to define concepts by its relationships with other concepts. Defining relationships are either supertypes (parents) or defining attributes. Defining attributes are specified as attribute–value pairs, where each attribute and value is itself a concept. Only relationships that are always true are used as defining relationships.

A concept is fully defined if its defining relationships are sufficient to distinguish it from all its supertype and sibling concepts. Primitive concepts do not have the unique relationships needed to distinguish them from their parent or sibling concepts.

A sufficient definition consists of a set of defining relationships (and relationship groups) which taken together imply a particular meaning. A necessary definition consists of a set of defining relationships (and relationship groups) that express all the attributes that are necessarily true about a concept. Other information, which is usually but not necessarily true, is outside the scope of SNOMED CT.

A lot of SNOMED CT is not yet fully defined.

Every active SNOMED CT concept (except the SNOMED CT root concept) has at least one supertype. Supertype relationships are used in subsumption testing, which allows users to identify whether a patient with a specific condition has a more general condition that subsumes the specific one. It allows one to answer questions such as: "Is angina pectoris a type of heart disease?"

This is useful in information retrieval, because most research, audit, and decision-support applications usually assume that a supertype includes all its subtypes (children and descendents). For example, a project may need to identify all patients with diabetes, which implicitly assumes that all types of diabetes will be included.

12.5.2 Qualifying Relationships

Qualifying attributes are used in post-coordinated expressions. They are optional nondefining relationships that may be applied by a user or implementer.

The possible values an implementer can select in assigning a qualifying characteristic to a concept are constrained by the SNOMED CT Concept Model.

12.6   Concept Model

The SNOMED CT Concept Model is the complete set of rules that govern the ways in which concepts are permitted to be modeled using relationships to other concepts.

The most common rules assert which attributes and values can be applied to a particular type of concept. For example, the Concept Model asserts that a concept that is a subtype of "clinical finding" can be related using the attribute "finding site" to a concept that is a subtype of either "anatomical structure" or "acquired body structure."

Other rules indicate whether particular relationships should be grouped together and whether the same attribute can be applied more than once to the same concept. These more complex rules are not discussed further here.

The Concept Model has around 50 attributes that may be combined with the various subtype hierarchies in a complex web of relationships. A machine-readable concept model (MRCM) is being developed to make this easier to use.

Each attribute has a domain and a range. The domain is the set of concepts (objects) to which this attribute may be applied; the range is the set of values which are allowed.

The Concept Model is too large and complex to describe in full here. See the SNOMED CT User Guide.

12.7   Clinical Findings

Clinical findings in SNOMED CT represent the result of clinical observations, assessments, or judgments and include both normal and abnormal clinical states; this covers a very broad range of concepts, with a similar range as the HL7 Observation (Fig. 12.4).

The default context for a clinical finding is that the finding has actually occurred, it relates to the subject of record (the patient), currently or at a stated past time.

The disease (or disorder) sub-hierarchy of clinical findings covers abnormal clinical states only.

Clinical finding allows the attributes including: finding site, associated morphology, associated with (including after, due to, and caused by), severity, and clinical course.

Finding Site specifies the body site affected by a condition and has values from either the body structure hierarchy. For example – appendicitis: finding site=appendix.

Associated Morphology specifies morphologic changes seen at the tissue or cellular level that are characteristic features of a disease and has values from the

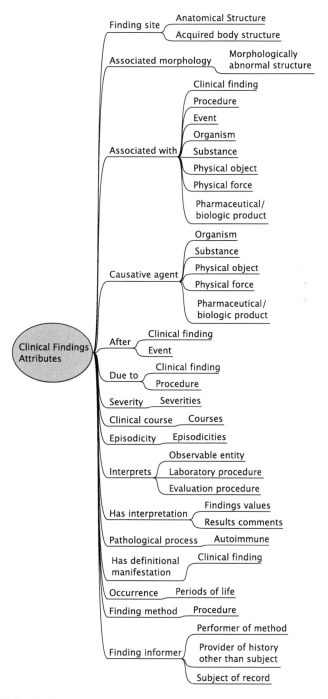

Fig. 12.4 Clinical Findings' Attributes

morphologic abnormality hierarchy. For example – Appendicitis: associated morphology = inflammation.

Associated With asserts that a clinical finding is associated with another clinical finding, procedure, pharmaceutical product, substance, organism, physical object, physical force, or event in some unspecified way. It has three subtypes: After, Due To, and Causative Agent. After is used when a clinical finding occurs after another clinical finding or procedure, emphasizing the sequence of events. Due To relates a clinical finding to its cause, which may be another clinical finding or an event. Caused By identifies the causative agent of a disease such as an organism, substance, pharmaceutical product, physical object, or force.

Severity is used to represent the severity level of a clinical finding.

Clinical Course represents the course and/or onset of a disease, such as acute or chronic.

Other attributes of clinical findings include episodicity, interprets, has interpretation, pathological process, has definitional manifestation, occurrence, finding method, and finding informer.

12.8   Procedure

In SNOMED CT the definition of a procedure is broader than the definition in the HL7 RIM. In SNOMED a procedure is broadly defined as including any type of action done intentionally as part of the process of delivering health care, including history taking, physical examination, testing, imaging, surgical procedures, disease-specific training and education, counseling, and administrative procedures (in HL7, the term procedure is limited in the main to surgical procedures).

The Procedure Model introduces the idea of direct and indirect attributes. A procedure may have a direct site or an indirect site. "Procedure site – direct" is used when a procedure is on the structure itself (e.g., excision of appendix), while "procedure site – indirect" is used when the procedure is on some other material such as a thrombus or removing a foreign body from the site.

The same idea is applied to morphology. An operation to remove a neoplasm uses the "direct morphology" attribute to link the procedure to neoplasm. While a procedure to remove stitches from a wound has "indirect morphology" link to the wound.

Procedure device has four subtypes: direct device (the subject of the procedure), indirect device (which is rarely used), using device (e.g., core biopsy needle), and using access device (e.g., endoscope).

Other procedure attributes include: approach, direct substance, priority, has focus, has intent, recipient category, revision status, route of administration, surgical approach, using substance, and using energy (Fig. 12.5).

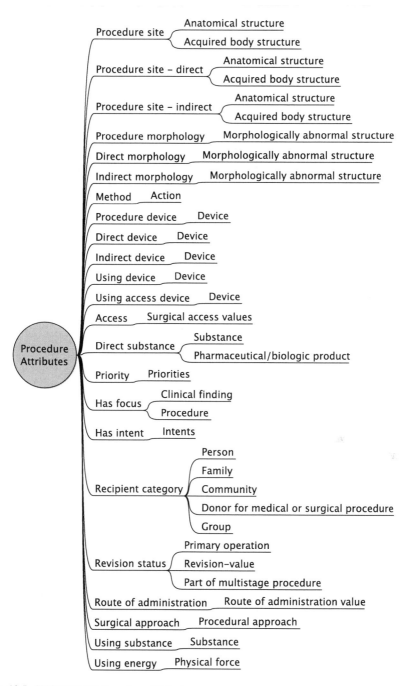

Fig. 12.5 SNOMED CT Procedure Attributes

12.9   Other Attributes

12.9.1   Observable

Observable entities (usually referred to as observables) are qualities or properties which can have values applied to them. When given a value, observables provide a specific finding or assertion about health-related information. Examples include the names of lab tests, physical exam tests, and dates of significant events.

A clinical finding can usually be modeled as an observable entity plus a value. One use is as headings on a template. For example, the concept "gender" is an observable entity, while the concept "female gender" is a clinical finding.

12.9.2   Event

Events are occurrences that happen which are not healthcare procedures or interventions, such as travel, earthquake, and death.

12.9.3   Situation with Explicit Context

Statements with explicit context are those that express something about who is the subject of the record (the patient or someone else), when the event took place (past, present, or future), whether a finding was present, absent, or unknown, and if a procedure was done, not done, or planned.

12.9.4   Staging and Scales

This hierarchy contains assessment scales and tumor-staging systems.

12.9.5   Specimen

Specimens are entities that are obtained, usually from a patient, for examination or analysis. They can be defined by attributes such as:

- Body structure from which they are obtained
- Procedure used to collect the specimen
- Source from which it was collected
- Substance of which it is comprised

12.9.6   Body Structure

Body Structure includes normal as well as abnormal anatomical structures. Normal anatomical structures can be used to specify the body site involved by a disease or procedure.

Body Structure has just one attribute, laterality (e.g., Left, Right, Left, and Right).

12.9.7   Organism

The organism hierarchy is limited to organisms of significance in human and animal medicine, including causes of diseases. Sub-hierarchies of organism include: animal, microorganism, and plant.

12.9.8   Pharmaceutical/Biologic Product

The SNOMED CT core distinguishes between medicinal substances, such as active ingredients and manufactured products.

Medicinal products have three distinct types:

- Virtual Therapeutic Moiety (VTM) is product name only (e.g., aspirin). The VMP is linked to the active ingredient substance.
- Virtual Medicinal Product (VMP) includes strength and form as used on a drug prescription (e.g., aspirin 75 mg tablet).
- Actual Medicinal Product (AMP) is a single unit dose of a marketed medicinal product and includes specific manufacturer and proprietary brand names. AMPs are often country-specific and are therefore found in national extensions, such as the NHS dictionary of medicines and devices (dm + d).

12.9.9   Physical Object

Physical Objects may be natural and man-made (e.g., a motor car).

12.9.10   Physical Force

Physical Force is used to represent forces which play a role in causing injuries.

12.9.11   Social Context

The Social Context includes social conditions and circumstances relevant to health care such as employment, education, housing, care provision, family relationships and lifestyle.

12.9.12   Environments and Geographic Locations

The Environments and Geographic Locations hierarchy includes types of environments as well as named places such as countries, states, and regions.

12.9.13   Qualifier Value

Includes concepts such as laterality.

12.9.14   Record Artifact

Used to refer to parts of electronic patient records.

12.9.15   Special Concept

One sub-hierarchy of Special Concept is Inactive concept, which is the supertype for all concepts that have been retired. Another is for special navigational concepts.

12.9.16   Linkage Concept

Linkage Concepts include SNOMED CT attributes used for defining concepts and in post-coordinated expressions.

12.10   SNOMED Expressions

Clinical records are created for the purpose of providing information about events or states of affairs. For example, a complete health record is a record artifact that also may contain other record artifacts in the form of individual documents or reports, which in turn may contain more finely granular record artifacts such as sections and section headers.

A SNOMED CT expression is a collection of references to one or more concepts used to express an instance of a clinical idea. An expression may be just a single conceptID (and optional term) or a combination of two or more concepts, which is known as a post-coordinated expression. The term expression is used to indicate that it expresses an instance of a real-world phenomenon (such as a headache), represented by a referenced concept occurring in a particular patient.

An expression is said to be pre-coordinated when a single concept identifier is used to represent a clinical idea. Including commonly used concepts in a pre-coordinated form makes the terminology easier to use (Fig. 12.6).

12.11 Post-Coordination

SNOMED CT allows the use of post-coordinated expressions to represent a meaning using a combination of two or more concept identifiers. Post-coordination describes representation of a clinical meaning using a combination of two or more codes. SNOMED CT allows concepts to be represented in a post-coordinated form. One form of post-coordination involves creating a single expression consisting of several concepts related by attributes.

Post-coordinated expressions may be single-level expressions or nested to any number of levels of detail. In a nested expression each attribute value is itself an expression, which can be single-level or nested.

Nested post-coordinated expressions provide a powerful but complex means to allow SNOMED CT to describe things in great detail and to cover unexpected requirements.

There are three main forms of post-coordination:

12.11.1 Subtype Qualification

Subtype Qualification is where the concept is elaborated (that is, linked with an attribute concept) in such a way as to result in a post-coordinated expression which is equivalent to a subtype of the unelaborated concept.

For example, the concept "Asthma" can be qualified with the attribute concept "Severe" to produce an expression that is the subtype of the concept "Asthma." Ideally, where expressions have been post-coordinated and saved in this way, at the point of retrieving the stored codes the application should be able to compute equivalence and, therefore, subsumption.

There are four types of subtype qualification: qualification; refinement of a defining attribute; addition of unsanctioned qualifiers; and addition of "nested" qualifiers.

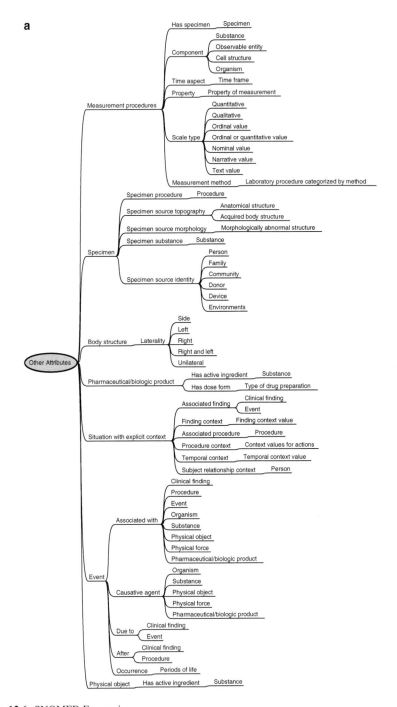

Fig. 12.6 SNOMED Expressions

b

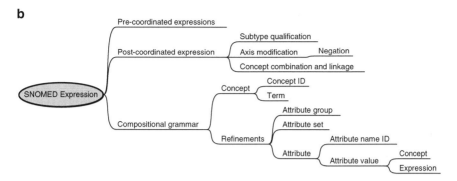

Fig. 12.6 (continued)

12.11.2 Axis Modification

Axis Modification is where the elaboration fundamentally changes the meaning of the concept, rather than simply qualifies or refines it. Such an elaboration of the concept results in it no longer being subsumed as a subtype of a parent concept. For example, if we elaborated the concept "Asthma" to associate it with a patient's mother, the meaning of the resulting expression would have a fundamentally different meaning, and therefore different clinical implications, from the noting of the concept of "Asthma" by itself. If the clinician were running a query of all instances of asthma in their practice, they would not expect the system to return instances where asthma is linked to a family member.

Additionally, concepts that are post-coordinated with a negation concept (such as "known absent"), have their meanings fundamentally shifted. A modified concept is not a subtype of the unmodified instance of the concept. For example, "Asthma not present" is not the subtype of the context-neutral concept, "Asthma." Instead, it is a type of "Explicit context." Negated concepts subsume in the opposite direction to their positive counterparts.

Whereas positive expressions are subsumed by more general instances, negated expressions are subsumed by more specific negative expressions. For this reason modified concepts need to be treated differently to concepts that have been refined through subtype qualification.

12.11.3 Concept Combination and Linkage

Concepts can be combined by way of a number of relationships, such as causal or temporal relationships. For example, one may post-coordinate the concept "Laparoscopic procedure" with the concept "Cholecystectomy," which is the canonical equivalent of the concept "Laparoscopic cholecystectomy." Concepts can also be linked together, for example, to indicate causality. In this way, the concept "Anemia" can be linked by the attribute "Due to" to the concept "Ascorbic acid deficiency." The resulting post-coordination is equivalent to the concept "Anemia due to ascorbic acid deficiency." In this example, the concept "Anemia" is the "base" concept, with "Due to" the attribute name, and "Ascorbic acid deficiency" the attribute value.

12.11.4 Compositional Grammar

SNOMED CT expressions are usually presented using a notation known as compositional grammar (IHTSDO 2008a).

Concept identifiers (ConceptID) are shown as a sequence of digits. Other SCTIDs are not usually shown in compositional grammar.

Display names (either FSN or preferred term) are delimited by a pair of pipe ("|") symbols following the concept identifier, e.g.,

87628006 | bacterial infectious disease |

Whitespace characters, such as space, tab, and linefeed, are ignored, except within a display name.

A colon (":") is used as a refinement prefix, between the concept and its refinement. A refinement consists of one or more attributes and/or attributes groups.

The equals sign ("=") is used as an attribute value prefix between the attribute name and its value. Each attribute consists of an attribute name and an attribute value.

The following example specifies a bacterial infectious disease caused by streptococcus pneumoniae.

87628006 | bacterial infectious disease |:

246075003 | causative agent |=9861002 | streptococcus pneumoniae |

When a refinement includes more than one attribute a comma (",") is used as the attribute separator.

The value of an attribute may be represented by a nested expression rather than a single concept identifier. In this case, the nested expression is enclosed in parentheses.

The following example specifies a bacterial infectious disease affecting the left upper lobe of the lung and caused by streptococcus pneumoniae. The nested expression localizes and lateralizes the site of the disease.

87628006 | bacterial infectious disease |:

246075003 | causative agent |=9861002 | streptococcus pneumoniae |,

363698007 | finding site |=(45653009 | structure of upper lobe of lung | :

272741003 | laterality |=7771000 | left |)

The plus sign ("+") is used to combine attributes to indicate that both apply to a concept. For example:

87628006 | bacterial infectious disease |+50043002 | disorder of respiratory system |

This means a disorder that is both a bacterial disease and disorder of the respiratory systems, for example, "bacterial pneumonia."

A stated definition view is the set of relationships (and groups of relationships) that an author has stated to be defining characteristics of a concept. An inferred definition view is derived from the stated concept definition by applying a consistent set of logical rules to the definition taking account of the definitions of related concepts. The standard SNOMED CT distribution includes the relationships table which represents an inferred view of the definitions of all active concepts, restricted to the proximal supertypes for each concept.

Another of these inferred concept definition views provides a comprehensive view of all supertype ancestors and is known as transitive closure. This includes a high-level of redundancy and when applied to the full content of SNOMED CT it results in tens of millions of relationships. However, a transitive closure table provides a direct way of checking whether any one concept is a subtype of any other and provides a means of high-performance subsumption testing. "A pre-computed transitive closure table appears to out-perform other options and is robust, flexible and easy to implement" (Fig. 12.7) (IHTSDO 2008b).

12.12   Extensions

When an organization creates an extension to SNOMED CT, the new components in the extension need to be identified as part of that particular organization's extension. SNOMED CT does this by allocating an identifier to the organization (the Namespace-identifier). The organization would include its namespace-identifiers as part of the identifiers originated in its namespace. The Namespace-identifier is part of the SCTID.

If no namespace is identified in a SCTID, it is assumed that the component is part of the International Release of SNOMED CT. In these cases, SCTIDs are used in an abbreviated form, without the seven-digit namespace-identifier.

12.13   Subsets

Subsets are key to the practical application of SNOMED CT. When using a system, a user is only interested in a tiny proportion of the whole of SNOMED CT and subsets provide one way of providing this. Subsets are used to specify picking lists for specific data entry fields, to provide priority search lists containing frequently used context-specific terms and for exclusions (terms and concepts that should not be used). Subsets are one of the keys to making SNOMED CT usable.

The number of members in a subset depends on its purpose. For example, a language subset will normally contain at least one description for every concept and so may have hundreds of thousands of members. A subset containing the concepts

a

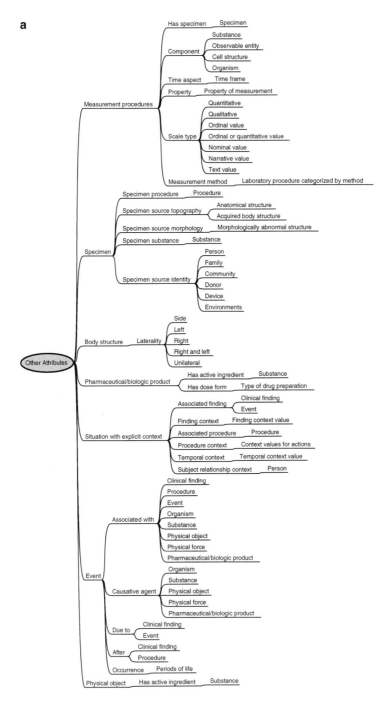

Fig. 12.7 SNOMED CT expressions

b

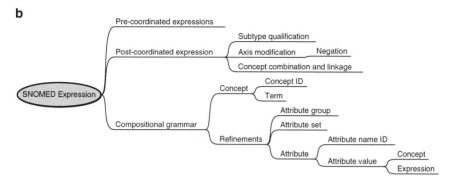

Fig. 12.7 (continued)

commonly used in a particular specialty may contain several thousand members, but the set of concepts or descriptions for a specific clinical protocol, template, or data entry field may only contain a few members (Fig. 12.8).

One way to think of a subset is as an index entry pointing to a set of pages relevant to a topic. A subset is simply a set of Concepts or Descriptions, or Relationships that are appropriate to a particular language, dialect, country, specialty, organization, user, or context. Subsets can be of any size, very large and very small. In its simplest form, a subset is a list of SNOMED identifiers (SCTIDs) each of which refers to a subset member, which is a SNOMED CT description or concept.

However, the subset mechanism provided in SNOMED CT appears complex, in part because the same mechanism is used to do several different jobs. Although subset members only have four fields, the use of three of these fields (MemberID, MemberStatus, and LinkedID) differs markedly depending on the type of subset.

There are eight types of subset

- Language Subset
- Navigation Subset
- Realm Concept Subset
- Realm Description Subset
- Realm Relationship Subset
- Context Concept Subset
- Context Description Subset
- Duplicate Terms Subset

Language subsets contain pointers to the terms (descriptions) used in a particular language or dialect; they are usually the largest. SNOMED CT can be translated into any language or dialect. Each translation uses existing concepts with new language-specific descriptions. A language subset is a set of references to the descriptions that make up that language edition and the Member status field indicates whether each description is the preferred term in that language.

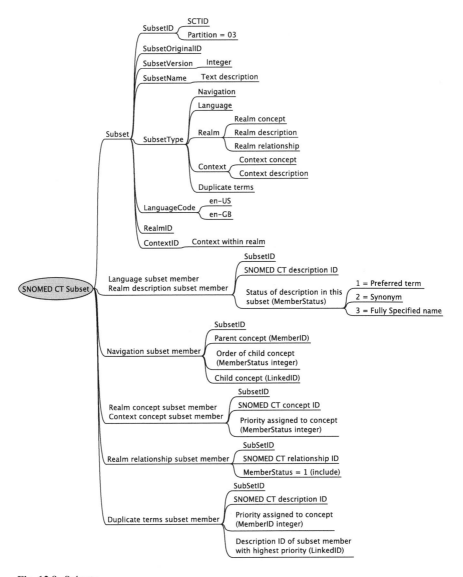

Fig. 12.8 Subsets

Navigation subsets provide an alternative tree-view of a set of terms in a specified order. Navigation hierarchies can reflect the way that people think when entering data, sometimes referred to as the model of use. Navigation hierarchies are useful for display, navigation, and data entry. These are usually handcrafted to limit the number of levels and the number of choices at each level, to list terms in a sensible order, and to ensure consistency over time. However, large numbers of handcrafted hierarchies are difficult to maintain. Each subset member includes a reference to the parent concept, a child concept, and the sequence order of that child.

Realm subsets are used for the terminology used in a specific area of expertise, preference, or authority. Examples of realms include: a specialty, a professional discipline, an organization, a country, or a specialty within a country (e.g., US dentists).

Context subsets are used for a specified part or field of a patient record, application, protocol, query message, or other communication specification.

Note that subsets are not necessarily mutually exclusive and the content of subsets may overlap.

Each subset comprises two logical tables: the Subsets Table provides metadata information with one row for each subset describing its scope, including an identifier for the whole subset, its name, version, type, and additional data such as language, realm, and context domain.

The subset members table contains one record for each subset member, which may refer to a concept, description, or relationship and assigns a member status to each.

The process of subset development and maintenance is challenging, time-consuming, and labor-intensive. It is no easier to develop and maintain a subset that has the support of a large clinical community than it is to develop any other consensus standard. Clinicians want subsets that meet their particular needs, complete and yet focused. Subset development is likely to remain a growth area for many years to come.

A typical subset development project is likely to involve the following steps:

- Establish scope and team
- Identify relevant terms from existing records and evidence base (literature)
- Extract terms and compare to SNOMED CT content
- Derive subsets, including hiding some of the complexity of SNOMED, allocating priorities, and the sequence of terms
- Validation using panels and in practice (comprehensiveness, relevance, reliability, usability)
- Implementation and deployment of software that enables users to achieve their goals
- Maintenance

A number of tools have been developed to help with the task of building, maintaining, and using subsets.

It is planned to replace the subset mechanism with a new Reference Set (RefSet) mechanism, which will better distinguish between the different purposes for which subsets are being developed.

12.14   Cross Mappings

Cross Mappings are used to reference other terminologies and classifications, such as the International Classification of Diseases (ICD). Cross mapping is needed to allow data collected for one purpose, such as clinical care, and to be used for another purpose such as reimbursement to avoid the costs and errors of having to reenter data. It is also needed when data need to be migrated to newer systems Fig. 12.9.

Ideally, computer programs will use the cross maps table to translate codes automatically, but unfortunately the rules of many coding systems, such as ICD-9 CM and ICD-10 are such that fully automated coding is not yet feasible.

The structure of the cross-mapping files allows a single SNOMED concept to be mapped to one or more target codes, with a stated level of precision.

Each cross map matches a SNOMED CT concept with another coding scheme (the target scheme).

The SNOMED CT structure to support Cross Mapping includes three tables:

• Cross Map Sets Table: Each row in this table represents a Target Scheme to which SNOMED CT is mapped (e.g., ICD-10).

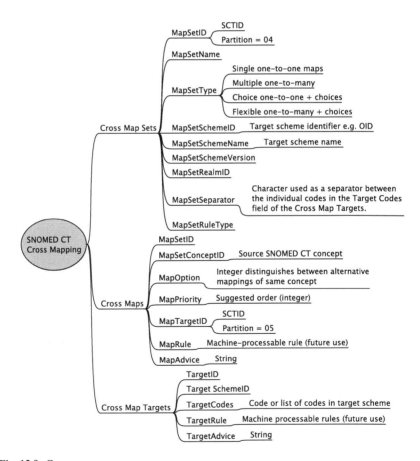

Fig. 12.9 Cross maps

- Maps Table (Cross Maps Table): Each row in this table represents one option for mapping a SNOMED CT Concept. This identifies the row in the Targets Table with the target codes for this SNOMED concept. Each concept may have one or more mappings to the Target Scheme.
- Targets Table (Cross Map Targets Table): Each row in this table represents a code or set of codes in the Target Scheme, which provides a mapping for one or more SNOMED CT Concepts.

Currently available cross maps include ICD-9CM, ICD-1,0, and the OPCS-4 classification of surgical procedures.

12.15 History Files

SNOMED CT includes component history files, which maintain a record of changes to existing components, in line with the principle of permanence.

12.16 Releases

The International Release consists of the Core, the IHTSDO's Specifications and other documents and software that the IHTSDO includes within the International Release.

The Core is the SNOMED CT content that is controlled, maintained, and distributed by the IHTSDO. The IHTSDO has the sole right to modify the Core.

The International Release is licensed by the IHTSDO, whether distributed on its own or as part of a Member's National Release (see below). Members' National Releases consist of the International Release plus National Extensions, Derivatives, and other documents and software that members choose to include within their National Releases.

Chapter 13
Using SNOMED and HL7 Together

One of the lessons of the past few years is that we cannot separate the issues of information structure from those of terminology. The idea that syntax and semantics are independent has been shown to be an oversimplification. We cannot slot any terminology into any data structure and expect it to work. Perhaps, it is surprising that for so many years, so many people thought that we could. After all, in every spoken language, such as English, the grammar (syntax) and words (terminology) have evolved together.

For reasons, which seemed good at the time, the standards development organization responsible for healthcare terminologies (such as SNOMED CT), message syntaxes (such as the HL7 V2 and V3) and information models, developed independently and in parallel. The main justification was the perceived need to interoperate with a wide range of legacy schemes and to meet the needs of different national requirements and languages. SNOMED CT was designed to be syntax-neutral, so it could work with any syntax. Reference models such as the HL7 RIM and EN 13606 set out to be terminology-neutral.

We now recognize that we need a special process called terminology binding, to specify how a specific terminology and a structural model shall be used for each use case (Markwell 2008). This is not straightforward because the flexibility built into both HL7 and SNOMED CT means that there is normally more than one way to perform the binding.

An important complication is that electronic information systems operate at two different levels, which Rector et al. (Rector et al. 2006) describe as "models of use" and "models of meaning."

13.1 Model of Use

The model of use describes how the system, such as an EHR, is actually used, and in particular the way that data are captured and displayed. The model of use represents the human interface. The same data could be captured in any number of different ways and the skill of the designer is to make this as easy and efficient as possible for each work process. Different use cases warrant different models of use.

T. Benson, *Principles of Health Interoperability HL7 and SNOMED*, HI,
DOI 10.1007/978-1-84882-803-2_13, © Springer-Verlag London Limited 2010

Data capture (the model of use) needs to be tuned to make individual work process as quick and easy as possible. Healthcare work is made up of a relatively small number of common high-volume processes, such as requesting tests, prescribing medication, and making referrals, intermingled with a much larger number of less common processes that are specific to the individual patient's condition, the location along their care pathway, and even the specialty of the clinician. The specifics of many tasks (such as patient assessment, diagnosis, and monitoring, and planning treatment, tests, and follow-up) differ greatly according to what is the matter with the patient.

One method of data capture is what we call ad hoc data entry in which the user simply types in the first few letters of the term in mind and the system responds with a list of matching terms. These terms are often organized hierarchically in a tree-structure, as exemplified by the Read Codes. The user can scan up and down the hierarchy, moving between levels of greater or lesser detail to find just the right term. The term selected is shown, providing the user with an opportunity to validate the choice. This method of data capture has been used successfully by almost all GPs in the UK for over 20 years, though there remain problems with the completeness and consistency of the data captured in this ad hoc way.

The practicality ad hoc data entry depends on keeping the size of the list of matching terms to a size that can be scanned quickly and easily. Psychological research has shown that the human eye can read about six lines of text of about 15 characters without moving the eye muscles. Anything more takes longer to read and increases the error rate.

One way to limit the number of options displayed is to provide subsets (value sets) for each task, which greatly restrict the number of options available for each task, or to display the most commonly used items first (known as velocity coding).

Structured data entry removes the requirement to type in the first few letters of the term, and the user simply points and picks with a mouse or on a touch screen, which can be very quick and easy. This works well when the work process has a narrow scope and clearly defined pathway; but the catch is, first of all, the user has to identify the specific work process. Every option is unambiguously defined in terms of the flow of questions, the terms used and the way that each item of data are recorded and coded. The computer protocol must follow the natural clinical order of the task. Items on picking lists need to be grouped in a natural order.

Another difficulty of data capture is the need to integrate data collection with the display of previous records and to integrate with clinical decision support warnings and alerts. At any one moment, the user's screen can only show a limited amount of information, although one patient's EHR may contain thousands of separate items of information. The solution is to provide multiple views into the record with almost instant switching between views.

Typical views are:

- Chronological. The most natural way to display information is in date/time accession order. Reverse order shows the most recent first. Data may be grouped by the clinically relevant date, so tests may be linked both to the date of sample, as well as to the report date.

- Summary views showing current demographics, clinical episodes or problem list. These summaries may be a starting point for further drill-down.
- Problem-orientation shows entries linked to a specific problem, along the lines of problem oriented medical records (POMR).
- Reminders and alerts for drug sensitivities, data that are missing from the records, etc.
- Clinician view allows users to remind themselves of the last entries they made for this patient.
- Notes type views provide a way to display information by type, to list separately the diagnoses, medication, operations, test results, and other classes of entry.
- Detailed flow charts and graphs can be provided for specific types of data, which need to be monitored and such as blood pressure, blood chemistry, and other numeric values.

Excellent work has been done on how best to capture and display data as part of the NHS Common User Interface project, undertaken in collaboration with Microsoft. This set out to deliver a consistent user experience across applications and devices, which would be useful, usable, and compelling to clinicians, thus encouraging increased adoption of health IT systems, improve patient safety, reduce the cost of adopting health IT systems, in terms of end-user training and support costs, and increase the productivity and effectiveness of clinicians.[1]

The work is presented in a number of documents:

- Terminology Matching[2]
- Terminology Elaboration[3]
- Display Standards for Coded Information[4]

The three main ways of entering SNOMED CT coded data are to use forms, single concept matching or text parser matching.

Forms are used where the user selects set options rather than entering text; here, an encoding interface is not needed, because the clinical codes should be embedded within the form itself.

In single concept matching, the user enters a note for a single clinical concept and selects an appropriate match returned by the SNOMED CT database and elaborates this as required.

---

[1] See www.mscui.net

[2] NHS CUI Design Guide Workstream – Design Guide Entry – Terminology – Matching, 2007. www.cuisecure.nhs.uk/CAPS/Clinical%20Noting%20and%20Terminology/Terminology%20-%20Matching.pdf

[3] NHS CUI Design Guide Workstream – Design Guide Entry – Terminology – Elaboration, 2007. www.cuisecure.nhs.uk/CAPS/Clinical%20Noting%20and%20Terminology/Terminology%20-%20Elaboration.pdf

[4] NHS CUI Design Guide Workstream – Design Guide Entry – Terminology – Display Standards for Coded Information, 2007. www.cuisecure.nhs.uk/CAPS/Clinical%20Noting%20and%20Terminology/Terminology%20-%20Display%20Standards%20for%20Coded%20Information.pdf

In text parser matching, the user enters notes as unconstrained free text and the system matches words and phrases against the SNOMED CT database. This requires the system to identify and match SNOMED CT concepts as well as build postcoordinated expressions based on sanctioned attribute relationships from within the text.

The first step in the process is to identify the context, so as to identify the appropriate form, navigation or other subset to constrain the options and simplify the task.

Having entered text, the system may present a set of choices, which can be refined or elaborated in various ways (Fig. 13.1):

- Adding unstructured text to the expression to give the expression further meaning.
- Browsing alternative matches and refining selected matches; this may include reviewing the parents, siblings, and child concepts in a navigation hierarchy or qualifying attributes.
- Matching a SNOMED CT expression from within a passage of text and leaving some of the text itself unencoded but associated with the encoded expression.

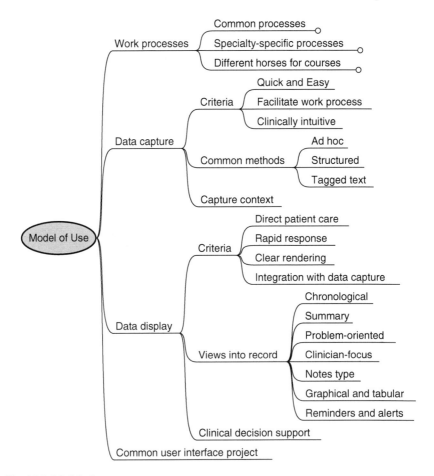

Fig. 13.1 Model of use

- Adding a qualifier to a SNOMED CT expression, using the qualifiers offered by the system, such as the severity of a condition. For example, the concept "Asthma" can be qualified with the attribute concept "Severe" to produce an expression that is the subtype of the concept "Asthma."
- Adding or selecting numerical or date and time values for a SNOMED CT expression. For example, the user should be able to add the value "38.9" and the unit "Degrees centigrade" to the concept of "Body temperature."

13.2 Model of Meaning

The model of meaning is a representation for reporting and analysis purposes, and represents our understanding of the world, so that we can reason about it in general and individual patients in particular. Computers are limited in their ability to process data and require information in a common, standardized format. The model of meaning provides such a format for data processing and reasoning. There is an enormous advantage for reporting and clinical decision support in working with a common model of meaning. This is the rationale for the development of reference models such as the HL7 RIM and the EN13606 (openEHR) reference model. Each model of use needs to be convertible into a model of meaning to make it computable.

The HL7 TermInfo report provides a set of recommendations on how to bind SNOMED CT with HL7 Version 3,[5] and expresses this requirement as follows:

> Every application has its own data entry screens, workflow, internal database design, and other nuances, and yet despite this, we talk of semantic interoperability. In order to achieve interoperability, and enable a receiver to aggregate data coming from any of a number of applications, it must be possible to compare data generated on any of these applications. In order to compare data, it helps imagine a canonical or normal form. If all data, regardless of how it was captured, can be converted into a common form, it becomes possible to compare.

This issue applies not only when we wish to exchange data between applications (semantic interoperability), but just as much within EHR systems, where a single system is used to support different models of use (semantic operability).

A number of suppliers have chosen to use a standard reference model as the basis of their applications architecture. The use of the HL7 RIM for this purpose has been termed RIMBAA (RIM-based Application Architecture). The EN 13606 (OpenEHR) reference model is also used in this way. It is also practicable to use a common proprietary architecture, which has a direct mapping to standards such as the HL7 RIM or EN 13606.

For storage and analysis, we need information to be in a form that allows it to be reused in a very wide range of different ways. The best way to do this is to store the data in a form that reflects the model of meaning. The storage system needs to keep information safe and secure, but the value of a system depends on what you can get out of it. The primary purpose is to enable questions to be answered accurately and efficiently. Accurate reports are precise and complete; efficient reports are quick and timely.

---

[5]HL7. Using SNOMED CT in HL7 Version 3; Implementation Guide. www.hl7.org/Special/committees/terminfo/index.cfm

Users need to be able to count and extract groups of patient records for innumerable reasons. The process of specifying a report involves:

- Selection and exclusion criteria to identify the records required. The first problem for the user is to identify what codes to use.
- The sort order in which to display the results.
- The content and format of each record displayed.
- The summary data at the top and bottom of the report (headings, totals, percentages).
- Where to send the report – screen, printer, or file.

Data retrieval for a user is particularly difficult if the underlying structure of the data is not the way that the user thinks it is, yet this is often the case. If the database is organized using a common model of meaning, then this has to be taught to everyone who wants to interrogate the data.

A second requirement is that users become familiar with the layout of their data collection screens and picking lists and may well regard this as "the way the system works." They reasonably expect to use the same lists and groups for their reports. The ability to report data in the way they are structured on data collection screens is a basic requirement. However, this can be quite awkward if the data are stored using a general-purpose model of meaning; system designers may need to go to some trouble to resolve this issue.

Another difficulty is the need for multidimensional analysis. A trauma surgeon may want to know:

- How many fractured shaft of femur did I see last year?
- How many open reductions and fixations did I perform (on any bone)?
- How many times did I use a locked intramedullary nail?

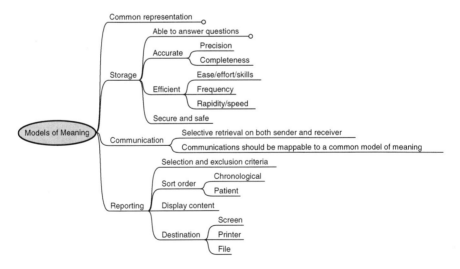

Fig. 13.2 Model of meaning

A simple code with a meaning such as "open reduction and fixation of fracture of the shaft of femur using a locked intramedullary nail" might appear at first sight to allow these questions to be answered, but in practice it is difficult to answer this sort of question in this way. This is why multiaxial coding systems such as SNOMED CT are needed, but they also have to be implemented properly in electronic patient record systems (Fig. 13.2).

13.3   Structural Models

In spite of the overlap between them, we need to bear in mind the fundamental differences between structural models such as HL7 RIM and clinical terminologies such as SNOMED CT.

The basic idea of a structural model is to provide a common framework that represents clinical information in a consistent standardized way, and relates each entry to common meta-data such as its subject, author, date/time, and location. Simple structural models can handle the basic structure of each entry quite easily, but become increasingly complex as the granularity of the data become finer and more detailed.

Structural models may be built around standardized reference models, such as the HL7 V3 RIM or the EN13606 Reference Models (including openEHR).

The basic structure of the HL7 V3 RIM is quite simple with its backbone of Act, Role and Entity, linked with ActRelationship and Participation association classes, although this top-level simplicity covers up a good deal of complexity. The HL7 Clinical Statement model provides a more refined pattern for representing clinical information, which is used in CDA Level 3.

The EN13606/OpenEHR reference model covers much the same domain as the HL7 Clinical Statement pattern, but is based on the traditional structure of medical records, with record components such as folder, composition, section, item, cluster, and element, as well as participants such as subject of care, healthcare professional, organization, and software or device. Many people find this easier to work with than having to translate these into the HL7 concepts of Act, Entity and Role. It is practicable to use EN13606 terms at the analysis level and to map these to the HL7 RIM-based artifacts as a subsidiary step.

EN 13606/OpenEHR Archetypes provide a standardized approach for representing and sharing clinical data specifications. Each archetype defines how the EHR reference model hierarchy is organized to represent the data for one clinical entry or care scenario. Because these archetype definitions are represented in a standardized form, using a formal language known as Archetype Definition Language (ADL), they can be shared and used across record-sharing communities to define how locally organized clinical data should be mapped consistently (even if the data originate from multiple systems).

EN13606/OpenEHR Templates are aggregations of constrained Archetypes, for a specific purpose. An Archetype usually contains a lot of detail that is not required in every use case. A Template contains just the functionality that is required.

The HL7 Clinical Statement pattern and the EN13606 reference models both contain a number of predefined attributes, which provide a structure to the model, but both allow the same information to be structured in more than one way. For example, any number of different coding schemes can be used and there is a good deal of flexibility in the way that data are handled. To take a simple example, both models allow the term "family history of asthma" to be handled either as a single concept, "family history of asthma," or as a composite of "family history" + "asthma."

13.4   Terminology Binding

Terminology binding is the process of establishing links between elements of a terminology such as SNOMED CT and an information model. Terminology binding is principally concerned with what can be said (concepts) – not how it is said (terms).

We often find situations where there are several possible ways to express the same meaning, due in part to the overlap between HL7 and SNOMED CT. It is impossible to draw a clean dividing line between the two.

The Terminfo Guide recommends:

The terminology should be used for specifying:

- Specific concepts and value sets
- Inclusion and exclusion constraints based on the SNOMED CT concept model
- Subsets/refsets including navigation hierarchies
- Simple semantic relationships, such as laterality
- Postcoordinated expressions at various levels of nesting

The structural information model should be used for specifying:

- Instance information and meta-data for any clinical statement such as dates and times, people and places, numbers and quantities
- Grouping and organization of the record framework including the record structure, the way that items should be grouped together, and anchors for terminology components, such as codes
- Differences due to the work process for a specific use case

There remain some grey areas, where the choices are not clear-cut, such as how best to handle issues such as context, negation, and uncertainty.

Recommendations should be widely understandable by implementers who are familiar with the use of SNOMED CT and HL7 V3; be able to be applied consistently and cover common scenarios.

Recommendations should result in instance representations that can be converted, by following a set of computational rules into a standard normal form.

We need to be able to confirm with tools that an instance conforms to the recommendations and that existing tools and applications, either in their current form or with reasonable enhancements, can produce the recommended instances.

In particular, the model should not require a combinatorial explosion of precoordinated concepts. For example, the model should not require the creation of the crossproduct of "Allergic to" and all drugs and substances.

Where more than one approach appears to be viable and broadly equal in respect of the criteria above a single approach is recommended to avoid unnecessary divergence. Where one approach has already been successfully implemented and the other has not, the implemented approach is recommended. Optionality is restricted where possible to simplify the delivery of semantic interoperability (Fig. 13.3).

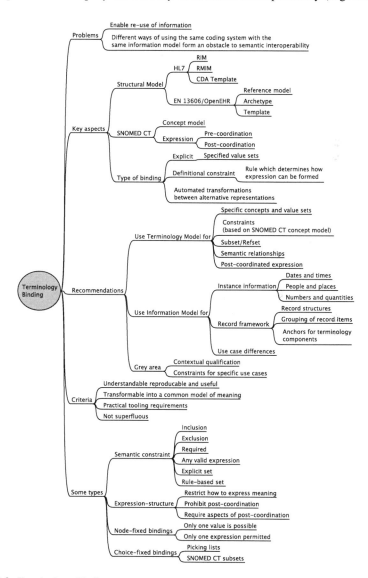

Fig. 13.3 Terminology binding

Glossary

The definitions in this Glossary are derived from the HL7 Glossary, SNOMED CT User Guide, 2008, CEN EN 13606, HIMSS Dictionary of Healthcare Information Technology Terms, Acronyms, and Organizations, 2006 and other sources.

Abstract message: The basic level definition of an HL7 V2 message associated with a particular trigger event. It includes the data fields that will be sent within a message, the valid response messages, and the treatment of application level errors.

Access control: Means of ensuring that the resources of a data processing system can be accessed only by authorized entities in authorized ways.

Accountability: Property that ensures that the actions of an entity may be traced uniquely to that entity

ACK: Acknowledgement message

ACR: American College of Radiology

Acronym: An abbreviation formed by using the initial components in a phrase or name.

Act: Any action of interest. Something that has happened or may happen.

Actor: An abstraction for entities outside a system that interact directly with the system. An actor participates in a use case or a coherent set of use cases to accomplish an overall purpose.

ActRelationship: A relationship between two Acts

ADT: Admission Discharge and Transfer

AFNOR: Association Francaise de Normalisation

AMIA: American Medical Informatics Association

ANSI: American National Standards Institute. ANSI represents US interests on International standards organizations such as ISO.

ANSI accreditation: ANSI accreditation dictates that any standard submitted to ANSI for approval, be developed and ratified by a process that adheres to ANSI's procedures for open consensus and meets a balance of interest requirement by attaining near equal participation in the voting process by the various constituencies that are materially affected by the standard (e.g., vendors, providers, government agencies, consultants, non-profit organizations). This balance of interest goal ensures that a particular constituency is neither refused participation nor is it allowed to dominate the development and ratification of a proposed standard.

Anonymization: Removal of identifiable personal elements from the data, making it less sensitive and potentially not subject to stringent regulations governing privacy of personal data – while retaining its value for legitimate secondary uses like research and reporting

API: Application Program Interface

Application: A software program or set of related programs that provide some useful healthcare capability or functionality.

Application layer: The seventh and highest layer of the OSI model. Provides resources for the interaction that takes place between a user and an application.

Application role: An abstraction that expresses a portion of the messaging behavior of an information system.

Archetype: Reusable, structured models of clinical information concepts that appear in EHRs, such as "test result," "physical examination," and "medication order," and are expressed in terms of constraints on the reference model.

Artifact: Any deliverable resulting from the discovery, analysis, and design activities leading to the creation of HL7 message specifications.

Architecture: A framework from which computer system components can be developed in a coherent manner and in which every part fits together without containing a mass of design detail

AS IS Model: Model of the present system as it is currently working

ASCII: American Standard Code for Information Interchange

Association: A reference from one class to another class or to itself, or a connection between two objects (instances of classes).

Association role name: A name for each end of an association. The name is a short verb phrase depicting the role of the class at the opposite end of the association from the perspective of the class adjacent to the role.

ASTM: American Society for the Testing of Materials

Attestation: Process of certifying and recording legal responsibility for a particular unit of information.

Attribute: Attributes express characteristics of concepts. SNOMED CT concepts form relationships to other SNOMED CT concepts through attributes. All of the attributes used in modeling SNOMED CT concepts are themselves SNOMED CT concepts and can be found in the Linkage concept hierarchy.

Attribute-value pair: The combination of an attribute with a value that is appropriate for that attribute. Example: FINDING SITE = Lung structure

Audit trail: Chronological record of activities of information system users which enables prior states of the information to be faithfully reconstructed

Authentication: Process of reliably identifying security subjects by securely associating an identifier and its authenticator.

Authorization: Authorization is the process of giving someone permission to do or have something. Authorization is sometimes seen as both the preliminary setting up of permissions by a system administrator and the actual checking of the permission values that have been set up when a user is getting access.

BCS: British Computer Society

Browser: A tool for exploring and searching the terminology content. A browser can display hierarchy sections and concept details (relationships between concepts, descriptions and Ids, etc.).

BSI: British Standards Institute. BSI represents British interests on International standards organizations such as CEN and ISO.

caBIG: Cancer Biomedical Informatics Grid

Canonical equivalence: When two SNOMED-CT concepts or post-coordinated expressions have the same meaning. Equivalence can occur when a post-coordinated expression has the same meaning as a pre-coordinated concept; or when two different post-coordinated expressions have the same meaning.

CAP: College of American Pathologists

Cardinality: Property of a data element (the number of times a data element MAY repeat within an individual occurrence of an object view) or column in the Hierarchical Message Description (the minimum and maximum number of occurrences of the message element).

Care Plan: A care plan is an ordered assembly of expected or planned activities, including observations, goals, services, appointments, and procedures, usually organized in phases or sessions, which have the objective of organizing and managing healthcare activity for the patient, often focused upon one or more of the patient's healthcare problems. Care plans may include order sets as actionable elements, usually supporting a single session or phase. Also known as Treatment Plan.

CCD: Continuity of Care Document

CCITT: Comité Consultatif International Télégraphique et Téléphonique

CCOW: Clinical Context Object Workgroup; HL7 standard for single sign on.

CCR: ASTM E2369 – 05 Standard Specification for Continuity of Care Record.

CD: Concept descriptor data type

CDA: Clinical Document Architecture

CDC: Centers for Disease Control

CDISC: Clinical Data Interchange Standards Consortium. CDISC mission is to develop and support global, platform-independent data standards that enable information system interoperability to improve medical research and related areas of healthcare.

CEN: Comité Européen de Normalisation (European Committee for Standardization

CENELEC: Comité Européen de Normalisation Electrotechnique

CEN/TC 251: CEN Technical Committee 251 responsible for standards within health informatics in Europe

Character Data: Text in a particular coding (e.g., ASCII), as distinguished from binary data.

Check-digit: SNOMED CT uses integers up to 18 digits in length as component identifiers known as SNOMED CT Identifiers (SCTIDs). The check-digit is the last digit of the SNOMED CT Identifier. It can be used to check the validity of SCTIDs. Clinical information systems can use the check-digit to identify SNOMED CT codes that have been entered incorrectly (typo errors, etc.).

Choice: A message construct that includes alternative portions of the message. For a choice due to specialization, the sender picks one of the alternatives and sends it along with a flag.

CIM: Constrained Information Model

Class: An abstraction of a thing or concept in a particular application domain.

Class: A class represents a concept within the system being modeled.

Classification: Classification is the systematic placement of things or concepts into categories which share some common attribute, quality, or property.

Clinical Decision Support (CDS): Clinical Decision Support (CDS) refers broadly to providing clinicians or patients with clinical knowledge and patient-related information, intelligently filtered or presented at appropriate times, to enhance patient care. Clinical knowledge of interest could range from simple facts and relationships to best practices for managing patients with specific disease states, new medical knowledge from clinical research and other types of information.

Clinical Document: A Clinical Document is a documentation of clinical observations and services, with the following characteristics:

- Persistence – A clinical document continues to exist in an unaltered state, for a time period defined by local and regulatory requirements.
- Stewardship – A clinical document is maintained by a person or organization entrusted with its care.
- Potential for authentication – A clinical document is an assemblage of information that is intended to be legally authenticated.
- Wholeness – Authentication of a clinical document applies to the whole and does not apply to portions of the document without the full context of the document.
- Human readability – A clinical document is human readable.

Clinical information: Data/information related to the health and healthcare of an individual collected from or about an individual receiving healthcare services. It includes a caregiver's objective measurement or subjective evaluation of a patient's physical or mental state of health; descriptions of an individual's health history and family health history; diagnostic studies; decision rationale; descriptions of procedures performed; findings; therapeutic interventions; medications prescribed;

description of responses to treatment; prognostic statements; and descriptions of socio-economic and environmental factors related to the patient's health.

Clone: A class from the Reference Information Model (RIM) that has been used in a specialized context and whose name differs from the RIM class from which it was replicated. This makes it possible to represent specialized uses of more general classes to support the needs of messaging.

Cluster: The means of organising nested multi-part data structures such as time series, and to represent the columns of a table.

CMS: Centers for Medicare and Medicaid Services

CNE: Coded No Exceptions

CMET: Common message element type (CMET) is a specialized message type in a Hierarchical Message Description (HMD) that MAY be included by reference in other HMD's.

Code: A fixed sequence of signs or symbols, alphabetic or numeric characters, serving to designate an object or concept.

Coding Scheme: A system of classifying objects or entities such as diseases, procedures, or symptoms, using a finite set of numeric or alphanumeric identifiers.

Component: An identifiable item in the main body of SNOMED CT, or in an authorized Extension. Each component is a uniquely identifiable instance of one of the following: Concept, Description, Relationship, Subset, Subset Member, Cross Map Set, Cross Map Target, History Component.

ComponentID: A general term used to refer to the primary identifier of any SNOMED CT Component. All ComponentIDs follow the form of the SCTID specification.

Composite data type: A data type assigned to a message element type that contains one or more components, each of which is represented by an assigned data type.

Composition: The set of information committed to one EHR by one agent, as a result of a single clinical encounter or record documentation session.

Concept: A clinical idea to which a unique ConceptID has been assigned in SNOMED CT. Each Concept is represented by a row in the Concepts Table.

Concept equivalence: When two SNOMED CT concepts or post-coordinated expressions have the same meaning. Concept equivalence can occur when a post-coordinated expression has the same meaning as a pre-coordinated Concept; or when two different post-coordinated expressions have the same meaning.

Concept Model: The SNOMED CT Concept Model is the complete set of rules that govern the ways in which concepts are permitted to be modeled using relationships to other concepts.

ConceptID: The unique identifier (code) for each SNOMED CT concept. Refer to the SNOMED Technical Reference Guide for a full explanation of how this identifier is structured.

Example: For the concept Pneumonia (disorder), the ConceptID is 233604007

Concepts Table: A table that includes all SNOMED CT concepts. Each concept is represented by a row.

Confidentiality: Property that information is not made available or disclosed to unauthorized individuals, entities, or processes.

Conformance Profile: A conformance profile is a constraint to either an underlying standard or another conformance profile. Normally, it specifies a single message or document.

Constraint: Narrowing down of the possible values for an attribute; a suggestion of legal values for an attribute (by indicating the data type that applies, by restriction of the data type, or by definition of the domain of an attribute as a subset of the domain of its data type). MAY also include providing restrictions on data types. A constraint imposed on an association MAY limit the cardinality of the association or alter the navigability of the association (direction in which the association can be navigated). A Refined Message Information Model (R-MIM) class MAY be constrained by choosing a subset of its Reference Information Model (RIM) properties (i.e., classes and attributes) or by cloning, in which the class' name is changed.

Context Model: A model that specifies relationships relating to semantic context that has been defined outside of the SNOMED-CT Concept Model.

Continua Alliance: Continua Health Alliance is a non-profit, open industry coalition of healthcare and technology companies joining together in collaboration to improve the quality of personal healthcare, such as those used in the home.

Control event wrapper: A wrapper that contains domain specific administrative information related to the "controlled event" which is being communicated as a messaging interaction. The control event wrapper is used only in messages that convey status, or in commands for logical operations being coordinated between applications (e.g., the coordination of query specification/query response interactions).

Core: A SNOMED CT Component released by the IHTSDO.

CPT-4: Current Procedural Terminology. Coding system used in the US as a guide to services for which patients may be billed.

Cross Map: A Cross Map links a single SNOMED CT concept to one or more codes in a target classification (such as ICD-9-CM) or terminology. Each Cross Map is represented as a row in the Cross Maps Table.

CRE: Care record element

CRS: Care Record Service (NHS)

CTS: Common Terminology Services. The CTS defines the minimum set of functions required for terminology interoperability within the scope of HL7's messaging and vocabulary browsing requirements.

CTV3: Clinical Terms Version 3 (Read Codes)

CTV3ID: A five-character code allocated to a concept or term in CTV3. For data compatibility and mapping purposes, SNOMED CT concepts include a record of the corresponding concept codes from the Clinical Terms Version 3 (CTV3, previously known as Read Codes) and SNOMED RT.

CUI: Microsoft Health/NHS CFH Common User Interface (CUI) provides user interface design guidance and toolkit controls that address a wide range of patient safety concerns for healthcare organizations worldwide, enabling a new generation of safer, more usable, and compelling health applications to be quickly and easily created [http://www.mscui.net]

CWE: Coded With Exceptions

DAM: Domain Analysis Model

Database: A collection of stored data typically organized into fields records and files and an associated description (schema)

Data type: The structural format of the data carried in an attribute. It MAY constrain the set of values an attribute may assume.

Delimit: To mark or set off. For example the day, month, and year in a string such as 2/5/2009 are delimited by the "/" symbol.

Description: A row in the Descriptions table. Each Description is assigned a unique DescriptionID and connects a Term and a Concept.

DescriptionID: An SCTID that uniquely identifies a Description. Refer to the SNOMED Technical Reference Guide for a full explanation of how this identifier is structured.

Diagnosis: The cause of a patient's problem. Various qualifiers such as provisional, working, primary, secondary, admitting, are applied to diagnosis. A differential diagnosis is a list of plausible possibilities as to the cause.

Dialect: A language modified by the vocabulary and grammatical conventions applied in a particular geographical or cultural environment.

DICOM: Digital Imaging and Communications in Medicine

Digital: Representation of an entity based on binary (on/off) signals.

DIN: Deutsches Institut fur Normung – the German national standards organization.

DH: Department of Health (UK)

DMIM: Domain Message Information Model

Domain expert: Individual who is knowledgeable about the concepts in a particular problem area within the healthcare arena and/or is experienced with using or providing the functionality of that area.

Domain Message Information Model (DMIM): A form of Refined Message Information Model (R-MIM) constructed to represent the totality of concepts embodied in the individual R-MIMs needed to support the communication requirements of a particular HL7 domain.

DRG: Diagnosis Related Group

DSTU: Draft Standard for Trial Use

DTD: Document Type Definition (XML)

EAI: Enterprise Application Integration

ED: Encapsulated Data Type

EDI: Electronic Data Interchange – based on electronic sending and receiving of messages

EDIFACT: Electronic Data Interchange For Administration, Commerce, and Transport – a set of rules and syntax for EDI maintained by the UN.

EDM: Electronic Document Management

eGIF: Electronic Government Interoperability Framework

EHR: Electronic Health Record. A comprehensive, structured set of clinical, demographic, environmental, social, and financial data, and information in electronic form, documenting the health care given to a single individual.

EHR-S FM: EHR System Functional Model (provides a reference list of over 160 functions that may be present in an Electronic Health Record System (EHR-S)

EHR System: The set of components that form the mechanism by which patient records are created, used, stored, and retrieved.

Element: The leaf node of the EHR hierarchy, containing a single data value

EN: Norme Europeene (European Standard) approved by CEN and which normally takes precedence over local or national standards.

Encounter: Encounter serves as a focal point linking clinical, administrative, and financial information. Encounters occur in many different settings - ambulatory care, inpatient care, emergency care, home health care, field, and virtual (telemedicine).

Entity: A person, animal, organization, or thing. Something that has separate and distinct existence and objective or conceptual reality. Something that exists as a particular and discrete unit. An organization (as a business or governmental unit) that has an identity separate from those of its members.

Entry: The information recorded in an EHR as a result of one clinical action, one observation, one clinical interpretation, or an intention. This is also known as a clinical statement.

ENV: Europaische Vornorm (European Pre-standard) – a standard that has yet to be put into a final and definitive form for approval as an EN.

EOM: End of Message

Eponym: The use of a person's name to describe an entity.

EPR: Electronic Patient Record (owned by the patient)

ESC: Escape

ETP: Electronic Transfer of Prescriptions

Expression: A collection of references to one or more concepts used to express an instance of a clinical idea. An expression containing a single concept identifier is referred to as a pre-coordinated expression. An expression that contains two or more concept identifiers is a post-coordinated expression. The concept identifiers within a post-coordinated expression are related to one another in accordance with rules expressed in the SNOMED CT Concept Model.

Extension: Extensions are complements to a released version of SNOMED CT. Extensions are components that are created in accordance with the data structures and authoring guidelines applicable to SNOMED CT.

FCE: Finished Consultant Episode (NHS)

Field: The smallest named unit of data in a database. Fields are grouped together to form records.

File: A collection of electronic data. A file has a name by which it is known to the computer and may contain, for example, data, records, text, image, etc.

Folder: The high level organization within an EHR, dividing it into compartments relating to care provided for a single condition, by a clinical team or institution, or over a fixed time period such as an episode of care.

FTP: File Transfer Protocol

Fully defined concept: SNOMED CT concepts are either primitive or fully defined. Fully defined concepts can be differentiated from their parent and sibling concepts by virtue of their relationships. Primitive concepts do not have the unique relationships needed to distinguish them from their parent or sibling concepts. A concept is primitive when its modeling (attributes and parents) does not fully express its meaning.

Fully Specified Name (FSN): A phrase that describes a concept uniquely and in a manner that is intended to be unambiguous.

Generalization: An association between two classes, referred to as superclass and subclass, in which the subclass is derived from the superclass. The subclass inherits all properties from the superclass, including attributes, relationships, and states, but also adds new ones to extend the capabilities of the parent class. Essentially, a specialization from the point-of-view of the subclass.

GOSIP: Government OSI Profile

GP: General Medical Practitioner

GP2GP: GP to GP record transfer service (NHS)

Graphical expression: A visual representation of a model that uses graphic symbols to represent the components of the model and the relationships that exist between those components.

HDF: HL7 Development Framework

HES: Hospital Episode Statistics (NHS)

Healthcare agent: Person, device, or software that performs a role in a healthcare activity

Healthcare organization: Organization involved in the direct or indirect provision of healthcare services to an individual or to a population. NOTE Groupings or subdivisions of an organization, such as departments, may also be considered as organisations where there is a need to identify them.

Health Care Party: Person involved in the direct or indirect provision of health-care services to an individual or to a population.

Health Care Professional: A person who is authorized by a nationally recognized body to be qualified to perform certain health duties.

Health Care Provider: A Health Care Provider is a person licensed, certified or otherwise authorized, or permitted to administer health care in the ordinary course of business or practice of a profession, including a healthcare facility.

Health Care Service: Service provided with the intention of directly or indirectly improving the health of the person or populations to whom it is provided.

Hierarchical Message Description: A specification of the exact fields of a message and their grouping, sequence, optionality, and cardinality. This specification contains message types for one or more interactions, or that represent one or more common message element types. This is the primary normative structure for HL7 messages.

Hierarchy: An ordered organization of concepts. General concepts are at the top of the hierarchy; at each level down the hierarchy, concepts become increasingly specialized. SNOMED CT concepts are arranged into Top-level hierarchies. Each of these hierarchies subdivides into smaller sub-hierarchies. Concepts are related by IS_A relationships to their more general parent concepts directly above them in a hierarchy. There is one concept from which the Top-level hierarchies descend called SNOMED CT concept or the "Root concept."

HIMSS: Healthcare Information and Management Systems Society

HIPAA: Health Insurance Portability and Accountability Act, 1996

HIS: Health (or Hospital) Information System

HITECH: Health Information Technology for Economic and Clinical Health Act

History Mechanism: SNOMED CT includes some information about the history of changes to concepts and descriptions.

HITSP: Health Information Technology Planning Panel

HL7: Health Level Seven (HL7) is an American National Standards Institute (ANSI) accredited, not-for-profit standards evelopment organization, whose mission is to provide standards for the exchange, integration, sharing, and retrieval of electronic health information; support clinical practice; and support the management, delivery, and evaluation of health services.

HMD: Hierarchical Message Description

Homonym: One term having two or more independent meanings

HTML: Hypertext Markup Language

HTTP: Hypertext Transfer Protocol

ICD: International Classification of Diseases

ICP: Integrated Care Pathway

ICPC: International Classification of Primary Care

ICPM: International Classification of Procedures in Medicine

ICT: Information and Communication Technology

Identifier: A piece of data that uniquely identifies an item, information, or a person as the subject of this identity within a given context

IEC: International Electrotechnical Commission

IEEE: Institute of Electrical and Electronics Engineers

IHE: Integrating the Health Environment

IHE (Integrating the Healthcare Enterprise) is an industry-led initiative to improve the way computer systems in healthcare share information. IHE promotes the coordinates use of established standards such as HL7 and DICOM to address specific clinical needs. http://www.ihe.net/

IHTSDO: International Health Terminology Standards Development Organization

IM&T: Information Management and Technology

IMIA: International Medical Informatics Association

Implementation Technology: A technology selected for use in encoding and sending HL7 messages. For example, XML is being used as an implementation technology for Version 3.

Implementation Technology Specification (ITS): A specification that describes how HL7 messages are sent using a specific implementation technology. It includes, but is not limited to, specifications of the method of encoding the messages, rules for the establishment of connections and transmission timing and procedures for dealing with errors.

Information Model: A structured specification, expressed graphically and/or in narrative, of the information requirements of a domain. An information model describes the classes of information required and the properties of those classes, including attributes, relationships, and states. Examples in HL7 are the Domain Reference Information Model, Reference Information Model, and Refined Message Information Model.

Integration Profile: An integration profile describes the workflow for a specific use case. It combines actors and interactions.

Interaction: A single, one-way information flow that supports a communication requirement expressed in a scenario.

Interface: A common boundary between two associated systems across which information may flow. The interface may filter or modify data as it passes across the boundary.

Interface Terminology: Interface terminologies are used to mediate between a user's colloquial conceptualizations of concept descriptions and an underlying reference terminology.

International Release: The required international components of the SNOMED CT terminology, along with related works and resources, maintained and distributed by the IHTSDO.

Internet: The International network of computers providing support for data exchange, Email and the World-wide Web.

IOM: Institute of Medicine

ISB: Information Standards Board (NHS)

ISO: International Organization for Standardization – the body overseeing endorsement and publication of international standards.

ISP: International Standardized Profile

IT: Information Technology

ITS: Implementation Technology Specification

ITU: International Telecommunications Union

IVR: Interactive Voice Response

LAN: Local Area Network

Language: For purposes of SNOMED CT translations, a language is a vocabulary and grammatical form that has been allocated an ISO639-1 language code. See also Dialect.

Language Subset: SNOMED CT can be translated into any language or dialect. These translations use existing SNOMED CT concepts, along with new language-specific descriptions. A language subset is a set of references to the descriptions that are members of a language edition of SNOMED CT. Additionally, this subset specifies the type of description (FSN, Preferred Term, or synonym).

LOINC: Logical Observation Identifiers Names and Codes

LR: Legitimate Relationship

LSP: Local Service Provider (NHS)

Mandatory: If an attribute is designated as mandatory, all message elements which make use of this attribute SHALL contain a non-null value or they SHALL have a default that is not null.

Mandatory association: An association with a multiplicity minimum greater than zero on one end. A fully mandatory association is one with a multiplicity minimum greater than zero on both ends.

Mapping Mechanism: SNOMED CT provides a mechanism for mapping concepts to other terminologies and classifications. This mapping mechanism consists of three tables: Cross Map Sets Table, Cross Maps Table, and Cross Map Targets Table

Markup: Computer-processable annotations within a document. Markup encodes a description of a document's storage layout and logical structure. In the context of HL7 Version 3, markup syntax is according to the XML Recommendation.

Master file: Common lookup table used by one or more application systems.

May: The conformance verb MAY is used to indicate a possibility.

MBDS: Minimum Basic Data Set

MeSH: Medical Subject Headings

Message: A package of information communicated from one application to another. See also message type and message instance.

Message element: A unit of structure within a message type.

Message element type: A portion of a message type that describes one of the elements of the message.

Message instance: A message, populated with data values, and formatted for a specific transmission based on a particular message type.

Message payload: Data carried in a message.

Message type: A set of rules for constructing a message given a specific set of instance data. As such, it also serves as a guide for parsing a message to recover the instance data.

Meta-model: A model used to specify other models. For example, the meta-model for a relational database system might specify elements of type "Table," "Record," and "Field."

MIB: Medical Information Bus

MIM: Message Implementation Manual published by NHS Connecting for Health.

MIME: Multipurpose Internet Mail Extension

MPI: Master Patient Index

MT: Message Type

Model: A semantically complete abstraction of a system

Multiplicity: In the information model, multiplicity is a specification of the minimum and maximum number of objects from each class that can participate in an association. Multiplicity is specified for each end of the association.

N3: National network for the NHS

Namespace or Namespace-identifier: When an organization creates an extension to SNOMED CT, the new components in the extension need to be identified as part of that particular organization's extension. SNOMED CT does this by allocating an identifier to the organization (the Namespace-identifier). The organization would include its namespace-identifiers as part of the identifiers originated in its namespace. The Namespace identifier is part of the SCTID. If no namespace is identified in a SCTID, it is assumed that the component is part of the International Release of SNOMED CT. In these cases, SCTIDs can be used in an abbreviated form, without the seven-digit namespace identifier.

Navigability: Direction in which an association can be navigated (either one way or both ways).

NCPDC: National Council for Prescription Drug Program

NDC: National Drug Code

Nested qualifiers: Where the value of a qualifier is a refinement of a refined concept.

NHS: National Health Service

NHSCR: NHS Central Register

NHS CFH: NHS Connecting For Health

NIST: National Institute for Science and Technology

NLM: National Library of Medicine

Node: One of the interconnected computers or devices linked in a communications network.

NPfIT: National Programme for Information Technology (NHS)

Null: A value for a data element which indicates the absence of data. A number of "flavors" of null are possible.

Object: An instance of a class. A part of an information system containing a collection of related data (in the form of attributes) and procedures (methods) for operating on that data

Object identifier: A scheme to provide globally unique identifiers. This object identifier (OID) scheme is an ISO standard (ISO 8824:1990).

ODA: Open Document Architecture

ODP: Open Distributed Processing (ISO/IEC 10746, used for describing distributed systems)

OHT: Open Health Tools is a community of open source developers, health professionals, and an ecosystem that brings together members from the health and IT professions to create a common health interoperability framework, exemplary tools, and reference applications to support health information interoperability. The fact that this software framework is available under a commercially friendly open source license means that anyone, any company, any hospital, whether or not they are a member, can build applications using this framework – without any payment required for the software.

OID: Object Identifier

OMG: Object Management Group

ONCHIT: Office of the National Coordinator for Health Information Technology

OpenEHR: OpenEHR is a not-for-profit foundation to make EHRs "adaptable and future-proof" through the use of a technology independent architecture.

OSI: Open Systems Interconnection

OWL: Web Ontology Language

PACS: Picture Archiving and Communication System

Participation: The involvement of a Role in an Act

Partition-identifier: The partition identifier is a two-digit number just to the left of the check-digit in the SCTID. The first of these two digits indicates whether the SCTID refers to a SNOMED CT Component in the International Release (indicated by a 0 as the first digit in the partition identifier), or a Component in an extension (indicated by a 1 as the first digit in the partition identifier). The second of the two digits in the partition identifier indicates which of the partitions of SNOMED CT the SCTID is identifying.

PAS: Patient Administration System

Patient: One who is suffering from any disease or behavioral disorder and is under treatment for it.

PC: Personal Computer

PDF: Portable Document Format

PDS: Personal Demographics Service (NHS)

PICS: Protocol Implementation Conformance Statement

PIM: Platform-Independent Model

PIN: Personal Identification Number

PKI: Public Key Infrastructure

PN: Person Name data type

POC: Point of Care

POMR: Problem-oriented medical record, originally developed by Dr Larry Weed.

Post-coordination: Representation of a clinical idea using a combination of two or more concept identifiers. A combination of concept identifiers used to represent a single clinical idea is referred to as a post-coordinated expression (see expression). Many clinical ideas can also be represented using a single SNOMED CT concept identifier (see pre-coordination). Some clinical ideas may be represented in several different ways. SNOMED CT technical specifications include guidance of logical transformations that reduce equivalent expressions to a common canonical form.

Pre-coordination: Representation of a clinical idea using a single concept identifier. A single concept identifier used to represent a specific meaning is referred to as a pre-coordinated expression (see expression). SNOMED CT also allows the use of post-coordinated expressions (see post-coordination) to represent a meaning using a combination of two or more concept identifiers. However, including commonly used concepts in a pre-coordinated form makes the terminology easier to use.

Preferred Term: The Term that is deemed to be the most clinically appropriate way of expressing a Concept in a clinical record. Preferred Term is one of the three types of terms that can be indicated by the DescriptionType field in SNOMED.

Primitive Concept: A concept is primitive when its modeling (attributes and parents) does not fully express its meaning. A concept definition is the list of its relationships to other concepts. Primitive concepts do not have the unique relationships needed to distinguish them from their parent or sibling concepts.

Privacy: Freedom from intrusion into the private life or affairs of an individual when that intrusion results from undue or illegal gathering and use of data about that individual.

Problem List: The problem list of a given individual can be described by formal diagnosis coding systems (such as ICD-10) or by other professional descriptions of healthcare issues affecting an individual. Problems can be short or long term in nature, chronic, or acute, and have a status. In a longitudinal record, all problems may be of importance in the overall long term care of an individual, and may undergo changes in status repeatedly. Problems are identified during patient visits, and may span multiple visits, encounters, or episodes of care.

Profile: A set of functions required in a particular setting or available as part of a particular system or component

PSIS: Personal Spine Information Service (NHS)

PSM: Platform Specific Model

QMAS: Quality Management and Analysis System (NHS)

QMR: Quick Medical Reference

QOF: Quality and Outcomes Framework (NHS)

QoS: Quality of Service

Qualifying attribute: Some SNOMED CT concepts can have Qualifying attributes, which are optional non-defining relationships that may be applied by a user or implementer in post-coordination. The qualifier value mechanism in SNOMED CT constrains the possible values an implementer can select in assigning a qualifying characteristic to a concept.

Query: Queries are the primary mechanism for retrieving information from computer systems. Many database management systems use the Structured Query Language (SQL) standard query format.

Realization: The relationship between a specification and its implementation.

Realm: A sphere of authority, expertise, or preference that influences the range of Components required, or the frequency with which they are used. A Realm may be a nation, an organization, a professional discipline, a specialty, or an individual user.

Receiver: The application fulfilling the Receiving Application role in an interaction

Receiver responsibility: An obligation on an application role that receives an interaction as defined in the interaction model.

Record: A writing by which some act or event, or a number of acts or events, is recorded.

Recursion: An association that leads from a class directly or indirectly back to that class.

Reference Information Model (RIM): The HL7 information model from which all other V3 information models (e.g., R-MIMs) and messages are derived.

Reference Terminology: A reference terminology is a terminology in which every concept designation has a formal, machine-usable definition supporting data aggregation and retrieval.

Refined Message Information Model (R-MIM): An information structure that represents the requirements for a set of messages. A constrained subset of the Reference Information Model (RIM) which MAY contain additional classes that are cloned from RIM classes. Contains those classes, attributes, associations, and data types that are needed to support one or more Hierarchical Message Descriptions (HMD). A single message can be shown as a particular pathway through the classes within an R-MIM.

Relationship: An association between two Concepts. The nature of the association is indicated by a Relationship Type. Each Relationship is represented by a row in the Relationships Table.

Relationship Type: The nature of a Relationship between two Concepts. The RelationshipType field indicates the ConceptID for the concept in SNOMED that forms the relationship between two other concepts (ConceptID1 and ConceptID2)

RelationshipID: A SCTID that uniquely identifies a Relationship between three concepts: a source concept (ConceptID1), a target concept (ConceptID2), and a relationship type.

Each row in the Relationships Table represents a relationship "triplet" (ConceptID1 – RelationshipType - ConceptID2) identified by a RelationshipID.

Relationships Table: A table consisting of rows, each of which represents a Relationship.

Release Version: A version of SNOMED CT released on a particular date. Except for the initial release of SNOMED CT that was called "SNOMED CT First Release," subsequent releases use the release data. Example: "SNOMED CT July 2008 Release"

Required: One of the allowed values in conformance requirements, it means that the message elements SHALL appear every time that particular message type is used for an interaction. If the data is available, the element SHALL carry the data, otherwise a null value MAY be sent.

Requirement: A desired feature, property, or behavior of a system.

RFID: Radio frequency identification (RFID) is a generic term that is used to describe a system that transmits the identity (in the form of a unique serial number) of an object or person wirelessly, using radio waves.

RIM: HL7 Reference Information Model

RHIO: Regional Health Information Organization

RMIM: HL7 Refined Message Information Model

Role: A part played by or the responsibility of an Entity

RoleLink: A relationship between two Roles.

Root Concept: The single Concept "SNOMED CT Concept" that is at the top of the entire SNOMED CT hierarchy of concepts.

SAEF: Services Aware Enterprise Architecture Framework. HL7's SAEAF defines the artifacts and specification semantics needed to support interoperability in healthcare, life sciences, and clinical research.

Sanctioned relationships: Relationships between SNOMED-CT concepts that are sanctioned by the SNOMED-CT Concept Model. Sanctioned relationships are specified in a row in the SNOMED-CT Relationships table, as opposed to "Allowable" relationships, which are a pattern in the Concept Model.

Scenario: A sequence of actions that illustrates behavior. A scenario may be used to illustrate an interaction or the execution of a use case instance.

Schematron: Schematron is an XML structure validation language for making assertions about the presence or absence of patterns in trees. It is a simple and powerful structural schema language.

SCR: Summary Care Record

SCT: SNOMED Clinical Terms

SCT Enabled Application: A software application designed to support the use of SNOMED CT.

SCTID: SNOMED Clinical Terms Identifier

SDO: Standards Development Organization

SDS: Spine Directory Service (NHS)

Section: EHR data within a composition that belongs under one clinical heading, usually reflecting the flow of information gathering during a clinical encounter, or structured for the benefit of future human readership.

Semantics: Meaning of symbols and codes

Semantic interoperability: Ability for data shared by systems to be understood at the level of fully defined domain concepts.

Sender: The application fulfilling the Sending Application role in an interaction.

Service: A consultation, diagnosis, treatment, or intervention performed for a person and/or other activity performed for a person. Includes health, goods, and support services.

Set: A form of collection which contains an unordered list of unique elements of a single type.

SGML: Standardized General Markup Language

Shall: The conformance verb SHALL is used to indicate a requirement.

Should: The conformance verb SHOULD is used to indicate a recommendation.

SIG: Special Interest Group

SMTP: Simple Mail Transport Protocol

SNOMED: An acronym for the Systematized Nomenclature of of Human and Veterinary Medicine originally developed by the College of American Pathologists.

SNOMED Clinical Terms (SNOMED CT): The clinical terminology maintained and distributed by the IHTSDO. The First Release of SNOMED Clinical Terms was the result of the merger of the CTV3 and SNOMED RT.

SNOMED Clinical Terms Identifier (SCTID): A unique identifier applied to each SNOMED CT component (Concept, Description, Relationship, Subset, etc.). The SCTID can include an item identifier, namespace identifier, a check-digit, and a partition identifier. It doesn't always include a namespace identifier.

SOA: Service Oriented Architecture provides methods for systems development and integration where systems package functionality as interoperable services. A SOA infrastructure allows different applications to exchange data with one another. Service-orientation aims at a loose coupling of services with operating systems, programming languages, and other technologies that underlie applications. SOA separates functions into distinct units, or services, which developers make accessible over a network in order that users can combine and reuse them in the production of applications. These services communicate with each other by passing data from one service to another, or by coordinating an activity between two or more services.

Specialization: An association between two classes (designated superclass and subclass), in which the subclass is derived from the superclass. The subclass inherits all properties from the superclass, including attributes, relationships, and states, but also adds new ones to extend the capabilities of the superclass.

Specification: A detailed description of the required characteristics of a product.

Standard: A document, established by consensus and approved by a recognized body, that provides, for common and repeated use, rules, guidelines, or characteristics for activities or their results, aimed at the achievement of the optimum degree of order in a given context.

Storyboard: Defines what happens from the users point of view. A narrative of relevant events defined using interaction or activity diagrams or use cases. The storyboard provides one set of interactions that will typically occur in the domain.

String: A sequence of text characters.

Stylesheet: A file that describes how to display an XML document of a given type.

Subclass: A class that is the specialization of another class (superclass).

Subset: A group of Components (e.g., Concepts, Descriptions, or Relationships) that share a specified common characteristic or common type of characteristic. Example: UK English Subset

Superclass: A class that is the generalization of one or more other classes (subclasses).

Swimlane: A partition on activity graphs for organizing responsibilities for activities, often corresponding to the organizational units in a business model.

Synonym: A term that is an acceptable alternative to the Preferred Term as a way of expressing a Concept. Synonyms allow representations of the various ways a concept may be described. Synonyms and Preferred Terms (unlike FSNs) are not necessarily unique. More than one concept might share the same Preferred term or Synonym.

Syntax: Rules for structuring words into sentences or computer commands or electronic messages.

System: A collection of connected units organized to accomplish a purpose.

Table view: An expression of the Hierarchical Message Description (HMD) common and message type definition condensed in size to fit on a printed page.

TC: Technical Committee

TCP/IP: Transmission Control; Protocol/Internet Protocol. A protocol for communication between computers, used as a standard for transmitting data over networks and as the basis for standard Internet protocols.

Template: A template is an RMIM which is used to constrain another model

Term: A text string represents the Concept. The Term is part of the Description. There are multiple descriptions per Concept.

Terminology: A terminology is a set of concepts designated by terms belonging to a special domain of knowledge, or subject field.

Terminology Binding: An instance of a link between a terminology component and an information model artefact.

Terminology server: Software that provides access to SNOMED CT (and/or to other terminologies). A Terminology server typically supports searches and Navigation through Concepts. A server may provide a user interface (e.g., a browser or set of screen controls) or may provide low-level software services to support access to the terminology by other applications.

Top-Level Concept: A Concept that is an immediate child of the root concept "SNOMED CT Concept" which is at the top of the entire SNOMED CT hierarchy of concepts.

Transaction: A complete set of messages for a particular trigger event, e.g., a message and a response.

Transport wrapper: A wrapper that contains information needed by a sending application or message handling service to route the message payload to the designated receiver. All HL7 Version 3 messages require an appropriately configured transport wrapper.

Trigger Event: Defines what causes a message to be sent. An event which, when recorded or recognized by an application, indicates the need for an information flow to one or more other applications, resulting in one or more interactions.

TRUD: Terminology Reference Data Update Distribution Service (NHS)

TSC: Technical Steering Committee (HL7)

UML: Unified Modeling Language

UMLS: Unified Medical Language System

UN/CEFACT: United Nations Centre for Trade Facilitation and Electronic Business

UKTC: UK Terminology Centre (NHS)

UPI: Unique Patient Identifier

Use case: The specification of sequences of actions, including variant sequences and error sequences that a system can perform by interacting with outside actors.

VA: Veterans Administration

Valid document: A document which meets all of the validity constraints in the XML specification.

Value set: A vocabulary domain that has been constrained to a particular realm and coding system.

View: Specific information displayed on a computer monitor after it has been filtered for a different user or purpose.

Vocabulary: The set of all concepts that can be taken as valid values in an instance of a coded attribute or field.

W3C: World Wide Web Consortium

WAN: Wide Area Network

WEDI: Workgroup on Electronic data Interchange

WHO: World Health Organization

Wrapper: The control or envelope information in which the message payload resides.

WWW: World Wide Web

XDS: Cross-enterprise Document Sharing

XML: Extensible Mark-up Language

XSL: Extensible Style sheet Language. The XSL family comprises three languages:

- XSL Transformations (XSLT): an XML language for transforming XML documents
- XSL Formatting Objects (XSL-FO): an XML language for specifying the visual formatting of an XML document
- XML Path Language (XPath): used to address the parts of an XML document

XSLT: Extensible Stylesheet Language Transformations (XSLT) is an XML-based language used for the transformation of XML documents into other XML or "human-readable" documents. The original document is not changed; rather, a new document is created based on the content of an existing one. The new document may be serialized (output) by the processor in standard XML syntax or in another format, such as HTML or plain text. XSLT is most often used to convert data between different XML schemas or to convert XML data into HTML or XHTML documents for web pages, creating a dynamic web page, or into an intermediate XML format that can be converted to PDF documents.

Bibliography

Papers and Chapters

Beeler W. HL7 Version 3 – An object-oriented methodology for collaborative standards development. *Int J Med Inform*. 1998;48:151-161.

Benson T. The message is the medium. *Health Serv J*. 1997;107(5538; IT update):4–5.

Benson T. Why general practitioners use computers and hospital doctors do not – Part 1: incentives. *BMJ*. 2002a;325:1086–1089. Available at: http://bmj.bmjjournals.com/cgi/reprint/325/7372/1086.pdf

Benson T. Why general practitioners use computers and hospital doctors do not – Part 2: scalability. *BMJ*. 2002b;325:1090–1093. Available at: http://bmj.bmjjournals.com/cgi/reprint/325/7372/1090.pdf

Benson T. Prevention of errors and user alienation in healthcare IT integration programmes. *Inform Prim Care*. 2007;15:1-7.

Berwick DM. Medical associations: guilds or leaders. *BMJ*. 1997;314:1564. Available at: http://www.bmj.com/cgi/content/full/314/7094/1564

Bleich HL, Lawrence L. Weed and the problem-oriented medical record. *MD Computing*. 1993;10:70.

Blumenthal D. Stimulating the adoption of health information technology. *N Engl J Med*. 2009;360:15.

Bos B. *XML in 10 Points*. W3C; 1999. Available at: www.w3c.org/XML/1999/XML-in-10-points

Chisholm J. The read clinical classification. *BMJ*. 1990;300:1092.

Cimino JJ. Desiderata for controlled medical vocabularies in the twenty-first century. *Meth Inform Med*. 1998;37:394-403.

Coiera E. Four rules for the reinvention of health care. *BMJ*. 2004;328:1197-1199.

DesRoches CM, Campbell EG, Rao SR, et al. Electronic health records in ambulatory care – a national survey of physicians. *N Engl J Med*. 2008;359:50-60.

Forrey AF, McDonald CJ, DeMoor G, et al. Logical Observation Identifier Names and Codes (LOINC) database, a public use set of codes and names for electronic reporting of clinical laboratory test results. *Clin Chem*. 1996;42:81-90.

Gibbons P et al. *Coming to Terms: Scoping Interoperability in Health Care*. Final. Health Level Seven EHR Interoperability Work Group; 2007.

Guyatt G, Cook D, Haynes B. Evidence based medicine has come a long way. *BMJ*. 2004;329:990-991.

Hammond WE, Cimino JJ. Standards in biomedical informatics. In: Shortliffe EH, Cimino JJ, eds. *Biomedical Informatics: Computer Applications in Health Care and Biomedicine*. 3rd ed. New York: Springer; 2006:265–311.

Hodge MH. History of the TDS Medical Information System. In: Blum BI, Duncan K, eds. *A History of Medical Informatics*. New York: ACM Press; 1990:328–344.

Jha AK, DesRoches CM, Campbell EG, et al. Use of electronic health records in US Hospitals. *N Engl J Med*. 2009;360.

Johansen I, Henriksen G, Demkjær K, Bjerregaard Jensen H, Jørgensen L. *Quality assurance and certification of health IT-systems communicating data in primary and secondary health sector.* Presentation at MIE 2003, 7 May 2003, St Malo.

Lindberg DA, Humphreys BL, McCray AT. The unified medical language system. *Methods Inf Med*. 1993;32:281-291.

Mandl KD, Szolovits P, Kohane IS. Public standards and patients' control: how to keep electronic medical records accessible but private. *BMJ*. 2001;322:283-287.

Mead CN. Data Interchange Standards in Healthcare IT – Computable semantic interoperability: now possible but still difficult, do we really need a better mousetrap? *J Health Inf Manag*. 2006;20:71-78.

MedCom – IT brings the Danish health sector together. November 2008. Available at: http://www.medcom.dk/dwn2440

MedCom – the Danish Health Care Data Network. A Danish health care network in two years. Odense, Denmark: Danish Centre for Health Telematics, 1996. Available at: http://www.medcom.dk/publikationer/publikationer/MedCom1-engelsk.pdf

O'Neil MJ, Payne C, Read JD. Read Codes Version 3: a user led terminology. *Methods Inf Med*. 1995;34:187-192.

Protti D, Johansen I. Further lessons from Denmark about computer systems in physician offices. *Electronic Healthcare*. 2003;2:36–43. Available at: http://www.itacontario.com/health care/2003/03ElectronicHC.pdf

Read J, Benson T. Comprehensive Coding. *Br J Healthcare Comput*. 1986;3:22-25.

Rector A, Nowlan W, Kay S. Foundations for an electronic medical record. *Methods Inf Med*. 1991;30:179-186.

Rector A, Solomon W, Nowlan A, Rush T, Claassen A, Zanstra P. A terminology server for medical language and medical information systems. *Methods Inf Med*. 1994;34: 147-157.

Rector AL, Qamar R, Marley T. Binding ontologies and coding systems to electronic health records and messages. In: *KR-MED 2006 Biomedical Technology in Action*. Baltimore; November 2006.

Schultz JR. A history of the PROMIS Technology: an effective human interface. In: Goldberg A, ed. *A History of Personal Workstations*. Reading, MA: Addison-Wesley; 1988.

Scott JT, Rundall TG, Vogt TM, Hsu J. Kaiser Permanente's experience of implementing an electronic medical record: a qualitative study. *BMJ*. 2005;331:1313-1316.

Selvachandran SN, Hodder RJ, Ballal MS, Jones P, Cade D. Prediction of colorectal cancer by a patient consultation questionnaire and scoring system: a prospective study. *The Lancet*. 2002;360:278-283.

Shannon CE. A mathematical theory of communication. *The Bell Syst Tech J*. 1948;27:379–423, 623–656.

Spackman K, Campbell K, Cote R. SNOMED RT: a reference terminology for health care. *Proc AMIA Symp*. 1997:640–644.

van der Vlist E. Using W3C XML Schema. October 21, 2001. Available at: http://www.xml.com/pub/a/2000/11/29/schemas/part1.html

Walker J, Pan E, Johnston J, Adler-Milstein J, Bates DW, Middleton B. The value of health information exchange and interoperability. *Health Affairs*, January 19 2005. Available at: http://content.healthaffairs.org/cgi/content/full/hlthaff.w5.10/DC1

Weed LL. Medical records that guide and teach. *NEJM*. 1968;278:593-599/652-657.

Westbrook J, Ampt A, Kearney L, Rob MI. All in a day's work: an observational study to quantify how and with whom doctors on hospital wards spend their time. *MJA*. 2008;188: 506-509.

Standards and Reports

ASTM. Specification for Continuity of Care Record, E2369-05, 2006.

ASTM E1238.88, 1988.

Beale T, Heard S, eds. *OpenEHR Architecture Overview*. Release 1.0.1, The openEHR Foundation, 2007.

CEN CR 12587:1996. *Medical Informatics - Methodology for the development of healthcare messages*. CEN Report, 1996.

CEN CR 1350:1993. *Investigation of syntaxes for existing interchange formats to be used in health care*. CEN Report, 1993.

CEN EN 13606-1. *Health informatics — Electronic health record communication — Part 1: Reference Model*.

CEN EN 13606-2. *Health informatics — Electronic health record communication — Part 2: Archetype Interchange Specification*.

CEN EN 13606-3. *Health informatics — Electronic health record communication — Part 3: Reference Archetypes and Term Lists*.

CEN EN 13606-4. *Health informatics — Electronic health record communication — Part 4: Security Features*.

CEN EN 13606-5. *Health informatics — Electronic health record communication — Part 5: Exchange Models*.

DH. *Delivering 21st century IT support for the NHS: National Strategic Programme*. Leeds, UK: Department of Health; 2002.

EU. *ICT standards in the health sector: current situation and prospects. A Sectoral e-Business Watch study by Empirica*. Special Study No. 1, 2008. Available at: www.ebusiness-watch.org/studies/special_topics/2007/documents/Special-study_01-2008_ICT_health_standards.pdf

HL7. *EHR System Functional Model and Standard Draft Standard for Trial Use (DSTU)*, 2004a.

HL7 EHR System Functional Model: A Major Development Towards Consensus on Electronic Health Record System Functionality. A White Paper, 2004b.

HL7. *Implementation Guide: CDA Release 2 – Continuity of Care Document (CCD)*, 2007.

HL7. *Using SNOMED CT in HL7 Version 3; Implementation Guide*, 2008.

HL7 Development Framework. Version 1.3, 2009

Høy A. *Guidelines for Translation of SNOMED CT*. Version 1, March 2009. Copenhagen: IHTSDO. Available at: www.ihtsdo.org/fileadmin/user_upload/Docs_01/SNOMED_CT/SNOMED_CT_Publications/IHTSDO_Translation_Guidelines_20090309_v1-00.pdf

IHE. *IT Infrastructure Technical Framework Volume 1 (ITI TF-1)*. Available at: www.ihe.net/Technical_Framework/upload/ihe_iti_tf_2.0_vol1_FT_2005-08-15.pdf

IHTSDO. *Compositional Grammar for SNOMED CT Expressions in HL7 Version 3. External Draft for Trial Use*. Version 0.06 December 2008.

ISO 13606-1:2008. Health Informatics – Electronic health record communication – Part 1: Reference Model

ISO Strategic plan 2005-2010: Standards for a sustainable world. Geneva: ISO 2004

ISO/IEC Guide 2:2004, definition 3.2

NHS CUI Design Guide Workstream - Design Guide Entry - Terminology – Display Standards for Coded Information, 2007. Available at: www.cuisecure.nhs.uk/CAPS/Clinical%20Noting%20and%20Terminology/Terminology%20-%20Display%20Standards%20for%20Coded%20Information.pdf

NHS CUI Design Guide Workstream - Design Guide Entry - Terminology – Elaboration, 2007. Available at: www.cuisecure.nhs.uk/CAPS/Clinical%20Noting%20and%20Terminology/Terminology%20-%20Elaboration.pdf

NHS CUI Design Guide Workstream - Design Guide Entry - Terminology – Matching, 2007. Available at: www.cuisecure.nhs.uk/CAPS/Clinical%20Noting%20and%20Terminology/Terminology%20-%20Matching.pdf

NHS CUI Design Guide Workstream - Design Guide Entry - Terminology - Post-coordination, 2007. Available at: www.cuisecure.nhs.uk/CAPS/Clinical%20Noting%20and%20Terminology/Terminology%20-%20Post%20Coordination.pdf

Markwell D. Terminology Binding Requirements and Principles. NPFIT-FNT-TO-SCG-0026 NHS Connecting for Health, August 2008.

Microsoft. *Connected Health Framework Architecture and Design Blueprint: A Stable Foundation for Agile Health and Social Care.* 2nd ed. March 2009.

NICE. *Improving Outcomes in Colorectal Cancers: Manual Update.* London/England: National Institute for Clinical Excellence; 2004.

Royal Society. *Digital Healthcare: The Impact of Information and Communication Technologies on Health and Healthcare.* London/England: Royal Society; 2006.

Schadow G, Russler D, Mead C, Case J, McDonald C. *The Unified Service Action Model: Documentation for the Clinical Area of the HL7 Reference Information Model.* Revision 2.6. Indianapolis, IN: Regenstrief Institute; May 2000. Available at: http://aurora.rg.iupui.edu/RIM/USAM-2.6.PDF

SNOMED CT Abstract Logical Models and Representational Forms. The International Health Terminology Standards Development Organisation, Copenhagen; 2008

SNOMED Clinical Terms User Guide. International Release, The International Health Terminology Standards Development Organisation, Copenhagen; 2009a.

SNOMED Clinical Terms Technical Reference Guide. International Release, The International Health Terminology Standards Development Organisation, Copenhagen; 2009b.

SNOMED Clinical Terms Technical Implementation Guide. International Release, The International Health Terminology Standards Development Organisation, Copenhagen; 2009c.

Spackman K. SNOMED User Group Meeting, Chicago, 2005

Spronk R. HL7 version 3: Message or CDA Document? Ringholm Whitepaper, version 1.2, 2007. Available at: http://www.ringholm.de/docs/04200_en.htm

Spronk R. The HL7 roadmap for CDA R3 and the CCD. Ringholm Blog, January 2009. Available at: http://www.ringholm.de/column/hl7_cda_r3_ccd_roadmap.htm

Tanenbaum A, *Computer Networks Second Edition.* Available at: http://en.wikiquote.org/wiki/Andrew_S._Tanenbaum

Wanless D. Securing our future health: taking a long-term view. Final report. London/England: HM Treasury; 2002.

Books

Ambler S. *The Elements of UML 2.0 Style.* Cambridge University Press; 2005.

Armour F, Miller G. *Advanced Use Case Modelling.* Reading, MA: Addison-Wesley; 2000.

Beck K. *Extreme Programming Explained: Embrace Change.* 2nd ed. Reading, MA: Addison-Wesley; 2005.

Benson T. *Medical Informatics: A Report for Managers and Clinicians.* Harlow, UK: Longman Health Services Management; 1991.

Benson T, Neame R. *Healthcare Computing: A Guide to Health Information Management and Systems.* Harlow, UK: Longman; 1994.

Blois MS. *Information and Medicine: The Nature of Medical Descriptions.* Berkeley, CA: University of California Press; 1984.

Blum BI, Duncan K, eds. *A History of Medical Informatics.* Reading, MA: Addison-Wesley; 1990.

Booch G, Rumbaugh J, Jacobson I. *The Unified Modeling Language User Guide.* Reading, MA: Addison-Wesley; 1999.

Brennan S. *The NHS IT Project: The Biggest Computer Programme in the World ... Ever!.* Oxford: Radcliffe; 2005.

Carrol L. *Through the Looking Glass and What Alice Found There.* London, UK. 1871:102.

Christensen CM, Grossman JH, Hwang J. *The Innovator's Prescription: A Disruptive Solution for Health Care*. New York: McGraw-Hill; 2009.

Cockburn A. *Writing Effective Use Cases*. Reading, MA: Addison-Wesley; 2001.

Cockburn A. *Agile Software Development*. Reading, MA: Addison-Wesley; 2002.

Coiera E. *Guide to Health Informatics*. 2nd ed. London/England: Arnold; 2003.

Collins T. *Crash: Ten Easy Ways to Avoid a Computer Disaster*. London/England: Simon and Schuster; 1997.

Coplien JO, Harrison NB. *Organizational Patterns of Agile Software Development*. Upper Saddle River, NJ: Pearson Prentice Hall; 2005.

Daschle T. *Critical: What We Can Do About the Health-Care Crisis*. New York: Thomas Dunne Books; 2008.

De Dombal FT. *Surgical Decision Making*. Oxford: Butterworth Heinemann; 1993.

Ellis D. *Medical Computing and Applications*. Chichester, UK: Ellis-Horwood; 1987.

Eriksson H-E, Penker M. *Business Modeling with UML: Business Patterns at Work*. New York: Wiley; 2000.

Evans E. *Domain-Driven Design: Tackling Complexity in the Heart of Software*. Reading, MA: Addison-Wesley; 2004.

Fowler M. *UML Distilled: A Brief Guide to the Standard Object Modeling Language*. 3rd ed. Reading, MA: Addison-Wesley; 2003.

Fowler M. *UML Distilled: a brief guide to the standard object modelling language*. 3rd ed. Reading, MA: Addison-Wesley; 2004.

Fox J, Das S. *Safe and Sound. Artificial Intelligence in Hazardous Applications*. Cambridge, MA: MIT Press; 2000.

Glushko RJ, McGrath T. *Document Engineering: Analyzing and Designing Documents for Business Informatics and Web Services*. Cambridge, MA: MIT Press; 2005.

Greenhalgh T. *How to Read a Paper: The Basics of Evidence Based Medicine*. 2nd ed. London/England: BMJ Books; 2001.

Hayes G, Barnett D, eds. *UK Health Computing: Recollections and Reflections*. Swindon, UK. BCS; 2008

Heitmann K, Bloebel B, Dudeck J. *HL7 Communication Standard in Medicine, Short Introduction and Information*. Koln, Germany: Verlag Alexander Mönch; 1999.

Henderson M. *HL7 Messaging, Version 2*. 2nd ed. Aubrey, TX: O'Tech Inc; 2007.

HIMSS Dictionary of Healthcare Information Technology Terms, Acronyms and Organizations. HiMSS, 2006

Hinchley A. *Understanding Version 3: A Primer on th eHL7 Version 3 Healthcare Interoperability Standard – Normative Edition*. 4th ed. Koln, Germany: Verlag Alexander Mönch; 2007.

Hohpe G, Woolf B. *Enterprise Integration Patterns: Designing, Building and Deploying Messaging Solutions*. Reading, MA: Addison-Wesley; 2004.

Institute of Electrical and Electronics Engineers. *IEEE Standard Computer Dictionary: A Compilation of IEEE Standard Computer Glossaries*. New York: IEEE; 1990.

Institute of Medicine. *Crossing the Quality Chasm: A New Health System for the 21st Century*. Washington, DC: National Academy Press; 2001.

Institute of Medicine. *The Computer-Based Patient Record: An Essential Technology for Health Care*. Revisedth ed. Washington, DC: National Academy Press; 1997.

Institute of Medicine. *Patient Safety: Achieving a New Standard for Care*. Washington, DC: National Academy Press; 2004.

ISO/IEC. *Open Distributed Processing – Reference Model: Overview*. ISO/IEC 10746-1, 1998.

Kleppe A, Warmer J, Bast W. *MDA Explained: The Model Driven Architecture: Practice and Promise*. Reading, MA: Addison-Wesley; 2003.

Kruchten P. *The Rational Unified Process: An Introduction*. 3rd ed. Reading, MA: Addison-Wesley; 2003.

Lamberts H, Woods M, eds. *ICPC: International Classification of Primary Care*. London/England: Oxford University Press; 1987.

Larman C. *Applying UML and Patterns: An Introduction to Object-Oriented Analysis and Design and Iterative Development*. 3rd ed. Prentice Hall; Upper Saddle River, NJ 2005

Marshall C. *Enterprise Modeling with UML: Designing Successful Software through Business Analysis*. Reading, MA: Addison-Wesley; 2000.

McLuhan M. *The Gutenberg Galaxy: The Making of Typographic Man*. Toronto, Canada: University of Toronto Press; 1962.

Mellor SJ, Scott K, Uhl A, Weise D. *MDA Distilled: Principles of Model-Driven Architecture*. Reading, MA: Addison-Wesley; 2004.

Negroponte N. *Being Digital*. London/England: Coronet Books; 1995.

Ogden CK, Richards IA. *The Meaning of Meaning: Study of the Influence of Language Upon Thought and of the Science of Symbolism*. Ark Paperbacks, London, UK.

Perry J. *OXMIS Problem Codes for Primary Medical Care. Oxford Community Health Project*. Oxford: OXMIS publications; 1978.

Pilone D. *UML Pocket Reference*. O'Reilly; 2003.

Preece J. *The Use of Computers in General Practice*. 4th ed. Edinburgh, UK: Churchill Livingstone; 2000.

Rosenberg D, Scott K. *Applying Use Case Driven Object Modelling with UML: An Annotated e-Commerce Example*. Reading, MA: Addison-Wesley; 2001.

Rumbaugh J, Jacobson I, Booch G. *The Unified Modeling Language Reference Manual*. Reading, MA: Addison-Wesley; 1999.

Simon HA. Designing organizations for an information-rich world. In: Greenberger M, ed. *Computers, Communication, and the Public Interest*. Baltimore, MD: The Johns Hopkins Press; 1971.

Straus SE, Richardson WS, Glasziou P, Haynes RB. *Evidence-Based Medicine: How to Practice and Teach EBM*. 3rd ed. Edinburgh, UK: Churchill Livingstone; 2005.

Sager N, Friedman C, Lyman MS. *Medical Language Processing: Computer Management of Narrative Data*. Reading, MA: Addison-Wesley; 1987.

Scott T, Rundall TG, Vogt TM, Hsu J. *Implementing an Electronic Medical Record System: Successes, Failures, Lessons*. Oxford: Radcliffe; 2006.

Seely Brown J, Duguid P. *The Social Life of Information*. Boston, MA: Harvard Business School Press; 2000.

Shapiro C, Varian HR. *Information Rules: A Strategic Guide to the Network Economy*. Boston, MA: Harvard Business School Press; 1999.

Shortliffe EH, Cimino JJ. *Biomedical Informatics: Computer Applications in Health Care and Biomedicine*. 3rd ed. New York: Springer; 2006.

Slack WV. *Cybermedicine: How Computing Empowers Doctors and Patients for Better Health Care*. San Francisco, CA: Jossey-Bass; 1997.

Slee V, Slee D, Schmidt HJ. *The Endangered Medical Record: Ensuring its Integrity in the Age of Informatics*. St. Paul, MN: Tringa; 2000.

Stokes AV. *OSI Standards and Acronyms*. 3rd ed. Manchester, UK: NCC Blackwell; 1991.

Sullivan F, Wyatt JC. *ABC of Health Informatics*. Oxford: Blackwell; 2006.

Taylor P. *From Patient Data to Medical Knowledge: The Principles and Practice of Health Informatics*. London/England: Blackwell; 2006.

Van de Velde R, Degoulet P. *Clinical Information Systems: A Component-Based Approach*. London/England: Springer; 2003.

Warmer J, Kleppe A. *The Object Constraint Language: Getting Your Models Ready for MDA*. 2nd ed. Reading, MA: Addison-Wesley; 2003.

Weed LL. *Knowledge Coupling: New Premises and New Tools for Medical Care and Education*. New York: Springer; 1991.

Wenger E, McDermot R, Snyder WM. *Cultivating Communities of Practice*. Boston, MA: Harvard Business School Press; 2002.

White SA, Miers D. *BPMN Modeling and Reference Guide: Understanding and Using BPMN*. Future Strategies; Lighthouse Point, FL. 2008.

Wyatt JC. *Clinical Knowledge and Practice in the Information Age: A Handbook for Health Professionals*. London/England: RSM Press; 2001.

Zielinski K, Duplaga M, Ingram D, eds. *Information Technology Solutions for Healthcare*. London/England: Springer; 2006.

On-Line Resources

Business Process Modeling Notation www.bpmn.org/
Canada Standards Collaborative www.infoway-inforoute.ca/lang-en/standards-collaborative
Common User Interface Project: www.mscui.net
Continua Alliance www.continuaalliance.org
Google Health http://code.google.com/apis/health/
HL7 Terminfo www.hl7.org/Special/committees/terminfo/index.cfm
HL7 (Health Level Seven) www.hl7.org
IHE (Integrating the Healthcare Enterprise) www.ihe.net
International Health Terminology Standards Development Organisation (IHTSDO) www.ihtsdo.org
Microsoft Health Vault http://msdn.microsoft.com/en-us/healthvault/default.aspx
NHS Connecting for Health. www.connectingforhealth.nhs.uk
NHS Common User Interface. www.cui.nhs.uk
Open Health Tools www.openhealthtools.org
OpenEHR Foundation www.openehr.org
UML Resource Page http://www.uml.org/
W3C World Wide Web Consortium - www.w3.org/BooksBibliographyBibliography

Index